UNIVERSITY OF NORTH CAROLINA AT CHAPEL HILL
DEPARTMENT OF ROMANCE LANGUAGES

NORTH CAROLINA STUDIES
IN THE ROMANCE LANGUAGES AND LITERATURES

Founder: URBAN TIGNER HOLMES
Editor: CAROL L. SHERMAN

Distributed by:

UNIVERSITY OF NORTH CAROLINA PRESS

CHAPEL HILL
North Carolina 27515-2288
U.S.A.

NORTH CAROLINA STUDIES IN THE
ROMANCE LANGUAGES AND LITERATURES
Number 267

THE CHARM OF CATASTROPHE:
A STUDY OF RABELAIS'S *QUART LIVRE*

THE CHARM OF CATASTROPHE:
A STUDY OF RABELAIS'S
QUART LIVRE

BY
ALICE FIOLA BERRY

CHAPEL HILL

NORTH CAROLINA STUDIES IN THE ROMANCE
LANGUAGES AND LITERATURES
U.N.C. DEPARTMENT OF ROMANCE LANGUAGES

2000

Library of Congress Cataloging-in-Publication Data

Berry, Alice Fiola.
 The charm of catastrophe: a study of Rabelais's Quart livre / by Alice Fiola Berry.
 p. cm. – (North Carolina studies in the Romance languages and literatures; no. 267).
 Includes bibliographical references.
 ISBN 0-8078-9271-8
 1. Rabelais, François, ca. 1490-1553? Gargantua et Pantagruel. 4e livre. I. Title.
II. Series.

PQ1694 .B46 2000
843'.3–dc21   00-045256

Cover design: Heidi Perov

Cover-figure from *Les Songes drolatiques*. Paris: Les Bons Libraires, 1869.

© 2000. Department of Romance Languages. The University of North Carolina at Chapel Hill.

ISBN 0-8078-9271-8

DEPÓSITO LEGAL: V. 4.198 - 2000

ARTES GRÁFICAS SOLER, S. L. - LA OLIVERETA, 28 - 46018 VALENCIA

*To my brother Henry
and to Marcel Tetel*

CONTENTS

	Page
INTRODUCTION: TEXTS AND CONTEXTS OF LE QUART LIVRE	11
CHAPTER ONE: PROLOGUES AND THE PROBLEM OF THE MIX	25
CHAPTER TWO: "L'ISLE MEDAMOTHI": RABELAIS'S ITINERARIES OF ANXIETY	47
CHAPTER THREE: INFERNAL BANQUETS	68
1. Points of Departure	68
2. Dindenault, Panurge, and the Death of the Lamb	75
3. Pigs in High Places: Les Chiquanous	82
4. Pigs and Snakes and the Reversible World: Les Andouilles of "l'isle Farouche"	91
5. The Hunger Artist: Messer Gaster	100
6. The Poet in the Kitchen	109
CHAPTER FOUR: THE BOOK OF THE DEAD: IMAGES OF READING AND WRITING IN LE QUART LIVRE	114
1. The Land of Death and of Writing	121
2. The Land of False Faith	126
3. Frozen Versus Thawed Words	132
4. "Le Mot de la Dive Bouteille"	139
CHAPTER FIVE: DARK BIRTHS: RABELAIS'S ENACTMENT OF MALE MATERNITY	142
1. Eating Wind: "l'isle Ennasin," "l'isle de Ruach" and Bringuenarilles...	147
2. Quaresmeprenant, Antiphysie, and "Les Andouilles"	151
3. Les Papefigues	157
4. The Carnival Child	160
CONCLUSION: THE CHARM OF CATASTROPHE	163
BIBLIOGRAPHY	166

INTRODUCTION

TEXTS AND CONTEXTS OF *LE QUART LIVRE*

IN *Le Quart Livre*, Pantagruel and Panurge undertake a sea voyage and a quest for a Word, "le mot de la dive Bouteille." However, though they set sail from France, the voyage quickly drops off the map to nowhere. Physis is pronounced dead in *Le Quart Livre*. The voyagers visit, one ofter another, islands inhabited by monsters who are "deperi(s) en nature" (718)¹ and who speak in often incomprehensible signs and sounds. These fragmented sites portray the collapse of nature, culture, language, even of self. This is a voyage to the lower depths. This is Rabelais's *Season in Hell*.

The terrible historical circumstances that prevailed during the period of *Le Quart Livre*'s composition may in part explain this extraordinary book. Indeed, by the 1540's, history had become a nightmare for Rabelais; all the young humanist's dreams were in shambles. The monk forbidden to study Greek in the twenties, the humanist-evangelical whose two "entertainments" were banned by the Sorbonne, must have been fortified to endure these crises by the faith that reason and right would ultimately prevail. But the forties were a decade of devastation and cruel disillusionment. The

---

¹ Unless otherwise noted, references to *Le Quart Livre* are drawn from *Rabelais: Oeuvres complètes*, ed. Mireille Huchon (Paris: Gallimard, 1994). They will be in parentheses and included in the text. Page numbers referring to the other books will be preceded by the following abbreviations: P (*Pantagruel*), G (*Gargantua*), TL (*Tiers Livre*).

The edition of Pierre Jourda was also consulted: *Oeuvres complètes*, 2 vols. (Paris: Garnier, 1962); as well as two editions of *Le Quart Livre*: by Gérard Defaux (Paris: Livre de Poche, 1994) and Robert Marichal (Geneva: Droz, 1947). References to these editions will be in the notes.

high scholarly and spiritual enterprises of the humanists had spawned only civil violence, and the Council of Trent was nullifying any prospect of compromise with the Reform by stiffening the orthodox doctrines the evangelicals had wanted to demote.² An increasing polarization between catholics and protestants left Rabelais almost alone in the center between the Scylla of his old enemies at the Sorbonne and the Charybdis of his old friends. On one side, he was attacked by such men as Gabriel de Puy-Herbault, Charles de Sainte-Marthe, and the theologian Galland;³ and on the other, there was Jean Calvin, once his ally, and André Tiraqueau's betrayal.⁴ Rabelais's perilous situation had forced him to flee to Metz after the publication of *Le Tiers Livre* where he remained in exile for two years.⁵ The prologue of 1548 and the letter to Odet de Chastillon of 1552 reveal his continuing precarious position, and his dread that consequences still graver than exile awaited him with the publication of yet another book.⁶ This book's humor is strained and black; it is gallows humor. Rabelais's characters wander through the wreckage that time and history have made of his life.

But history has a mythic as well as a personal and political dimension in *Le Quart Livre* and in all of Rabelais's four books. Taken

---

² The Council of Trent sat first in December of 1545 and again in late 1551 to early 1552. At the beginning of the tempest scene (ch. 18), the voyagers encounter nine boatloads of monks on their way to the Council, which Rabelais calls "de Chesil," a Hebrew word for "madmen." They intend to "grabeler les articles de la foy contre les nouveaulx haereticques" (581). *Grabeler*, according to Randle Cotgrave, means "to garbell spices, etc." and also "to examine precisely." *A Dictionarie of the French and English Tongues* (London, 1611; rpt. Columbia: U of South Carolina P, 1950).

³ See Jean Plattard, *François Rabelais* (Paris: Boivin, 1932), 277-79, 285-86.

⁴ Rabelais and Calvin had been evangelists together, and in *De Scandalis* (1550), Calvin reproached Rabelais for falling into disbelief and materialism after having "tasted" the Scriptures (Plattard 301). André Tiraqueau's sins toward his old friend were sins of omission. In the 1545 edition of *De Legibus Connubialibus*, he eliminated both the praise of Rabelais and the *pièces liminaires* by Pierre l'Amy and Rabelais that he had included in the 1524 edition. Also, in *De Nobilitate* of 1549, he did not mention Rabelais when listing illustrious doctors (Plattard 286-7).

⁵ Rabelais's exile in Metz ended in 1548 when he accompanied Jean Du Bellay to Rome (Plattard 261-6).

⁶ Rabelais evokes the possibility of his own execution in the Letter to Odet de Chastillon. If he were in reality guilty of heresy as accused, "(p)ar moymesmes, à l'exemple du Phoenix, seroit le bois sec amassé et le feu allumé, pour en icelluy me brusler" (520). Dolet's execution in 1546 must have been a terrifying example. We must also remember that many others of Rabelais's generation had not survived the 1540's. Francis I died in 1547, Marguerite de Navarre, in 1549, Geofroy d'Estissac and Guillaume Du Bellay, in 1543. Clément Marot died in exile in Turin in 1544.

together, these stories trace the old plot of the heroic life. After the hero's birth, childhood, and youthful exploits narrated in the *Pantagruel* and repeated in the *Gargantua*, *Le Tiers Livre* explores the crises and perplexities of middle age, the issues of governance and marriage above all. *Le Quart Livre* develops the last phase of that life, the cycle of old age and decline. This book is a descent into the underworld,[7] but as for Orpheus, Dante, Aeneas, Jason and so many other heros, the terrible voyage is undertaken in quest of a treasure and healing secret, the elixir that will renew the self and the world. Rabelais calls it "le mot de la dive Bouteille."

On "l'isle Medamothi," the narrator gives a portrait of the heroic life in its full sweep as he describes Pantagruel's purchase of seventy-eight tapestries depicting the life of Achilles from before his birth to after his death, his appearance in the nether regions (541). In 1532, at the end of the first book, Alcofribas had projected a similar biography for Pantagruel, forecasting his marriage as well as that of Panurge, and a quest for "la pierre philosophale" which would lead the giant to the underworld (as well as to the moon).[8] However, as we know, it took many years for Rabelais to pursue this itinerary; he hesitated on the threshold of every phase of Pantagruel's life. In 1534, rather than completing the story outlined by Alcofribas in 1532, he repeated the youthful cycle and retold the story of the father Gargantua. There followed a silence of twelve years and, when *Le Tiers Livre* appeared in 1546, the issue of marriage was displaced from Pantagruel and centered entirely on Panurge. *Le Quart Livre* of 1548 began to recount the sea voyage forecast in

---

[7] Bakhtin also makes this point: "(A)ccording to Rabelais's initial plan the novel's central topic was to be the search for the underworld and Pantagruel's descent into hell (Dante's topic presented on the comic level) . . . . (A)lthough the novel was written over a period of twenty years and with considerable interruptions, Rabelais did not digress from his original plan and indeed almost fulfilled it. Thus the journey into the underground was in the novel from its conception and was elaborated in every detail." *Rabelais and His World*, trans. Hélène Iswolsky (Cambridge, MA: MIT, 1968) 370.

My discussion of the cycles of the heroic life is indebted to Joseph Campbell's *The Hero with a Thousand Faces* (Princeton: Princeton UP, 1949).

[8] In chapter 34 of the *Pantagruel*, the narrator promises that the rest of the story will appear at the Frankfurt fair, "et là vous verrez comment Panurge fut marié, et cocqu dès le premier moys de ses nopces, et comment Pantagruel trouva la pierre philosophale . . . et comment il naviga par la mer Athlantique . . . et conquesta les isles de Perlas. Comment il espousa la fille du roy de Inde nommé Presthan. Comment il combatit contre les diables et fist brusler cinq chambres d'enfer . . . et comment il visita les regions de la lune . . ." (336).

1532, but was broken off abruptly, in the middle of a sentence at the outset of the *escale* on "l'isle des Macraeons," the land of death. The episode and the voyage to the underworld are not completed until 1552.

As Dante needed Virgil to guide him into the *Inferno*, so Rabelais needed predecessors to help him write the story of Pantagruel's middle and later years. Indeed, he had also required a model to compose the saga of the giant's early life. From beginning to end, these books show a very complicated intertextual history. As the narrator himself reveals in the Prologue to the *Pantagruel*, the first book was written in imitation of the anonymous *Grandes et inestimables Chronicques de l'enorme geant Gargantua*,[9] and with the publication of his own *Gargantua*, Rabelais forever appropriated the story of the father as his own creation. *Les Tiers et Quart Livres* also have predecessors which triggered their composition and were all but effaced by the brilliance of the "imitation." However, the relation of the two later books to their pre-texts is more complex, because the models Rabelais is following were initially imitating *him*. During the twelve-year silence after the *Gargantua*, two books appeared which were clearly inspired by the program Alcofribas had set forth in the last chapter of the *Pantagruel*: an anonymous chapbook published in 1538, *Le Voyage et Navigation que fist Panurge, Disciple de Pantagruel*[10] and *Le Songe de Pantagruel* by François

---

[9] In his prologue, Alcofribas extravagantly praises *Les Chroniques* and says that, with the *Pantagruel*, he is offering his readers "un aultre livre de mesme billon" (215). For a discussion of the several editions and titles of this text, see Huchon's "Notice" 1171-83.

[10] 1538 is printed on the first dated edition, but the initial publication may have been earlier. The complete title as it appeared in the 1538 edition is: *Le Voyage & Navigation que fist Panurge, Disciple de Pantagruel aux Isles incongneues & estranges, et de plusieurs choses merveilleuses difficiles à croyre qu'il dict avoir veues, dont il faict Narration en ce present Volume, & plusieurs aultres Joyeusetés pour inciter les lecteurs & auditeurs à Rire.* For a review of the theories regarding the authorship of this book, see Guy Demerson's and Christiane Lauvergnat-Gagnière's introduction to the critical edition (Paris: Nizet, 1982), esp. viii-xiv. Some, including Abel LeFranc insisted that Rabelais wrote the book since it was sometimes published with his works, but Demerson and Lauvergnat-Gagnière do not accept this theory. They are rather swayed by the hypothesis that the author of the *Disciple* is Jean D'Abundance (xii-xiv). Nemours H. Clement, *The Influence of the Arthurian Romances on the Five Books of Rabelais* (New York: Phaeton, 1970) 166-68, suggests that Jean Quentin is the author, the same man whom Rabelais mentions as one of the physicians taking part in "la morale comédie de celui qui avoit espousé une femme mute" (TL, ch. 34).

Habert which appeared in 1542. *Le Songe*, as its title indicates, recounts a lengthy dream in which Pantagruel's father appears to give him spiritual and moral advice and to urge him to marry. Generally considered to be the most direct inspiration for *Le Tiers Livre*, this book brings Rabelais back to the theme of marriage and gives him many other ideas which he developed in his book.[11] *Les Navigations* carries forth the sea voyage suggested by Alcofribas in 1532 (although Pantagruel is mysteriously absent), and *Le Quart Livre* owes much to this book in its details as well as its overall design. In greatly modified and elaborated form, many episodes and characters have their source in *Les Navigations*, including Bringuenarilles, "l'isle Farouche" and "les Andouilles," "les Ennasins," and "l'isle de Ruach."[12]

However, if *Les Navigations* provided the impetus for the voyage of *Le Quart Livre*, it is certainly not the book's only predecessor. To the contrary, the *Fourth Book* is a compendium of all the sea voyages, real and imaginary, that Rabelais knew. The *Odyssey* stands behind this book, as does another written in self-proclaimed imitation of Homer, Lucian's *True History*.[13] Allusions to Virgil's *Aeneid*

---

[11] See the edition of *Le Songe de Pantagruel*, published with an introduction by John Lewis in *Etudes rabelaisiennes* 18 (1985): 103-62. In an introductory passage, Pantagruel invites several wise men to a banquet to discourse on the nature of truth, a structure which forecasts the symposium of *Le Tiers Livre*. Panurge also appears to Pantagruel in a dream and, as he recounts his adventures, he praises the link between debtors and creditors in an abbreviated form of what will become "l'éloge des dettes." Additionally, Gargantua's advice to Pantagruel about the sort of woman he should marry prefigures Hippothadée's view of virtuous women.

Le Songe may also have had an influence on *Le Quart Livre*. As we will discuss, the dream structure is also important for this book, and Rabelais also remembered Gargantua's lengthy digression on Pan the Great Shepherd when he composed the episode on "l'isle des Macraeons." Though Plutarch's *De defectu oraculorum* (419 b-d) is the most direct source for the Pan story, Rabelais's reading of *Le Songe* is also echoed there.

[12] Five chapters (4-8) of *Le Disciple* are devoted to Bringuenarilles whose importance to *Le Quart Livre* we will subsequently discuss. Rabelais's Andouilles are a combination of "Les Farouches," a people "velus comme rats" (22) who eat fish "à la moustarde comme nous faisons les andouilles" (25); and the 12-foot long and edible Andouilles who throw themselves into a river of mustard to flee the voyagers' attack. The Andouilles are given to pulling the noses off their enemies, thus suggesting to Rabelais the idea of the "Ennasins." An island of wind is also visited in *Le Disciple*, "les isles Eolides desquelles Eolus est seigneur & maistre" (81), which is the forerunner of "L'isle de Ruach."

[13] "Many... have written about imaginary travels.... Their guide and instructor in this sort of charlatanry is Homer's Odysseus.... I did wonder, though, that they thought that they could write untruths and not get caught at it. Therefore, as I

are present from the outset of the voyage,[14] and Rabelais's reading and enjoyment of Folengo's *Baldus* are apparent as well.[15] *Les Argonautiques orphiques* also influenced the elaboration of *Le Quart Livre*,[16] and *The Travels of Saint Brendan*, whose popularity was widespread during the middle ages, is another important source. In quest of the Earthly Paradise, Saint Brendan also set out on a long voyage to the Northwest and visited strange islands along the way.[17] Additionally, Rabelais interwove the contemporary voyages of discovery with these legendary travels. The itinerary he sets forth in the first chapter of *Le Quart Livre* traces the one that Cartier followed in search of the Northwest Passage in 1534 and 1535-36.[18]

---

myself, thanks to my vanity, was eager to hand something down to posterity . . . , I took to lying. But my lying is far more honest than theirs, for though I tell the truth in nothing else, I shall at least be truthful in saying that I am a liar." *A True Story*, trans. A. M. Harmon, *Lucian*, vol. 1 (Cambridge: Harvard UP, 1913) 251-3. The tone as well as the content of this passage show Rabelais's debt to Lucian, a debt recognized by such contemporaries as Pasquier, Calvin, Henri Estienne and also Joachim Du Bellay who in his *Deffence et Illustration* alludes to Rabelais as "celuy qui (. . .) faint si bien le nez de Lucien." Quoted by Paul J. Smith, *Voyage et écriture: Etudes sur Le Quart Livre de Rabelais* (Geneva: Droz, 1987) 28. See his discussion of Lucian's influence on the *Fourth Book*, 28-30.

[14] At the end of *Le Tiers Livre* (ch. 47), as Panurge is pleading with Pantagruel to undertake the quest for "la dive Bouteille," he promises to play Achates to the giant's Aeneas (494). Screech suggests that the departure of the voyagers "au jour des festes Vestales" (537) is also an allusion to the *Aeneid*, for on this day Aeneas arrived in Italy from Troy. *Rabelais* (Ithaca: Cornell UP, 1979) 300.

[15] The Dindenault episode and also, perhaps, the tempest and the combat with the whale also stem from the *Baldus*. For a discussion of Folengo's influence on Rabelais, see Marcel Tetel, "Rabelais and Folengo," *Comparative Literature* 15 (1963): 357-64.

[16] In her "Notice" to *Le Quart Livre*, Mireille Huchon argues persuasively for the influence on Rabelais of Orpheus' account of the Argonauts' navigation home after the conquest of the Golden Fleece, a text which was printed in Greek and Latin several times at the beginning of the 16th-century. See esp. 1461-4.

[17] For a discussion of the *Navigatio Sancti Brendani*, see Bahktin 398-9 and Clement 206-7. On one island, deep silence reigns and lamps are shown at the time of the holy office. The old man described in this legend is much like the old Macrobe on Rabelais's "l'isle des Macraeons" (Bakhtin 309).

[18] Bakhtin describes the intermingling of the real voyages of discovery with the imaginary ones of the Celtic tales, especially that of St. Brendan. Cartier's northwestern itinerary, he points out, was also the legendary route to hell and paradise (397-8). Smith, as others before him, including Abel LeFranc, stresses the similarity between the route described in chapter one of *Le Quart Livre* and that of Cartier. He notes the mention, in chapter two, of Canada as well as many other allusions that link *Le Quart Livre* to Cartier's *Brief recit*, including the similarity between its opening lines and the first chapter of Rabelais's odyssey (35-42).

INTRODUCTION   17

Dream voyages also stand behind the sea quest of *Le Quart Livre*, for water is the element of dream. In chapter sixty-three, near the end of the voyage, we see Pantagruel sleeping on the deck of *La Thalamege* and are told that he fell asleep while reading a book, "un Heliodore Grec" (687).[19] This portrait of the sleeping giant recalls Habert's adventure; indeed the whole *Quart Livre* could be construed as another "Songe de Pantagruel." The *Hypnerotomachia* remains present in *Le Quart Livre* as it has been since 1534 in the *Gargantua*.[20] However, of all the dream voyages, Dante's is the most influential. Though Rabelais never mentions the *Divine Comedy* directly, he would surely have encountered it in Rome.[21] As in Dante,

---

Frank Lestringant in "L'Insulaire de Rabelais, ou la fiction en archipel (pour une lecture topographique du *Quart Livre*)," *Rabelais en son demi-millénaire* (Geneva: Droz, 1988) 249-274, also comments on the mixture of the real and the imaginary in Rabelais's voyage as in all "récits par îles": "D'une manière générale l'Insulaire naît de la rencontre, en bien des points fortuite, d'un espace géographique, fictif ou réel, et d'un espace purement linguistique. Y compris dans les insulaires qui prétendent décrire le monde réel, l'on découvre des archipels suscités par une prolifération des noms sans objets" (251). However, Lestringant does not agree that Jacques Cartier's *Brief recit* was the primary influence on Rabelais's voyage. He stresses instead the points of similarity with the *Carta Marina et Descriptio septentrionalium terrarum* of Olaus Magnus, published in Venice in 1539 (262-4).

[19] If Pantagruel is reading Heliodorus in Greek, he is reading the *editio princeps* of the *Aethiopica* published in Basel in 1534. Jacques Amyot's translation with a laudatory and instructive preface appeared in 1547, which Rabelais would also have certainly read. Amyot's edition both popularized Heliodorus' romance and posited it a model of literary creation. See Gerald N. Sandy, *Heliodorus* (Boston: Twayne, 1982) 97-102, and Robert Marichal, "Quart Livre: Commentaires," *Etudes rabelaisiennes* 5 (1964): 144.
    Why is Pantagruel reading this book? Marichal suggests that his falling asleep is a sign of derision: "A juger par ce passage il a dû trouver (les *Aethiopiques*) ennuyeuses!" (144). But the giant's choice of this romance, even to drowse over, is significant. This story of young lovers so often separated may be linked in Rabelais's mind to Poliphilo's search for his beloved in the *Hypnerotomachia*–and to the quest for a wife which generated *Le Quart Livre* and which is reintroduced in this same episode with the discussion of Panurge's future wife (693). Moreover, as we will argue in Chapter Four, the giant's sleep over this book also carries forth the "reading lesson" elaborated in relation to the anecdote of the "sureau sauvage" recounted at the end of Gaster, the immediately preceding episode.

[20] In this work, Poliphilo searches for his beloved in a dream where he passes through architectural designs covered with hieroglyphs, and it is in the context of Egyptian hieroglyphs that Rabelais mentions this work: in chapter nine of the *Gargantua* (29) and in an entry to the "Briefve Declaration" relevant to "l'isle des Macraeons" (598 & 708).

[21] Rabelais made three trips to Rome with Jean Du Bellay: in 1534, in 1535-36, and in 1548-50, the period during which he was writing the second *Quart Livre*. Rabelais also spent 1540-43 in Turin with Guillaume Du Bellay and was present, as he

the *escales* are islands of the mind, inhabited by monsters that embody and isolate a moral or spiritual vice. And, as in the *Inferno*, the vices become ever more hellish, the creatures more demonic. *Le Quart Livre*, too, spirals downward toward a terrible Ninth Circle.

But of all his models, the Bible is perhaps the most important. It was the Old Testament above all which provided Rabelais with stories to help him cross the last threshold of Pantagruel's life and enter the terrifying realm of death and cosmic catastrophe. *Le Quart Livre* expresses the pain of Old Adam cast out of Eden and separated from creation; of Noah on the ark of self floating over the debris of a dark, ruined universe; of Israel's scattered tribes in exile from the Old Kingdom, not yet attaining the new. But above all, this book speaks of Jonah cast into the belly of the whale, and of Moses discovering in the desert the mountain of God and bringing down the Word revealing the world's new order. We will discuss these stories separately in order to reveal their relevance to the voyage of Rabelais's *Quart Livre*.

JONAH

The story of the descent into the whale combines several of Rabelais's sources. In the *True History* (285-305), Lucian and his companions were swallowed into the maw of a gigantic sea monster and they met many creatures and had many adventures in the belly of the whale before they were disgorged. In the *Disciple*, Bringuenarilles plays the role of the whale. A huge giant encountered at sea, he eats men and boats at a gulp, and thus carries living creatures in his belly. But unlike Lucian, the *Disciple* tells of the effect of this indiscriminate swallowing on the whale. Suffering repeated bouts of indigestion, Bringuenarilles frequently requires the services of a "ramoneur"-*cum*-physician who enters his belly and sweeps it out. Consequently, the creatures within the giant are liberated – through his anus, his mouth, or his nose.[22]

---

says on "l'isle des Macraeons" (602-3), at the statesman's death there. Du Bellay's death is also described in chapter 21 of *Le Tiers Livre*.

For another discussion of the influence of Dante on Rabelais, see François Rigolot, *Le Texte de la Renaissance* (Geneva: Droz, 1982) 155-170.

[22] See especially chapters 4-8 of the *Disciple* (10-21).

As we know, in composing this story, the author of the *Disciple* was imitating Rabelais, who had enacted a similar version of the Jonah story at the end of the *Pantagruel*. In chapter thirty-two, Alcofribas entered and explored the world in the mouth of his creation, and in chapter thirty-three, was swallowed into the giant's sick belly with other voyager-physicians, "avallés comme pillules" (335). There they find an olympian case of constipation, "une montjoye d'ordure" (335). They hack and hew and clean the intestine, and finally Pantagruel is cured by a victorious movement wrought by their labor. The doctors, too, are restored as Pantagruel vomits them back into the world: "Il me souvenoit quand les Gregeoys sortirent du cheval en Troye" (335).

In transforming the story of Jonah into a medical myth, both Rabelais and the author of the *Disciple* understood what may be its essential meaning. This fable speaks of the "regulation of life," of the relationship of death to life. It is a myth of bodily death and regeneration.[23] The physician as Jonah is swallowed into the suffering body of self and of the world, and he experiences death in the belly as tomb and bodily grave. He, in his turn, harms the whale as a disease, a foreign object within its body, and he aggressively attacks the creature from within, hews and cuts it in an effort to remove the sickness. But the prophet is also re-created in the belly as womb, reborn as the whale spews him out. By the same gesture, the whale is likewise healed and the integrity of the body reestablished. The story of Jonah embodies what Foucault called "the true archeology of the medical point of view."[24]

In *Le Quart Livre*, the writer-physician once again enters the sick body of self and of the world in order to heal it, and the voyage takes place in two phases as in the *Pantagruel*. The events of the 1548 edition are situated "in the mouth": the encounters with Din-

---

[23] The phrase "regulation of life" is taken from Bakhtin 70. The most evocative essays on the Jonah story are: Gaston Bachelard, "Le Complexe de Jonas" in *La Terre et les rêveries du repos* (Paris: Corti, 1948) 128-82, and Joseph Campbell, "The Belly of the Whale," in *The Hero with a Thousand Faces* 90-4. Both Bachelard and Campbell stress that this is a myth of death and rebirth, and we recall that Christ compares himself to Jonah as he promises his resurrection: "For as Jonas was three days and three nights in the whale's belly; so shall the Son of man be three days and three nights in the heart of the earth" (Matthew 12: 40; see also Luke 11: 29-32).

[24] *The Order of Things* (New York: Pantheon Books, 1970) 15.

denault, Panigon, the red-snouted Chicquanous, the Ennasins, and with "Slitnose" Bringuenarilles all occur in the head if not in *la gueule*, and explore the oral activities associated with the banquet —chewing and swallowing, drinking and speaking. The 1552 edition descends to a lower psychic and physical level. The whale is sighted, it is killed, and its belly is slit open. The voyagers penetrate into the belly, the domain of Messer Gaster, the bodily hell where the serpent resides. There they do battle with the intestine, "l'être andouillicque," and cut it into sausage meat. But in the end, as in the *Pantagruel*, the book is purged of disease and fear. Panurge descends into the ship's hold, the lowest point of the voyage, and there he loses control of his anal sphincter and dirties himself. However, he is reborn as Jonah was reborn, by climbing up and out of "(l)es cuisines d'Enfer" (698). As he emerges from the darkness, he ends Rabelais's *odyssée du ventre* with a call to fresh life and further voyages. "Beuvons" is the book's last word.

Moses

Jonah's medical journey into the body is also a cosmic passage, and Rabelais explicitly designates the map on which the larger voyage should be traced. In chapter one, Pantagruel interrupts the departure festivities to preach a sermon from the Bible "sus l'argument de navigation" (538) and then Psalm 114 is sung, "le psaulme du sainct Roy David, lequel commence: *Quand Israel hors d'Ægypte sortit*" (539). Thus the Exodus story is linked to the voyage of Panurge and Pantagruel. The epic of Moses, "noble prophete" (616), "chevalereux capitaine . . . conducteur du peuple Israelicque" (625) is the second Biblical myth underlying *Le Quart Livre*.

The allusion to Exodus confers many tragedies on this book. Just as Moses and the Israelis wandered in the desert, Pantagruel and Panurge journey from island to island, in exile from the old order and still in quest of the new. Moses' story evokes the sense of transcendental homelessness which is the underlying emotion of *Le Quart Livre*. It also evokes a more archaic emotion: cosmic terror, the fear that the immeasurable and infinitely powerful material masses of the world will rise up in anger against its human inhabitants.[25] In this book, as in Exodus, the world is pitched back into "l'antique Cahos, on quel estoient feu, air, mer, terre, tous les elemens en refraictaire confusion" (582), but in *Le Quart Livre*, that chaos is given a Christian explanation. On "l'isle des Macraeons," we are told that it is nature's mourning for the death of the long hoped-for Redeemer, Pan-Christ who finally came to the world only to be betrayed by those who should have served Him. With His death, the new world is thrown back into the terrors of the old, and no promise of resurrection is offered on "l'isle des Macraeons."

The tragedies enacted in Exodus and in *Le Quart Livre* take place in the City as well as in the cosmos and in nature. Indeed, Moses' story is in many ways a tale of two cities. It traces the passage away from the corruption of Egypt toward Jerusalem, the new community to be founded on God's word, and Pantagruel's voyage follows the same itinerary. He too leaves behind a woeful city held by a tyrant-monster "avid for the greedy rights of 'me and mine,'"[26] and in *Le Quart Livre*, that tyrant is the Pope and his clergy. In Rabelais's eyes, this evil sovereign has betrayed the Christian community and installed *philautia*, self-love, to govern in place of Christ's *caritas*. *Philautia* has turned the City into a wilderness where men prey on other men and the islands of *Le Quart Livre* reflect this shattered community. They are lands of egotistical self-aggrandizement inhabited by monsters who fight among and always *for* themselves.

Land of idolatry and false faith, Egypt is also the land of the lie, and the breakdown of language is, as Montaigne argued in *Du Dementir*, both cause and reflection of civic catastrophe:

> Nostre intelligence se conduisant par la seule voye de la parolle, celuy qui la fauce trahit la societé publique. C'est le seul util par le moien duquel se communiquent nos volontez et nos pensées,

---

[25] We recall the second strophe of Clément Marot's translation of Psalm 114:
> Le mer le veit, qui s'enfuyt soudain
> Et contremont l'eau du fleuve Jourdain
> Retourner fut contraincte.
> Comme moutons montaignes ont sailly
> Et si en ont les costeaux tresailly
> Comme aigneletz en craincte.

Oeuvres de Clément Marot, ed. Georges Guiffrey and Jean Plattard (Paris: Schmeit, 1931), v, 283-84.

[26] Campbell 15.

> c'est le truchement de nostre ame: s'il nous faut, nous ne nous tenons plus, nous ne nous entre-connoissons plus. S'il nous trompe, il rompt tout nostre commerce et dissoult toutes les liaisons de nostre police.[27]

It is just such a dissolution which is displayed in the the warring islands of *Le Quart Livre*. Isolated by self-interest, their inhabitants are also isolated by their perverted use of language. They so twist and falsify the common meaning of words for their own ends that words lose their link to a shared and comprehensible reality. The result is the failure of expression and communication that plagues the book.

Moses' quest is linked to this linguistic failure as well as to the civic and spiritual catastrophes. Prophet and city father, he is also a logotherapist, for the Word that he found in the desert healed words. In giving the Law on which Jerusalem could be founded, the *Logos* brought language back to the fundamental relation it should bear to reality and truth. And Pantagruel strives to emulate Moses' achievement. Wandering in the desert of afflicted language, he too seeks a Hebrew word, "l'oracle de la dive Bouteille Bacbuc" (537), the Word that will heal the world. The outcome of his quest remains in question at the end of *Le Quart Livre*, but for one brief moment in the Frozen Sea, Pantagruel allows himself to hope that he too has been called to Sinai, to "le manoir de Verité" where "les Parolles" exist in full and perfect relation to "les Idées, les Exemplaires et protraictz de toutes choses passées et futures" (668). Significantly, Panurge responds to this possibility by recalling Moses on the mountain:

> Mais en pourrions nous veoir quelqu'une? Me soubvient avoir leu que l'orée de la montaigne en laquelle Moses receut la loy des Juifz, le peuple voyoit les voix sensiblement. (669)

To hear the Word and then to inscribe it, "sensiblement" so that human language and culture may return to the origins of life and experience a renascence, a true second chance–this is the deepest yearning of *Le Quart Livre* and, perhaps, its most tragic impossibility.

---

[27] *Oeuvres complètes de Montaigne*, ed. Albert Thibaudet and Maurice Rat (Paris: Gallimard, 1962) 650.

These, then, are the stories which enabled Rabelais, after many hesitations, to penetrate into the evening and night of Pantagruel's biography. The sea and dream voyages of many prior books and the biblical myths of Jonah and Moses served him as an Ariadne's thread into a bodily zone of darkness and danger which is also a woeful city of lying words. This perilous journey is undertaken for medical purposes, to heal the cosmic, social, spiritual, and linguistic diseases the book has explored. It is a quest for an elixir, "le mot de la dive Bouteille," which will return the flow of life to the self and to the world. In the end, however, we must ask if this quest succeeds. Is the secret brought back? Is the world renewed? We will further ponder these questions as we proceed from island to island of Rabelais's enigmatic book.

Chapter One

PROLOGUES AND THE PROBLEM OF THE MIX

THE prologue of 1548 has the dubious distinction of being the only chapter in all of Rabelais's four books which he repudiated in its entirety. Though the other episodes of the first edition of *Le Quart Livre* were extensively revised and expanded, they were nonetheless retained as *escales* in the full sea voyage of 1552.[1] However, the first introduction to that voyage was banished from the book. In its place Rabelais substituted not one but two new prologues: the true prologue of 1552 as well as a "pre-prologue" in the form of a letter to his patron, Odet de Chastillon. These three prefaces to *Le Quart Livre* face each other as in a labyrinth of mirrors where they distort and also reflect each other truly, and this chapter will explore the relationships between them. But we will begin by interrogating the cast-off prologue of 1548, and will return to it in the end in an effort to penetrate the secret that Rabelais desired to hide from posterity and even, perhaps, from himself.

This Old Prologue does not begin auspiciously, and we are thrown into confusion from the first paragraph. To our amazement, we discover that our "Ambassadeur" has appeared before the writ-

---

[1] *Le Quart Livre des faictz et dictz Heroiques du noble Pantagruel. Composé par M. François Rabelais, Docteur en Medicine, et Calloier des Isles Hieres* was published in Lyon in 1548. It consists of a prologue and eleven chapters comprising seven episodes: the departure, Dindenault, "l'isle Ennasin," "l'isle de Chely," "les Chiquanous," Bringuenarilles and the tempest. An eighth episode on "l'isle des Macraeons" is begun but is less than one page long and is broken off in mid-sentence. See Jean Plattard's critical edition, *Le Quart Livre de Pantagruel (édition dite partielle, Lyon, 1548)* (Paris: Champion, 1909).

er to plead with him on our behalf.[2] We are not told the substance of his plea, but to our increasing perplexity, Rabelais does offer this odd little "summary":

> Le sommaire de sa proposition, je reduis en trois motz, lesquelz sont de tant grande importance, que jadis entre les Romains par ces trois motz le Preteur respondoit à toutes requestes exposées en jugement:
> ... "Vous donnez, vous dictes, vous adjugez." (715)

Strangest of all, and most significant, we find that Rabelais has misquoted the Roman magistrate who never said "vous." He rather spoke in the first person: *do, dico, addico*.[3] In this way, from the outset of the prologue of 1548, "I" and "thou" are confused, judge and judged, subject and object–all the categories are confounded.

Indeed, confusion must be called the structural principle of the "Ancien Prologue," for all of its subsequent anecdotes and arguments are built around this juridical formula and these mistaken pronouns. As a consequence, its most crucial relationships are thrown into disarray. The relationship between writer, reader, and text is profoundly altered and the medical relationships are also confused–the connection between "François Rabelais, docteur en medicine," the author of this book, and his reader-patients. We will discuss the impact of the "mixed" pronouns on these two sets of relationships in the old prologue as well as in the "Lettre à Odet" and the new prologue of 1552 which represent Rabelais's unsuccessful attempts to separate and clarify the relationships he had, to his peril, confounded in 1548.

In accordance with the first term of the judgment, a text is "given," the story of the war between the jays and the magpies and of the hero-bird Goitrou who led the jays to victory with his rousing

---

[2] "Beuveurs trèsillustres, et vous, goutteurs tres precieux, j'ay veu, receu, ouy, et entendu l'Ambassadeur que la seigneurie de voz seigneuries ha transmis par devers ma paternité, et m'a semblé bien bon et facond orateur" (715).

[3] "Le prêteur, les jours fastes, après l'audition des parties et des témoins, prononçait, en cas de demande justifiée, les trois mots suivants: *do* (*do iudicem* «je désigne un juge»), *dico* (*dico ius* «je dis l'acte juridique en cause»), *addico* (*addico litem* «j'assigne l'objet en litige»). Avec cette formule, les parties se retrouvaient devant le juge" (Huchon 1592 n. 4).

war cry, "Crocquez pie."[4] Though this tale does not equal the vivacity of Rabelais's prior prologues, his manner of presenting and describing the story follows a formula he has used before. Like the silenus box and the marrowbone of 1532, and like Diogenes' Tub of 1546, the prologue of 1548 is also made into a container with an inside and an outside; it is presented as a breviary in the form of a bottle. Also in the manner of Socrates' artifact, "figures joyeuses et frivoles" (5) are engraved on the outside: ". . . les reigletz, la rose, les fermailz, la relieure, et la couverture: en laquelle je n'ay omis à considerer les Crocs et les Pies, peintes au dessus, et semées en moult belle ordonnance . . . . (comme si fussent lettres hieroglyphicques) . . ." (715). Once again, the reader's task is to imitate the philosophic dog–and Goitrou–and crack the ciphers, "crocquer" the bone-bottle-keg in order to extract the wisdom which lies on the inside of the story. And again, outside and inside merge in the call to drink of Rabelais's wine, for "crocquez la pie" means not only to "croake, creake, cracke, crash, crackle . . ." the magpie, it also means "to wet the whistle . . . throughly; to drinke hard."[5]

However, despite these similarities, the reversed pronouns of the first paragraph have generated one astonishing dissimilarity between the fable of 1548 and the prologues of 1534 and 1546–we *readers* give this story! We are transformed into the *writers* of the fable of the jays and the magpies, and François Rabelais plays the part of the reader here. All of the problems and paradoxes of reading that were turned against us in 1534 and 1546 are, in 1548, turned back upon the writer as he interprets "our" story and strives to extract "our" hidden meanings:

> Aussi bien à quel propos me feriez vous present d'un breviaire? . . . Sus ce doubte ouvrant ledict breviaire, j'apperceu que c'estoit un breviaire, faict par invention mirificque, et les reigletz touts à propos avec inscriptions opportunes. Doncques vous voulez qu'à prime je boyve vin blanc: à tierce, sexte et nonne, pareillement: à vespres et complies, vin clairet. Cela vous appelez crocquer pie. (717)

---

[4] For a discussion of this expression, see Paul J. Smith, "'Croquer Pie': *Quart Livre*, Ancien Prologue," *Rabelais-Dionysos: vin, carnaval, ivresse,* ed. M. Bideaux (Paris: Jeanne Laffitte, 1997) 97-108.

[5] Randle Cotgrave's definition, *A Dictionarie of the French and English Tongues* (London, 1611. Rpt. Columbia: U of South Carolina P, 1950).

Vous donnez? *Vous* voulez? *Vous* appelez? The wine of this prologue is indeed "mixed" as never before. For while it is true that we have seen Alcofribas Rabelais reading his own book, in the first chapter of *Gargantua*,[6] we readers have never before been implicated in its writing. Furthermore, to our best knowledge, no writer before Rabelais had ever involved the reader so deeply and so strangely in the fictional process. To find anything comparable, we must wait at least fifty years for the second part of the *Quixote* which incorporates the reactions of its readers to the first part of the book. Or, we must wait until the eighteenth century, when writers were experimenting with new and ironic roles for the readers of the long prose forms we now call novels: Diderot's *Jacques le fataliste*, for example, or Laurence Sterne's *Tristram Shandy* in whose autobiography pages are left blank for the reader to "put his own fancy in."[7]

But in France at the time Rabelais was writing, the traditional pedagogic relationship between reader and writer still prevailed. However much prose writers may have desired to please and surprise their readership, their most fundamental aim was to instruct–at least in the sense that they gave the reader to know something he or she had not known before.[8] The fable of the jays and the magpies could have conveyed no moral to Rabelais's audience, for by implying that the writer "reads" and above all that the reader "writes," he had turned the pedagogic roles topsy-turvy. This prologue must have been incomprehensible to his contemporaries. Indeed, there is a good possibility that their distaste and confusion, directly expressed, caused Rabelais to banish this prologue from the book.

If he had no literary precedents for this fictional game, what then caused him to play it in this manner? It is possible that this "mixing" of reader and writer was generated by Rabelais's increasing awareness of his medium–in the 1540's he writes *books, Les*

---

[6] Whereas Alcofribas is the eyewitness chronicler of the *Pantagruel,* he rather designates himself as reader and translator of the *Gargantua*. The book, found buried, is written in incomprehensible script and Alcofribas is called to the rescue: "Je (combien que indigne) y fuz appellé: et a grand renfort de bezicles, practicant l'art dont on peut lire lettres non apparentes, comme enseigne Aristoteles, la translatay . . ." (10).

[7] Quoted by Walter J. Ong, "The Writer's Audience is Always a Fiction," *PMLA* 90 (1975): 17. In this article, Ong explores the effect of print on fictional relationships in general and on reader roles in particular.

[8] Ong 15.

Tiers et Quart Livres. Though he characteristically writes his books in an oral style, Rabelais has come to understand that written communication establishes relationships between reader, audience, and story that are very different from those established by the spoken word, and he attempts to duplicate those relationships here. Story*telling* takes place in the present and has its meaning established by the live interaction of the teller and his audience. But story*writing* and reading occur in solitude and in the mutual absence of writer and reader: "O gens de bien," laments Rabelais in the 1548 prologue, "je ne vous peulx voir" (715). Written words are what he says they are, "lettres hieroglyphicques"; their meaning is latent and must be deciphered and reconstructed. As a result, the reader acquires a control over the meaning of a written story that the listener of an oral tale simply does not possess–the book is, figuratively as well as literally, in the reader's hands. It is the reader's power over the text and his or her participation in the creation of its meaning that Rabelais means to express when he calls us "writer" of the fable of the jays and the magpies.

Rabelais also means to express the reader's power over the writer as well as over the book, for is it not the presence of the man that we seek in his hieroglyphs? Rabelais had indicated this to be true in the prologue of 1534 where he compared the reading of the book to the reading of a man: Socrates, Gargantua, Alcofribas. And we ourselves constantly affirm what Montaigne called the "consubstantiality" of the book and its author[9] by the turn of phrase which permits us to say that we are "reading Rabelais," the book and the man, the man become book, the man become words. As we read Rabelais's text, Rabelais-as-text, we create him as we want him to be. It is the essential nature of the written word to cast this god-like power upon us.

Here is the heart of the matter and the most crucial issue, not only of the prologue of 1548 but also of the prologues of 1552–this power of the reader over the text and its author. For Rabelais's main purpose in writing these three introductions to *Le Quart Livre* was to defend himself against his bad readers, "calumniateurs de mes escripts" (718) who had abused their creative powers to falsify the meaning of his text and to cast a disfiguring face upon his face.

---

[9] *Oeuvres complètes de Montaigne*, ed. A. Thibaudet and M. Rat (Paris: Gallimard, 1962) 648.

They said that his books were "farciz d'heresies diverses" (519), which was to place his life in grave peril, for heresy was a capital crime. To create this similacrum, Rabelais's enemies had only to twist his language and use his own writing against him:

> . . . d'heresies poinct: sinon perversement et contre tout usaige de raison et de languaige commun, *interpretans* ce que, à poine de mille fois mourir, si autant possible estoit, ne vouldrois avoir pensé: comme qui pain *interpretroit* pierre: poisson, serpent: oeuf, scorpion. ("Lettre à Odet" 520, my italics)

To forestall such malicious misreadings and to place limits on the reader's power over the book and its author, Rabelais will add a glossary to *Le Quart Livre* of 1552, "La Briefve declaration d'aulcunes dictions plus obscures." But in 1548, his defensive strategy is not limited to definitions, although they do play their part in this prologue.[10] Here he rather concentrates on the larger role that a good reader should play, and it is to teach us our proper role that Rabelais plays the part of reader of our text. We must act as his alter ego and read in the spirit in which he writes, as "Pantagruélistes," members of that generous-minded and open-hearted fraternity he describes in the prologue to *Le Tiers Livre*, "(qui) jamais en maulvaise partie ne prendront choses quelconques ilz congnoistront sourdre de bon, franc et loyal couraige" (351).

Similarly, and more important perhaps, we must read as "Beuveurs," as banqueteers, eaters and drinkers and above all, as talkers. This is the meaning of Rabelais's description of his book as a bottle and of his constant injunction to drink of its wine–we are to put the book "in our mouths"–*talk* it. For Rabelais the spoken word is the ultimate guarantor of truth and in his lexicon, the word "lecture"

---

[10] Rabelais begins the "Vous adjugez" section of the prologue by attacking names which have no definitions: ". . . Caphards, Cagotz, Matagotz, Botineurs, Papelards, Burgotz . . . . Je n'y ay entendu que le hault Allemant, et ne sçay quelle sorte de bestes comprenez en ces denominations . . . . (M)aintenant est deperie en nature, . . . et ne sçavons quelle en soit la diffinition: comme vous sçavez que subject pery, facilement perit sa denomination" (717-18).

This passage is followed by Rabelais's definition of calumny (cited below) the essence of which is to falsify and obliterate the relationship between words and their references. These reflections must surely have inspired Rabelais to add "La Briefve declaration" to the 1552 edition and are part of a continuing concern in both *Quart Livres* to discern the nature of the relationship between words and things.

means reading aloud. It is when we talk the book and hear it, "oyans en mon absence la lecture de ces livres joyeulx" (719),[11] that the writer resurges among us to banish the absence of writing and to correct the error and illusion it generated.

These are some of the truths of writing that Rabelais explores when he mixes the roles of reader and writer in the prologue of 1548. But the strangest truth of the "mix" is this: that Rabelais himself is both reader and writer of the fable of the jays and the magpies. Writing drives a wedge of absence between the author and himself as well as between him and his true audience. This book is both part of him and "other," a mystery, a hieroglyph to be deciphered. Rabelais too had to "read Rabelais" and he was as ill-equipped as the other readers of his time to confront this text and understand it. It may have been his own anxiety, as well as theirs, which caused him to suppress this troubling prologue.

And when we proceed to the "vous dictes" and "vous adjugez" sections of the prologue of 1548, the graver consequences of the mistaken pronouns become apparent. For, by mixing the roles of reader and writer, Rabelais sabotaged his main and most substantive arguments against his enemies, the medical arguments. The remainder of the prologue is devoted to Rabelais's contention that he does truly write as a *docteur en medicine,* that his books and stories are remedies to heal the body as well as the mind of the reader. The validity of this contention will be subsequently weighed, but what is important here is to understand that the medical arguments depend for their efficacy on the clear distinction of the very roles that Rabelais had confounded in the preceding fable–the writer must be in control of the story as the physician who dispenses the medicine of his words to heal his reader-patients. By jumbling these roles, he had undermined his main defense even before he had offered it, and his very life was at stake in purifying the mixed wine of the prologue of 1548.

Therefore, in 1552, he proceeds with caution and in a very different manner. He composes a new fable, the wondrous story of Couillatris and his lost ax. Like the fable of 1548, it is meant to be a

---

[11] The definition of "lecture" as oral reading is also given in the "Lettre à Odet": ". . . de telles calumnies avoit esté le defunct roy François d'eterne memoire, adverty: et curieusement aiant par la voix et pronunciation du plus docte et fidele Anagnoste ("Lecteur," BD 703) de ce royaulme ouy et entendu lecture distincte d'iceulx livres miens . . . n'avoit trouvé passaige aulcun suspect . . ." (520).

lesson in good reading and interpretation, but in 1552, Rabelais conducts the lesson in the traditional manner; the writer *qua* writer tells the reader how to extract the moral from the story. Although it is a medical moral–moderation, "médiocrité," is the condition of good health–Rabelais does not mix medicine with fiction as he had done in 1548. The medical arguments are rather set forth in the "Lettre à Odet de Chastillon" which precedes the prologue, and in the letter, Rabelais takes every precaution to convince us of his sincerity. This is a historical document, fact not fiction, truth not illusion. It is signed by a well-known and universally-respected physician and is postmarked: "De Paris ce.28 de Janvier .1552" (521). The letter alludes to people, places, and events that can be objectively verified and it advances the medical arguments most systematically, arguments which are buttressed by the highest authorities of antiquity: Hippocrates, Galen, Plato, Aristotle. Even more crucial perhaps, the letter is not addressed to the reader, that troubling "vous" of 1548. The "I" here is clearly Rabelais, and the "vous" is one specific individual, Odet de Chastillon, who had proven himself to be a good reader and friend of Rabelais. Although we are allowed to read this private correspondence, as "Beuveurs et Pantagruélistes," we are not allowed to intervene. The reader is present in the Letter only in the third person, a weakened and ineffectual "eux."

But Rabelais's strategies of separation and suppression failed. They failed because the "mix" he had concocted in 1548 expressed problems and paradoxes endemic to the acts of reading and writing, and these perplexities continue to plague him in 1552. Additionally, he came face to face with a "mix" inherent in the idea of logotherapy, the very tradition upon which he relies to clarify and justify his enterprise. The medical categories, like the fictional ones, collapse on him and in the end, these prologues are forced back into the labyrinth from whence they struggle to escape.

It is time that we do justice to Rabelais's claim that his books and stories have therapeutic powers, for it is based on the authentic medical doctrine of the ancients.[12] The conviction that words are a

---

[12] My presentation of the history of logotherapy is drawn from Pedro Laín Entralgo, *The Therapy of the Word in Classical Antiquity*, trans. J. Rather and J. M. Sharp (New Haven: Yale UP, 1970).

medicine indispensable to the proper execution and success of the therapeutic procedure can be traced back to Homer and followed in an unbroken line down to the last half of the sixth and the first half of the fourth centuries B.C.[13] This is the period of the Sophists, notably Gorgias and Antiphon,[14] as well as of Hippocrates, Plato, and Aristotle whom, with Galen, Rabelais cites as his main authorities. As a humanist-scholar, he had studied and commented these texts,[15] and as a writer-physician he strives to put their doctrine of the therapy of the word into practice:

> Seulement avois esguard et intention par escript donner ce peu de soulaigement que povois es affligez et malades absens, lequel voluntiers, quand besoing est, je fays es presens qui soy aident de mon art et service. (517)

Rabelais relies most heavily on the authority of Hippocratic medicine in the prologues to the *Quart Livre*, but we must rather turn to Plato and Aristotle to understand his logotherapy. For while it is true that Hippocrates and Galen were both aware of the psychosomatic efficacy of words and advocated that speech be used on occasion to exhort or cheer their patients,[16] neither propounded

---

[13] See the *Odyssey* (Book 19, 455-60) where the sons of Autolykos bind Ulysses' wound and "singing incantations over it, stayed the black blood"; and the *Iliad* (Book 15, 392-94) where Patroklos treats the fallen Eurypylos with cheering speech as well as with herbs, "making him glad with talk." Consult Laín Entralgo's discussion of the therapeutic word in the Homeric epic, 1-31. See also 31-107 where Orpheus, the tragedians, Pythagoras, Empedocles, Anaxagoras and Democritus are discussed.

[14] Laín Entralgo gives considerable weight to the logotherapy of the Sophists, especially the writings of Gorgias (91-105).

[15] As Plattard notes in *François Rabelais* (Paris: Boivin, 1932), the humanists repudiated Arab medical doctrine, Avicenne in particular, in favor of the Greeks, and Rabelais distinguished himself very early in his medical career as a scholar of ancient Greek texts (116). For his "cours de stage" at Montpellier in 1532, he explicated Hippocrates' *Aphorisms* and Galen's *Ars Parva* (115). In 1532, the year of the *Pantagruel*, Rabelais published the *Aphorisms* in Greek with his philological commentary (131). In 1537, when he returned to Montpellier for his "license," he explicated the Greek text of Hippocrates' *Prognostics* (217). In this same year, Rabelais also conducted in Lyon one of the first public dissections of a cadaver in France (215-16).

[16] In Book Four of *On Diet*, for example, Hippocrates recommends to patients afflicted with melancolia that they attend theatrical productions, especially those that cause laughter. See: *Oeuvres Complètes d'Hippocrates*, ed. E. Littré, vol. 6 (Paris: Baillière, 1849) 649-51. In Book Six of the *Epidemics*, Hippocrates describes the psychic causes of certain diseases (vol. 5, 349) and he also prescribes

any systematic use of the techniques of verbal psychotherapy. Insofar as their medicine was scientific, it was somatic, putting faith in treatment by diet, drugs, and surgery.[17] Hippocratic medicine, in fact, broke with the long tradition of logotherapy which preceded it, and transformed healing into the *muta ars* that Virgil called it (*Aeneid*, XII, 396-97). Medicine remained mute for some twenty-five centuries until Freud and the introduction of psychiatry into the medical curriculum only a few generations ago.

But the somatic bias of Hippocratic medicine did not go unchallenged by the ancient doctors. Plato chides Hippocrates by name in the *Phaedrus* (270c) for understanding the two-fold nature of man only somatically, and he persistently argues throughout the dialogues that the correct use of the psychologically effective word is the physician's most crucial art, that without it, his knowledge of herbs, diet, and surgery is ineffective. In the *Charmides,* to cite the most explicit example, Socrates is called "physician" (155b) and he agrees to heal the young boy of a persistent headache. He offers Charmides a medicinal herb, but explains that the plant alone will not suffice:

> For all good and evil, whether in the body or in the whole man, originates . . . in the soul, and overflows from thence, as if from the head into the eyes. And therefore, if the head and body are to be well, you must begin by curing the soul–that is the first and essential thing. And the cure of the soul, my dear youth, has to be effected by the use of certain charms, and these charms are fair words, and by them temperance comes and stays, there

---

these necessary "complaisances pour les malades": "les visites, les discours, la tenue, l'habit, la chevelure, les ongles, les odeurs . . ." (309). He also speaks of "Paroles, silence, dire ce qu'on veut, paroles prononcées à haute voix, ou nombreuses, viridiques ou mensongères" (347). Rabelais refers to Book Six of the *Epidemics* in both the prologue of 1548 and the Letter of 1552.

We know, too, of the influence on his imagination of the apocryphal Hippocratic novel included in the supplements to the Hippocratic anthology which circulated extensively in the sixteenth century. See Mikhail Bakhtin, *Rabelais and His World*, trans. Hélène Iswolsky (Cambridge: MIT, 1968) 360-61.

[17] J. M. Rather makes the point in his preface to the *Therapy of the Word*, xix. See also chapter iv, "The Word in Hippocratic Medicine," esp. 161-170. Laín Entralgo does not deny that Hippocratic medicine advocated the occasional use of the therapeutic word. He rather comments on the paucity and vagueness of the psychotherapy, especially in comparison with Plato.

health is speedily imparted, not only to the head, but to the whole body. (156e-157b)[18]

Freud could not have put it more succinctly! This passage from the *Charmides* constitutes the essential credo of verbal psychotherapy, and is the main premise of Rabelais's medico-literary enterprise. Though he cites Hippocrates and Galen most often, he also cites Plato, and he had been reading Plato since the 1520's, more than ten years before he went to medical school.[19] It seems likely that his reading of their texts was colored by his prior reading of the philosopher, for it is the Platonic principle of logotherapy which

---

[18] This designation of the word as "charm" is ubiquitous in the dialogues. See, for example, the *Euthydemus* (289e-290a) and the *Phaedrus* (267d). In both dialogues, speechmakers are said to cast spells and practice the enchanter's art. But Socrates too is called "spellbinder" and "enchanter"–in the *Meno* (80a) and in Alcibiades' famous speech in the *Symposium* (215-216c).

Most interesting is Socrates' commentary in the *Phaedo*. After Cebes asserts that the fear of death is a childish fear, Socrates concludes that we must daily enchant ourselves, or find an enchanter, until the charm has extinguished the fear in us (77a-78a). In the final pages of the dialogue (114a-d), the dying Socrates identifies that charm as myth, a beautiful and persuasive tale, which acts against the childish fear of death.

The *Phaedo* is crucial to Laín Entralgo's analysis of Platonic logotherapy. He argues that Plato rationalized the charm so that it lost the negative connotation of supernatural magic or enchantment and became consonant with the term *logos* in its double sense of "reasoning" and "the word": "The *epôdê*, which began as a conjuration or magical charm, has become (in the *Phaedo*) reasoning or a tale against harmful emotions" (113).

[19] The fact that Rabelais received his "baccalauréat" just six weeks after enrolling in medical school (Plattard 112), and that he gave his "cours de stage" on Hippocrates and Galen (see n. 15), would indicate that he had been studying Greek medicine for some time prior to his arrival in Montpellier. However, it seems certain that his study of Plato would predate his work on Hippocrates and Galen, for in the early Renaissance, the humanists customarily learned Greek in order to read (and often, *by* reading) Plato. We possess Rabelais's copy, with *ex-libris*, of the first edition of Aldus' Greek text (1513). Additionally, we know that Ficino's Latin translation was in the library at Fontenay-le-Comte, and we may speculate that Rabelais began with the translation and continued to consult it as he was learning to read the dialogues in the original. See Abel LeFranc, "Le Platon de Rabelais," *Bibliothèque du Bibliophile et du Bibliothécaire* (1901): 105-14, 169-81. We also possess Rabelais's copy of Ficino's translation of Dionysius the Aeropagite, found in 1932, with an *ex-libris* dated 1521 as well as an inscription mentioning Pico della Mirandola, the great Florentine Neo-platonist and friend of Ficino. See Robert Marichal, "L'Attitude de Rabelais devant le Néo-platonisme et l'italianisme," in *François Rabelais: Ouvrage publié pour le quatrième centenaire de sa mort* (Geneva: Droz, 1953) 181.

In sum, Rabelais's study of Plato and the Neo-platonists may be situated, with fair certainty, in the very early twenties, perhaps even in the late teens.

underlies his argumentation and which Hippocrates and Galen are called upon to substantiate.

An Aristotelian idea of logotherapy also intervenes in the prologues to *Le Quart Livre*, the notion of *katharsis* above all. We must be reminded that this doctrine has its roots in medical practice as well as in ritual and religion–it is "purgation" as well as "purification."[20] *Katharsis* may be described as a homeopathic technique whereby the emotions of pity and fear are brought to a paroxysm so that they may be suddenly exorcised. And in the *Poetics*, Aristotle diverges on a significant point from Plato, his teacher, and Rabelais follows him in this divergence, for both believe that the restoration of the body and the mind to their original equilibrium may be achieved by entering the world of "imitation life" or art. Aristotle's treatise on comedy is unfortunately missing, but for the Renaissance, he was the philosopher who had praised laughter as the essential characteristic of man.[21] It seems certain that Aristotle would have described comic *katharsis* just as he did the tragic, for the expulsion of fear and melancolia is audible in the *Ha, Ha* that Rabelais so often writes into his stories.

Plato too spoke of *katharsis* and, though he spurned the poet's arts of illusion in favor of philosophy, he often characterized the process like Aristotle. In the *Sophist* (229d-230e), for example, the Stranger describes the power of the educative word to cleanse the soul of discord, and thereby restore it to that "temperance" which Socrates had designated in the *Charmides* as the essence of good health (see citation above). But earlier in the *Sophist* (226c-228a), the Stranger spoke differently of *katharsis*, putting the emphasis less on purification *by* the word than on purification *of* the word. For, from the remotest origins of verbal psychotherapy, it had been recognized that the persuasive powers of language could be turned to evil as well as to good, and the word *pharmakon* means

---

[20] Laín Entralgo's discussion of the *Poetics* and of *katharsis* as a medical procedure is found 183-239.

[21] As we remember, Aristotle's famous formula (*De partibus animalium* III, 10) concludes Rabelais's introductory poem to the *Gargantua* (3):

> Mieux est de ris que de larmes escripre.
> Pource que rire est le propre de l'homme.

According to Bahktin, this formula "enjoyed immense popularity and was given a broader interpretation; laughter was seen as man's highest spiritual privilege, inaccessible to other creatures" (68).

both "remedy" and "poison."[22] Plato was obsessed with separating the remedy from the poison in the structure of the *pharmakon* because the sophists, his most pernicious enemies, called themselves healers just as Socrates did, and in the *Gorgias* (456b), we hear the speech-maker boasting that he is a more efficient doctor than his brother who is a physician. Socrates will not hear of it in the *Gorgias* and in the *Sophist,* the Stranger strives to distinguish once and for all between the just logos of the philosopher-physician and the unjust logos of sophistry. He applies the term *katharsis* to this process of separation, which he classifies as a technique of "diacritics," of "division," and which he defines as the "art of discerning or discriminating" better from worse, good words from bad (226c, d).

Rabelais's exposition of the therapeutic powers of his books and stories relies on the principles of both Platonic and Aristotelian logotherapy and both concepts of *katharsis* underlie his argumentation. Following Aristotle, Rabelais insists that his words are meant to purge his patients of melancolia,[23] and his therapy relies on theatrical techniques and concepts. The practice of medicine, as he describes it both in the Old Prologue and in the "Lettre à Odet," is an *art de paraître*. In order to generate the laughter that heals, the physician must engage in "prosopopée," defined in "La Briefve declaration" as "Desguisement. Fiction de personne" (703). His person must be masked, his clothing bright and cheerful, his face composed into a smile. There are no more pernicious doctors in Rabelais's book than those who tell the sufferer the brutal truth of his condition and several humorous examples are given of doctors who did so, thereby frightening their patients to death on the spot.[24] The

---

[22] Laín Entralgo makes this point while discussing the sophist Gorgias (93-95), but he does not dwell on the duplicity of the *pharmakon*. Jacques Derrida, to the contrary, builds his entire analysis of the *Phaedrus* around the *pharmakon* in its double sense of "remedy" and "poison"; "La Pharmacie de Platon," *La Dissémination* (Paris: Seuil, 1972) 69-197.

[23] In the first paragraph of the "Lettre à Odet," Rabelais suggests that melancolia or depression is the malady which troubles his patients: "... plusieurs gens *languoureux, malades,* or autrement *faschez et desolez* avoit à la lecture d'icelles, trompé leurs *ennuictz,* temps joyeusement passé, et repceu alaigresse et consolation nouvelle" (517, my italics).

[24] I cite only one of several "case studies" given in the "Lettre à Odet": "Pareillement est de Cl. Galen, *lib.* 4, *comment. in 6 Epidemi.* grandement vituperé Quintus son praecepteur en medicine, lequel à certain malade en Rome, homme honorable, luy disant: 'Vous avez desjeuné, nostre maistre, vostre haleine me sent le vin': arroguamment respondit: 'La tienne me sent la fiebvre: duquel est le flair et l'odeur plus delicieux, de la fiebvre ou du vin?'" (519).

good physician, to the contrary, cultivates the beneficient lie, the healing illusion. Indeed, so crucial is illusion to the physician's success that in the "Letter to Odet," Rabelais moves the whole therapeutic enterprise into the theatrical arena. The practice of medicine in his opinion takes place "in lusio," in the game:

> ... Hippocrates en plusieurs lieux, mesmement on sixiesme livre des *Epidemies*, descrivant l'institution du medicin son disciple: Soranus Ephesien, Oribasius, Cl. Galen, Hali Abbas, autres auteurs consequens pareillement, l'ont composé en gestes, maintien, reguard, touchement, contenence, grace, honesteté, netteté de face, vestemens, barbe, cheveulx, mains, bouche, voire jusques à particularizer les ongles, comme s'il deust jouer le rolle de quelque Amoureux ou Poursuyvant en quelque insigne comoedie, ou descendre en camp clos pour combatre quelque puissant ennemy. Defaict la practique de Médicine bien proprement est par Hippocrates comparée à un combat et farce jouée à trois personnages: le malade, le medicin, la maladie. (517-18)

Medicine depends on "conduites masquées"[25] and it is a game of love and war. Eros and Logos rediscover their traditional unity in Rabelais's doctrine,[26] and the physician plays an androgynous part in the play. On one hand, a male and aggressive warrior in the *agon* of love, his words strive to penetrate "to the inside," "descendre en camp clos pour combatre," and in both the prologue of 1548 and

---

[25] A phrase used by Jean Starobinski in his study of "Stendhal pseudonyme," *L'Oeil vivant* (Paris: Gallimard, 1961) 191.

[26] See Laín Entralgo's discussion of Pleithô, goddess of amorous seduction and persuasive speech, whom Aeschylus called Aphrodite's daughter (64-67).

For the union of Eros and Logos in Socrates' nature, see "La Pharmacie de Platon," esp. 133-36. Derrida reminds that, in the *Phaedrus*, Socrates is seduced by Eros to speak of love and he discerns Socrates' features in Diotima's portrait of the god of love in the *Symposium* (203c-e). We also recall Alcibiades' famous final speech of this dialogue where, in order to express Socrates' seductive powers and the erotic mania he incites, Alcibiades compares the effect of his words to the music of Marsyas, the satyr:

> Now the only difference, Socrates, between you and Marsyas is that you can get the same effect without any instrument at all—with nothing but a few simple words, not even poetry.... For the moment I hear (Socrates) speak I am smitten with a kind of sacred rage, worse than any Corybant, and my heart jumps into my mouth and the tears into my eyes.... (215c-e)

Trans. Michael Joyce in *The Collected Dialogues of Plato*, ed. Edith Hamilton and Huntington Cairns (Princeton: Princeton UP, 1973) 567.

the letter of 1552, Rabelais cites Plato and Averroes as authorities for this penetration–healing words should operate a "transfusion des esperitz . . . du medicin *en la persone* du malade" (519, my italics). But on the other hand, the physician must also play a seductive, feminine role in the game and in the same paragraph as the above citation, Rabelais compares his own wiles to those of Julia, lascivious daughter of Octavian Augustus. For the efficacy of words derives from their ancient and mysterious power to charm and seduce the mind of the patient, to beguile him or her back to good health.

But seduction implies deceit and betrayal, and at this point in Rabelais's argumentation, the Platonic concept of *katharsis* becomes crucial. He is now faced with Plato's task of distinguishing the good medicine of the philosopher-physician from the poisonous words of those sixteenth-century sophists at the Sorbonne. And Rabelais's enterprise of separation is doomed to failure just as Plato's was and for the same reason–the sophists are "in lusio" with him and their tactics are identical to his own. They too put on the smiling face of virtue and good will; like his words, their words are masked. "Cafards, Cagotz, Matagotz, . . ." (717)–all these epithets are variations on the single theme of hypocrisy, and the essential strategy of the hypocrite is to use words to create the appearance of virtue where there is only vice, of truth where there is only the emptiness of the lie. Neither is hypocrisy a secular vice nor a minor sin in Rabelais's mind–to the contrary, it is the very essence of evil. When we use words to deceive and destroy, we imitate the Betrayer himself who shattered paradise with his lies:

> Car en Grec calumnie est dicte diabole. Voyez combien detestable est devant Dieu et les Anges, ce vice dict Calumnie (c'est quand on impugne le bien faict, quand on mesdit des choses bonnes) que par iceluy non par autre, quoy que plusieurs sembleroient plus enormes, sont les Diables d'enfer nommez et appellez. (718)

Rabelais is on the side of the angels, we never have any reason to doubt that. But from the outside, his good medicine bears a dangerous resemblance to the Devil's poison. Both depend on the art of "semblance-making" (*Sophist* 235d-236b) to create illusions and manipulate appearances, both engage in "conduites masquées," both lie. How then may the beneficient lie be distinguished from the evil one? What may be used as a *katharmos* to separate the remedy from the poison in the structure of the *pharmakon*?

As Derrida argued in "La Pharmacie de Platon," Plato's solution in the *Phaedrus* was to strive to confer the terrible mind-darkening powers on the written word, which he associates with fraud and the mask, forgetfulness, oblivion, and death.[27] Speech is posited as the remedy to this poison, the oral dialectic of the philosopher-physician. Plato's valorization of the spoken word over writing became an instinctive mode of Western thought and Rabelais's prologues to *Le Quart Livre* show its influence. As was argued with the fable of the jays and the magpies, he is very troubled by the written word, by its endemic error and illusion which intrude to corrupt the medicine of his stories. For this reason, he constantly exhorts us to bring his writing back to its source of truth in speech. Like Plato, Rabelais ascribes the paternal position to the spoken word–he calls it "father" of the printed book, "ma paternité."[28] Writing is, in his mind, the dangerously prodigal son.

---

[27] The fulcrum of Derrida's analysis of the *Phaedrus* is the myth of Theuth (274c-75b), the god of number and calculation, geometry and astronomy, draughts and dice, and above all, of writing. He offers his latest and most wonderful invention to King Thamus as a *pharmakon*, a "remedy" for memory and wisdom. But the king refuses the gift, and in so doing, he too uses the word *pharmakon* to condemn writing as a "poison":

> If men learn this, it will implant forgetfulness in their souls; they will cease to exercise memory because they rely on that which is written, calling things to remembrance no longer from within themselves, but by means of external marks. What you have discovered is a recipe (*pharmakon*) not for memory but for reminder. (275. Trans. R. Hackworth, *Collected Dialogues* 520)

Derrida reproaches translators for using a word (here, "recipe") which does not take into account the duplicity of the *pharmakon*:

> Quand un mot s'inscrit comme la citation d'un autre sens de ce même mot, quand l'avant-scène textuelle du mot *pharmakon*, tout en signifiant *remède*, cite, ré-cite et donne à lire ce qui *dans le même mot* signifie, en un autre lieu et à une autre profondeur de la scène, *poison* (par exemple, car *pharmakon* veut dire encore d'autres choses), le choix d'un seul de ces mots français par le traducteur a pour premier effet de neutraliser le jeu citationel, "l'anagramme," . . . (111)

See esp. 84-133 of "La Pharmacie de Platon" for Derrida's exploration of the myth of Theuth.

[28] See the citation, note 2 above, from Rabelais's prologue of 1548. See also Derrida 84-95, where he argues that in Plato's dialogues the spoken word is characteristically designated as the father of language and the origin of value.

Yet, Rabelais was also a man of his own time and the very concept of "Renaissance" is bound into a praise of the written word–it is "la restitution des bonnes *lettres*" (29, my italics), to use Rabelais's own definition. No epoch of human history has loved books and writing as much as the Renaissance, for had not the written word miraculously preserved intact, for some twenty centuries or more, the wisdom of the ancients whom the humanists so cherished? And of all the ancients, they were most dazzled by Plato whose dialogues had been almost lost to the Western world for many centuries.[29] Therefore, in great part because of Plato, Rabelais's logocentrism could not have been as vigorous and he was hence forced to openly confront the duplicity which Plato submerged in the *Phaedrus*: that writing as well as speaking can be used to teach and to heal and, conversely, that speech can deceive and destroy. In his earlier books, Rabelais, like Plato, had strived to push evil to the outside of the magic circle of the book-bottle-barrel, he had banished his enemies' bad words to the chaos beyond the safekeep of Thelema.[30] But by 1548-52, evil has seeped into the inside. Rabelais's enemies are now "in lusio" with him, and he does not know how to push them away.

Nonetheless, Rabelais does offer one valid touchstone for separating the good medicine of the logotherapist from the poison of sophistry–the ineffable and elusive quality that we call "intention." The good doctor is motivated by love, *caritas*, and all his games of illusion and appearance are mounted for the sole purpose of giving aid and succor to his fellow creatures:

---

[29] It is true that the Latin Middle Ages were imbued with Platonic and Neo-platonic conceptions. However, this knowledge was gained indirectly through such writers as St. Augustine, Johannes Scotus Erigena and Boethius. Medieval readers had direct knowledge of just one dialogue, the partial version of the *Timaeus*. See Raymond Klibansky, *The Continuity of the Platonic Tradition* (London: The Warburg Institute, 1939) 21-37.

[30] We recall the inscription on the "Abbaye de Thélème" which refuses entry to the hypocrites and bigots who use words falsely and which invites inside those who strive toward the right use of words:

> Cy entrez vous qui le sainct evangile
> En sens agile annoncez, quoy qu'on gronde,
> Ceans aurez un refuge et bastille
> Contre l'hostile erreur, qui tant postille
> Par son faux stile empoizonner le monde:

(143)

> Semblablement pourroit le medicin ainsi desguisé en face et habitz, . . . respondre à ceulx qui trouveroient la prosopopée estrange: "Ainsi me suis je acoustré, non pour me guorgiaser et pomper; mais pour le gré du malade, lequel je visite: auquel seul je veulx entierement complaire: en rien ne l'offenser ne fascher." (518)

Bad doctors, to the contrary, are motivated by *philautia,* self-love, self-interest. The arts of sophistry are arts of gain and self-aggrandizement and, as Rabelais stipulates in the prologue of 1552, *sanita et guadain* (535) are antithetical values. *Philautia* causes one to harm, even to kill, others and as Couillatris' imitators learn to their chagrin, it is ultimately a self-destructive motivation.

Indeed, the purpose of the prologue of 1552 is to display the many nefarious effects of self-love. When we ponder the fable of Couillatris, we understand that Rabelais conceives of *philautia* as a political as well as a personal vice. It is the fatal disease of the city. At the beginning of the story, Jupiter as king grieves over the state of his kingdom which is besieged by enemies from without and from within. Of the two, however, the enemy within is the more pernicious, and Jupiter and his court chastise Rameau and Galland for their "petites philauties," ". . . lesquelles, viventes allumoient couillonniquement le feu de faction, simulte, sectes couillonniques et partialté" (528) in the land.[31]

Panurge, we remember, painted a similar portrait of a sick society in 1546. "Un monde sans debtes" (TL, ch. 3) is a world without *caritas* where people refuse to help one another, thus precipitating corporeal, civil, and cosmic catastrophe. Even farther back, in his

---

[31] Edwin Duval, *The Design of Rabelais's* Quart Livre *de* Pantagruel (Geneva: Droz, 1998) 49-63, places the anecdote of Rameau and Galland–not the story of Couillatris–at both the figurative and literal center of the 1552 prologue. Rather than the issue of "mediocrité," Duval feels that the new prologue focusses on "the problem of stalemate, of the irreducible antagonism between diametrically opposed factions" (58). The emblem of Rameau and Galland's stalemate is offered by Priapus' fable of the dog destined to take the fox who is, in its turn, destined never to be captured. Priapus' solution to the insoluble dilemma of Pierre Rameau and Pierre Galland is to petrify them, make them into "pierres mortes" cemented into Notre Dame de Paris. They stand as an "obvious negative counterpart to the 'lapidus vivi' or 'pierres vives' that Saint Peter would like to see 'built up' . . . into a 'spiritual house of God' . . . . Thanks to Priapus' burlesque and punning wit, the emblem of all irreducible antagonisms highlighted at the center of the prologue is specifically valorized as an emblem of *anticaritas* . . ." (60).

introduction to the medical letters of Jean Manardi published in 1532, Doctor Rabelais offered this diagnosis of the ills of France:

> Si je soumets la chose dans son ensemble à un examen attentif, et si je la pèse . . . , cette Odyssée d'erreurs ne me semble pas avoir d'autre origine que cette honteuse "philautie" tant blâmée par les philosophes . . . . (980)

This citation could stand as the epigraph of *Le Quart Livre*, "l'Odyssée d'erreurs" of 1548-52. *Philautia* has shattered what should be a community of citizens held together by mutual care and respect into the islands of self-interest which the *escales* represent.

"For what ought we to admire a poet?" Aeschylus asks in Aristophanes' *Frogs*. ". . . (B)ecause we make people in the cities better," answers Euripides.[32] It is a very ancient function of the logotherapist to heal the city, and with the fable of Couillatris, Rabelais offers comedy's traditional remedy to urban ills—the green world, Couillatris' forest and his garden. The woodsman's *mediocrité* is expressed, of course, by asking for the return of just his own humble ax. But it is also expressed by his using the profits from the sale of the gold and silver axes to buy a farm.[33] Couillatris becomes a *planteur de choux*. In Rabelais's world, the cultivator is a recurrent figure of sanity and health, and agriculture is a main metaphor of *caritas* and "exchange," of giving back to the earth all that one takes from it and providing nourishment for other humans. Agriculture is also a metaphor of sexual exchange, of what Panurge called in *Le Tiers Livre*, "le debvoir de mariage" (367), and Priapus, "guardian des jardins en terre" (530) is present in the Prologue of 1552 to remind the Gods, and us, that "il faut cultiver notre jardin."[34] The creation of human life and its sustenance de-

---

[32] *The Comedies of Aristophanes*, trans. W. J. Hickie (London: George Bell, 1893) 583. Laín Entralgo cites this passage during his discussion of Aristotle whom he calls a "theoretician of urban life" (197) and in whose writings the bond between tragedy and the *polis* is constantly affirmed. See esp. 204-11.

[33] "Il en achapte force mestairies, force granges, force censes, force mas, force bordes et bordieux, force cassines: prez, vignes, boys, terres labourables, pastis, estangs, moulins, jardins, saulsayes; beufz, vaches, brebis, moutons, chevres, truyes, pourceaulx, asnes, chevaulx, poulles, cocqs, chappons, poulletz, oyes, jars, canes, canars, et du menu" (532).

[34] The phrase, of course, comes from Voltaire's *Candide*. In the 1552 prologue, the link between the forest, garden, and sexuality is affirmed by Priapus' pun on the

pends on this affectionate giving of "real money": one's substance, one's self. Love, *Eros* as well as *Agape*, is the medicine contained in the fable of Couillatris, the antidote for the poison of *philautia* which was despoiling the city and its inhabitants.

Yet, if this is so, if the philosopher-physician is motivated by love and if he dispenses love as a medicine to others, how is it that Rabelais could compare himself to "Timon le Misanthrope" at the end of the 1548 prologue (719-20)? Timon hated men and withdrew from the community, and in both "l'éloge des dettes" and in "La Briefve Declaration," the misanthrope is chastised for these vices.[35] And how is it that the book, offered so insistently as a remedy, can be offered by Timon as a rope so that his enemies may kill themselves on his fig tree, "(se) pendre et estrangler" (720)? Rabelais's medical arguments come full circle in the prologues to *Le Quart Livre*. He becomes what he hates.

The problem of Timon and his rope takes us back to the end of *Le Tiers Livre*, to the description of the disturbingly ambiguous "Pantagruélion" (chapters 49-52), Rabelais's image of the *pharmakon*. He must have chosen *cannabis* as the book's emblem because of its double nature. On the one hand, since antiquity, *cannabis* had been the remedy of all remedies, cureall for every ailment of the body and mind, "l'Idée et exemplaire de toute joyeuse perfection" (506).[36] But on the other, rope is made from hemp,

---

word "coingnée": "Roy Juppiter, on temps que . . . j'estois guardian des jardins en terre, je notay que ceste diction Coingnée est equivocque à plusieurs choses. Elle signifie un certain instrument, par le service duquel est fendu et couppé boys. Signifie aussi (au moins jadis signifioit) la femelle bien à poinct et souvent gimbretiletolletée. Et veidz que tout bon compaignon appelloit sa guarse fille de joye, ma Coingnée" (530).

[35] In chapter 3 of *Le Tiers Livre*, Panurge names Timon among those "briguans, assassineurs, empoisonneurs" (363) whose misanthrophy will throw the world into chaos. Timon is also castigated in the "Briefve declaration" in an entry for the "Lettre à Odet": "*Misanthropes*. Haissans les hommes. Fuyans la compaignie des homes. Ainsi feut surnommé Timon Athenien. Cic. 4. *Tuscul*." (703).

[36] Rabelais enumerates the medicinal properties of the "Pantagruélion" in chapter 51 of the *Tiers Livre*:

> . . . le jus d'icelle exprimé et instillé dedans les aureilles tue toute espece de vermine, qui y seroit née par putrefaction, et tout aultre animal qui dedans seroit entré . . . Et est l'eaue ainsi caillée (du jus du Pantagruélion) remede praesent aux chevaulx coliqueux, et qui tirent des flans. La racine d'icelle, cuicte en eaue, remollist les nerfz retirez, les joinctures contractes, les podagres sclirrhotiques, et les gouttes nouées. Si promptement voulez guerir une bruslure, soit d'eaue, soit de feu, applicquez y du Pantagruelion crud . . . (507)

such as Timon's rope, and rope *kills*.³⁷ It is, of course, meant to kill "them" and cure "us," but the *pharmakon* is unstable and unpredictable, and there is always the grave and essential danger of achieving the result opposite to that desired and expected.³⁸ For Rabelais's enemies seem to have thrived on what was meant to be a "poison" for them. And his friends, himself, were gravely menaced by the "remedy."

Rabelais was deeply troubled by the menacing duplicity of his *pharmakon* for, significantly, he brings the entire edifice of "le Pantagruélion" to bear on the problem of *katharsis* in the Platonic sense, the problem of "diacritics":

> Verité vous diray. Mais pour y entrer, car elle est d'accés assez scabreux et difficile, je vous demande. Si j'avoys en ceste bouteille mis deux cotyles de vin, et une d'eau *ensemble bien fort meslez, comment les demesleriez vous? comment les separeriez vous* ? de maniere que vous me rendriez l'eau à part sans le vin, le vin sans l'eau, en mesure pareille que les y auroys mis . . . . comment en housteriez vous l'eau entierement? *Comment les purifieriez vous?*
> . . . Respondez. Par ma figue, vous seriez bien empeschez. (509-10, my italics)

The prologue of 1548 takes up where "le Pantagruélion" left off in 1546, with the "mixed wine," red and white, of the fable of the jays and the magpies and the problem of purification which it poses. Rabelais struggled for four more years, from 1548 to 1552, to operate the *katharsis*, to clearly distinguish the opposites which he

---

Many of these same medicinal virtues are listed in Pliny's *Natural History*, XX, xcvii.

³⁷ See chapter 51 of the *Tiers Livre*: "Aultres avons ouy sus l'instant que Atropos leurs couppoit le fillet de vie, soy griefvement complaignans et lamentans de ce que Pantagruel les tenoit à la guorge. Mais (las) ce n'estoit mie Pantagruel. Il ne feut oncques rouart, c'estoit Pantagruelion, faisant office de hart, et leurs servant de cornette . . ." (506).

³⁸ Consider the fate of Couillatris' imitators in the 1552 Prologue. Consider also the sad case of Bringuenarilles, "avalleur de moulins à vent" (578). Though the giant fell seriously ill of indigestion caused by eating "paelles, paellons, chaudrons, coquasses, lichefretes, et marmites . . . en faulte de moulins à vent" (578), he would have survived were it not for the good doctors who proposed a more natural regimen. He died of their "remedy": "Le bon Bringuenarilles (helas) mourut estranglé mangeant un coing de beurre frays à la gueule d'un four chauld, par l'ordonnance des medicins" (581).

had confounded: I/thou; reader/writer; remedy/poison; good/bad; love/hate. But despite all his efforts, the categories collapse back into one another, and the wine of these prologues remains "mixed." Indeed, it is true that we are "empeschez" by *Le Quart Livre*: we, the reader and the writer, the reader-writer, François Rabelais, *docteur en medicine*.

CHAPTER TWO

"L'ISLE MEDAMOTHI": RABELAIS'S ITINERARIES
OF ANXIETY

As the first port of call of the 1552 *Quart Livre*, "l'isle Medamothi" deserves our particular attention–it stands at the beginning of Pantagruel and Panurge's sea voyage, and of their quest for "le mot de la dive Bouteille." Yet it is a difficult episode to pay attention *to*. Medamothi means Nowhere, "Nul lieu en Grec" (BD 705), and the island seems well-named, for on Nowhere nothing much happens. The voyagers land there after four days out to sea and find a market filled with "choses": paintings and tapestries and animals. Each buys a "thing" or two. Then Gargantua's envoy arrives bringing "things" from the father to his son: a bird, a letter, and "quelques livres joyeulx" (544). Pantagruel composes a letter of reply, and sends his father the "belles et rares choses" (545) he has purchased (chapters 2-4). This seems an unadventurous beginning for an adventure story.

But this rather dull episode acquires an intense interest if we look at it in relation to *Le Quart Livre* of 1548, for there is no Medamothi episode in the first version of the story.[1] The 1548 *Quart Livre* was abandoned by Rabelais in the most astonishing fashion–halfway through the voyage, at the beginning of the episode on "l'isle des Macraeons," and in the middle of a sentence. Four years later, Rabelais picked up that sentence where he had left it and carried the story forward. But he also went back and extensively revised all that he had written in 1548. As discussed in Chapter One, he suppressed the old prologue and added two new ones

---

[1] References from the 1548 edition are taken from the Plattard edition, *Le Quart Livre de Pantagruel (édition dite partielle, Lyon, 1548)* (Paris: Champion, 1909).

in its place: the true prologue of 1552 and a pre-prologue in the form of a letter to his patron, Odet de Chastillon. He added a glossary of terms, "La Briefve declaration d'aulcunes dictions plus obscures," and he expanded the 1548 episodes so greatly that most are doubled, and some are tripled, in length in the 1552 version. Yet the kernel of the old story still shows through into the new and the 1548 sequence of *escales* is retained–with the single exception of Medamothi. What happened that caused Rabelais to add this new episode? Why must the voyage of 1552 go to Nowhere, and why must it go there first?

To my mind, the answers to these questions must be sought in the presence of Gargantua on Medamothi, for the father is absent from the first version of the book. In the 1548 departure, "Pantagruel (prend) congé du bon Gargantua son père" (Plattard 71), and he also takes leave of all that Gargantua represents, the medieval tradition of storytelling from which these books were born, and Rabelais's own past books which are still so closely tied to that tradition. By the chanting of Psalm 114, "Quand Israel hors d'Ægypte sortit,"[2] Pantagruel expresses his ambivalence toward the Gargantuan past. On the one hand, the Exodus is a going into exile; it is an act of distress. Pantagruel seems filled with regret for the fatherland he is leaving behind, and with dread of the "voyes perilleuses" (537) that lie before him. The Exodus evokes that profound sense of transcendental homelessness which, we repeat, is an underlying emotion of *Le Quart Livre*.[3] But on the other hand, the Exodus is an act of liberation–leaving a land of captivity to find one's own place, to found one's own home–and the fearful seas on which the voyagers sail are also the seas of poetic discovery, the seas of the modernist enterprise.[4] Though dread and desire remain mixed in the departure of 1548 and both past and future exert their pull, the episode comes to rest on the itinerary of discovery, the modernist itinerary.[5] Pantagruel leaves the lands of Gargantua behind and

---

[2] The full title of the psalm, as quoted here, was not given until 1552. In 1548, Rabelais gives this truncated version: "Quand Israel, etc." (Plattard 73).

[3] For the importance of the Exodus story to *Le Quart Livre*, see the discussion in our Introduction, 20-2 and in Chapter 4, esp. 114-21.

[4] Margaret Ferguson makes a similar point about Joachim Du Bellay's use of the sea as a metaphor for poetic discovery, "The Exile's Defense: Du Bellay's *La Deffence et illustration de la langue françoyse*," PMLA 93 (1978): 278.

[5] My sense of "itineraries" has been influenced by my reading of Thomas M. Greene, *The Light in Troy: Imitation and Discovery in Renaissance Poetry* (New

goes in quest of the future and the new. He is seeking his own logos which he calls "le mot de la dive Bouteille."

But this quest falters and fails and is abandoned in 1548, for past will not stay behind Pantagruel, it will not stay in the past. The voyagers have five adventures and they survive a fearful tempest at sea,[6] but only to land in another country of the old, "l'isle des Macraeons," the land of "Gens qui vivent longuement," as Rabelais will explain in 1552 (BD 708). In the 1548 fragment, upon arriving on the island, the voyagers meet an old man, "un vieil Macrobe." As he steps forward to greet them, the shadow of the past once again falls on the book and an old drama threatens to be reenacted[7]–the drama of the father who has been reborn or resurrected in every book of a cycle clearly intended at the outset to belong to the son. It is to forestall the resurgence of that tenacious, intrusive ghost that Rabelais throws down his pen in 1548 and cuts off the book: "Vray est que / *quia plus n'en dict*." "I am at a nonplus (Cotgrave) and say no more."[8]

By suppressing the resurrection of the old in his book, however, Rabelais also suppresses the birth of the new he is seeking. Thus he is led to repentance, to "pentimento," as the painters say, and in

---

Haven: Yale UP, 1982), Terence Cave, *The Cornucopian Text: Problems of Writing in the French Renaissance* (London: Oxford UP, 1979) and David Quint, *Origin and Originality in Renaissance Literature: Versions of the Source* (New Haven: Yale UP, 1983). All three explore what Greene calls the "double bind" (193) of the Renaissance artist who simultaneously undertook two contradictory "voyages": moving back to the source to sketch a myth of origins and also moving forward to assert one's freedom from the past by sketching a modernist myth of growth away from origins. (See esp. Greene 14-19, 194-196; Quint's preface ix-xii, and first chapter, 1-31; and Cave, esp. the chapters on "Copia" 3-34 and "Imitation" 35-77.)

[6] The sequence of episodes in the 1548 edition, after the departure of chapter 1, is as follows: Dindenault (chs. 2-3); "l'isle Ennasin" (ch. 4); "l'isle de Chely" (ch. 5); "les Chicquanous" (ch. 6); Bringuenarilles (ch 7); the tempest (chs. 8-10); "l'isle des Macraeons" (ch. 11).

[7] I intend this reading to apply only to the 1548 version of "l'isle des Macraeons," just a dozen lines long, and not to the episode as it came to be developed in 1552. On the relation of the two versions, I share Jean Plattard's point of view: "Il est possible . . . qu'en 1548, rien n'existait encore du développement sur les héros de l'isle des Macréons" (53).

[8] Duval suggests a very different interpretation of this expression, based on his conviction that *quia* should not be read as one word: "The original printer's accidental conjoining of 'qui' and 'a' has led to a common misreading of this line first proposed by Plattard in his edition of the incomplete *Quart Livre* of 1548 . . . . The phrase obviously means that there is more to the book than what appears here but that the author (or printer) will not (or cannot) produce the rest: 'He who has it says no more', or 'Let him who has it say no more'" (*Design* 17 n. 3).

1552 he lays a centripetal itinerary over the centrifugal one he had inscribed in 1548. He returns to the beginning of the book, to his own beginnings, and writes Gargantua into the voyage. The first signs of this repentance appear in the 1552 departure which casts a retrospective eye on the 1548 book at its point of rupture on "l'isle des Macraeons,"[9] and a significant repair is made to forestall the recurrence of that rupture. Panurge or Xenomanes (but not Pantagruel, it is important to note) leaves Gargantua an itinerary of the voyage: "Icelluy *pour certaines et bonnes causes* avoit à Gargantua laissé et signé en sa grande et universelle Hydrographie la route qu'ilz tiendroient visitans l'oracle de la dive Bouteille Bacbuc" (537 my italics). Gargantua follows the map and comes to Medamothi, the place especially prepared to receive him in 1552. He comes inscribed in writing, as a text carried to his son by a messenger called Malicorne.

But Gargantua is not allowed to come immediately, for he is not the only father of Rabelais's books. The drama of origins that occurs on Medamothi is complicated because these stories have two genealogical lines, two sets of precursors. Side by side and interwoven with the medieval sources represented by Gargantua, the classical sources, the humanist influences, have always been present in Rabelais's books. And these paternal presences also play their part in the drama that occurs on Medamothi. This is a Greek island, with Greek kings. The things purchased in the markets of Medamothi are classical things—images and animals and, above all, books from antiquity are found there, books that stand in opposition to Gargantua's "livres joyeulx."

It is thus a double drama of influence which is enacted on Medamothi. On this island, Rabelais struggles to work out his relationship with both sets of fathers, to resolve the burden of the double heritage, classical and medieval, that haunts him. And in the midst of these two pasts, he strives to carve out an imaginative space of his own, a space of originality. He calls this space Nowhere, he calls it Medamothi.[10]

---

[9] "Car sans naufrage, sans dangier, sans perte de leurs gens, en grande serenité (exceptez un jour prés l'isle des Macreons) feirent le voyage de Indie superieure en moins de quatre moys . . ." (539-40).

[10] Certainly the most important study of the son's relationship with the father and with "parent" texts is that of Carla Freccero, *Father Figures: Genealogy and Narrative Structure in Rabelais* (Ithaca: Cornell UP, 1991). While she concentrates

As Paul Smith has pointed out (165-78), two related concepts underlie the first chapter of Medamothi: the Horatian affirmation of *ut pictura poesis* and the doctrine of the imitation of the ancients. This island, "belle à l'oeil et plaisante" (540), is dominated by the desire for vision, and the desire is double. The king of Medamothi, Philophanes, is not only "couvoiteux de veoir" like his brother Philotheamon–he is also eager to be seen, to give vision as well as to achieve it. Philophanes is "couvoiteux de veoir et estre veu" (BD 706). And in the markets of his kingdom, visual images are for sale: paintings and tapestries and animals that are said to be "au vif painct(s)", "selon le naturel representé(s)" (540-1). However, these things do not represent nature directly, they rather imitate nature as it has already been imitated in art. They are copies, "transumpts" is Rabelais's word (541), of originals that are named or clearly implied in the text, and with the exception of Frère Jean's purchases, these originals are found in the literature of the ancients. This seems a double exercise in the kind of imitation called *ekphrasis*: written stories are first depicted as paintings and then translated back into words.

But a knot of complexity surrounds the idea of imitation as it is developed on Medamothi. Philophanes, "desirous of seeing and being seen," is absent from the island. His allegiance to his brother, who only wants to see, has led the king elsewhere; Philotheamon has married the daughter of Nearby (540) "l'Infante du royaulme des Engys" ("Auprès," BD 706), and Philophanes has gone to the wedding. Until the king of sight returns–or is brought back–we cannot see the pictures for sale in his markets. The first things purchased, by Frère Jean, Panurge, Epistemon, and Rhizotome, offer only flashes of vision, incomplete images. Like the text found buried with Gargantua's book (G, ch. 1), these things are "fanfreluches," texts with holes in them. And these holes, as well as the transfer of vision away from Medamothi and its deferral to the future, are complexities stemming from the idea of the "transumpt," the kind of copy these things are.

---

on the ambivalent relationship of Pantagruel with Gargantua and does not discuss the classical inheritance, the thesis of her study is similar to my own in this chapter: that "the story of the son inaugurates the new and repudiates the past. But only in part, for the story of the son turns to the father to find both its origin and the terms of its difference" (2-3). See especially chapters 2 and 3 (8-89) where the problems of genealogy and filial succession in the *Pantagruel* and the *Gargantua* are discussed.

According to Cotgrave, "transumpt" is a legal term meaning "an exemplification; the copie of a Record." But *transumptio*, or *metalepsis*, is also a rhetorical trope, one which "transfers," "takes across" from an earlier word, image, or fable to a later figure.[11] As all forms of imitation, transumption involves a diachronic and allusive relationship between texts; it is technique of "echoing" the past, according to Hollander, "a representation set against time" in Bloom's words.[12] The rub, however, is that transumption is elusive as well as allusive. The movement across tropes or texts used tropically involves the suppression of logically necessary intermediate figures—one moves from A to C, for example, without stating B—so that an absence is created at transumption's center, a missing link which must be recovered by interpretation. Transumption thus operates by a "rhetorical sleight of hand, . . . a momentary sinking out of sight of the normal chain of signification or filiation; when meaning emerges it has been transformed."[13]

But no meaning emerges from the first things purchased on Medamothi, for they do not complete the act of transumption. Not only does the chain of filiation sink out of sight momentarily, it is

---

[11] For a history of the trope of transumption, see John Hollander's appendix to *The Figure of Echo: A Mode of Allusion in Milton and After* (Berkeley: U of California P, 1981) 133-49. Quintilian in *Institutes* 8. 6 37-39 was the first to describe transumption and he treats it dismissively, as a kind of phonetic punning:

> It is the nature of *metalepsis* to form a kind of intermediate step between the term transferred and the thing to which it is transferred, having no meaning in itself, but merely providing a transition. It is a trope with which to claim acquaintance, rather than one which we are ever likely to require to use. The commonest example is the following: *cano* is a synonym for *canto* and *canto* for *dico*, therefore *cano* is a synonym for *dico*, the intermediate step being provided by *canto*. We need not waste any more time over it. (Quoted by Hollander, 135)

The trope continued to cause disapproval and perplexity during the Middle Ages and the Renaissance and then fell largely into disuse. It was Angus Fletcher who, in a long footnote on Milton, first called modern critical attention to this trope in *Allegory: The Theory of a Symbolic Mode* (Ithaca: Cornell UP, 1964) 241. Harold Bloom appropriates transumption as a name for the ultimate trope of revision, *A Map of Misreading* (London: Oxford UP, 1973) esp. 101-03. Hollander devotes two chapters of *The Figure of Echo* to transumption, "Echo Metaleptic" (113-32) and the appendix cited above. Leonard Barkan in *Transuming Passion: Ganymede and the Erotics of Humanism* (Stanford: Stanford UP, 1991) uses the term to describe the "belated re-imaginings" (48) of the myth of Ganymede in particular, and in general, the ways in which images of past culture are incorporated into present art and thought.

[12] *Map of Misreading* 103.
[13] Barkan, *Transuming Passion* 44.

snapped off altogether. A past text or painting is evoked, and the promise of vision in the future is held out—like Philophanes, it seems tantalizingly Nearby. But the present, the *ekphrasis* itself, is erased, and we are given no means of recovering it, no ground for interpretation. It is not until we reach the things purchased by Pantagruel that transumption is completed and a positive strategy of imitation emerges. Pantagruel's things repair the holes of vision and bring the king of sight back to his island.

Frère Jean begins the cycle of blindness by buying two tableaux: "en l'un des quelz estoit au vif painct le visaige d'un appellant: en l'aultre estoit le protraict d'un varlet qui cherche maistre . . . . painct(s) et inventé(s) par maistre Charles Charmois" (540-1), a contemporary painter. But here is the hole: though we are told that the depiction of these figures was accomplished "en toutes qualitez requises," we are not told how—which "gestes, maintien, minois, alleures, physionomie, et affections" (541) they exhibit. And thus like "le Faquin" who pays for the smell of roast beef with the sound of money (TL, 469-70) Frère Jean buys these paintings with counterfeit coin, "monnaie de singe," gestures and grimaces which degrade them and express his scorn for imitation as a servile and simian thing.[14]

The tableau purchased by Panurge recedes farther from our grasp. He buys the copy of a copy that has its original in Ovid:

> un grand tableau painct et transumpt de l'ouvrage jadis faict à l'aiguille par Philomela exposante et representante à sa soeur Progné, comment son beaufrere Tereus l'avoit despucellée: et sa langue couppée, afin que tel crime ne decelast. (541)

This description, like that of Frère Jean's paintings, omits details of the image, but the account of Panurge's tableau goes one step farther into negativity. The narrator himself intervenes to express how

---

[14] As R. Wittkower notes, "Imitation, Eclecticism, and Genius," *Aspects of the Eighteenth Century*, ed. Earl R. Wasserman (Baltimore: Johns Hopkins UP, 1965) 146-47, the ancient phrase "Ars simia naturae" ("Art the ape of nature") was a "title of honor" in anecdotes used by Pliny and other ancients to praise works so faithful to nature that they deceived the beholder. The phrase continued to be a positive judgment until the sixteenth century. At this time, "a differentiation became common between *imitatio sapiens* and *imitatio insipiens*. The ape now symbolized the foolish, faithful imitation of nature . . ." (146).

the representation was *not* accomplished: "Ne pensez, je vous prie, que ce feust le protraict d'un homme couplé sus une fille . . . . La paincture estoit bien aultre, et plus intelligible" (541). Then, with a gesture that forecasts the resolution of this episode, the narrator leaps over this blank present to promise vision in a place that is both past and future, Gargantua's place: "Vous la pourrez veoir en Theleme à main guausche entrans en la haulte guallerie" (541).

The holes in these "fanfreluches" continue to widen with the purchases of Epistemon and Rhizotome. Epistemon buys a painting "on quel estoient au vif painctes les Idées de Platon, at les Atomes de Epicurus" (541). Once again, the negating voice of the narrator intervenes, by his entries in the "Briefve declaration" for "Idées" et "Atomes," to stress the impossibility of depicting entities which are by their essence beyond sensory perception: "invisibles, imaginées" (706). And Rhizotome purchases the final mysterious painting of this first series, the most complex and perhaps the most revealing of the problem of imitation as it has been explored by these first images. He buys a tableau "on quel estoit Echo selon le naturel representée" (541).

Rhizotome's tableau of Echo is an *impossibile* like the things pictured in Epistemon's painting, for sound cannot be expressed by the "silent art" of painting. But Echo also exists as words, as Philomela exists, in Ovid's *Metamorphoses*, and their stories are similar. Both are "language-denying metamorphoses,"[15] accounts of young women whose powers of speech were violated, whose personal voices were taken away. Philomela, however, triumphs over the muteness to which she is condemned. She first uses her hands in place of her tongue and weaves her story in a tapestry, and then she is given song.[16] Echo has a more difficult task, for she is condemned to *repetition*, never to be the originating voice, always to

---

[15] Leonard Barkan, *The Gods Made Flesh: Metamorphosis and the Pursuit of Paganism* (New Haven: Yale UP, 1986) 247.

[16] Barkan's discussion of Shakespeare's use of the story of Philomela in *Titus Andronicus* and *Cymbeline* is relevant to my argument (*Gods* 243-51). In his view, Ovid offered Shakespeare and other Renaissance writers a series of paradigms for the act of communication and for the struggle to invent new languages, a struggle in which these authors themselves were engaged. Philomela's mutilation was of special interest because it required her to create a new medium, a composite of words and pictures. Her tapestry thus becomes "a metonym for the whole history of the book in which Shakespeare found her story" (247)–and perhaps of Renaissance books in general, where words and visual images are so often intertwined.

repeat the words of others. As such, she is the figure of imitation [17] and of the fear of imitation underlying this first series of images–the fear of finding oneself to be only a replica, a simian copy and counterfeit as in Frère Jean's imagery, doomed always to be inferior to the real coin of the original.[18]

Echo is imprisoned in repetition, however, only if she repeats the words of a single strong originating voice, and the things of the first series share this characteristic: they are copies of a only one original. But when Echo hears many anterior voices, she can emulate Philomela and weave the sounds together in a web of resonances that transcends any one of the sounds heard alone.[19] Such is the strategy of imitation propounded by Pantagruel. He purchases the life of Achilles in seventy-eight tapestries which weave together many models in a kind of imitation called "eclectic."[20] By multiplying and fragmenting the originals, the writer can avoid being trapped by the prestige of any one of them[21] and can thus assert his independence and seek his own personal style.

---

[17] In a discussion of the myth of Echo and Narcissus (*Gods* 48-52), Barkan too suggests that the nymph is a figure of imitation: "Echo's metamorphosis from normal, articulate woman to echo imprisons her in herself: she cannot initiate or even experience a fruitful sexual union because she is trapped in imitation and reflection" (48).

[18] See Quint's discussion of the counterfeit and the forgery in relation to the Renaissance dilemma of origins versus originality (1-31).

[19] I am thinking here of the tradition that associates Echo with Pan rather than with Narcissus and that describes her as a singer and musician beloved of the Muses. In Longinus's version, for example, Pan becomes angry with Echo, and he causes the shepherds to tear her to pieces, and scatter her still singing limbs all over the earth. They were preserved by the Muses and Echo's fragments continue to imitate "all things now as the maid did before, the Gods, men, organs (instruments), beasts." (Quoted by Hollander 7-8. See the whole chapter "Echo Allegorical" 6-22.)

[20] This term was not coined until the 18th century (Wittkower 151), but is nonetheless commonly used by critics to discuss the Renaissance theory that advocated the imitation and reinterpretation of many ancient writers. Partisans of eclectic imitation stood in opposition to those who advocated the imitation of single models. As Greene discusses in his chapter "Sixteenth-Century Quarrels" (171-196), the conflict began in 1512, with an exchange of letters between Pietro Bembo, who defended the imitation of one author, and Gianfrancesco Pico, a proponent of eclectic imitation. The argument waged throughout the century and involved its most influential voices including Erasmus, Etienne Dolet, Joachim Du Bellay and other French theorists of the 1540's and 1550's. (Cave also describes these quarrels in his chapter on imitation 35-77.) There can be little doubt that Rabelais was aware of this controversy.

[21] Cave makes this point xi.

> Pantagruel par Gymnaste feist achapter la vie et gestes de Achilles en soixante et dixhuict pieces de tapisseries à haultes lisses, . . . toute de saye Phrygienne, requamée d'or et d'argent. Et commençoit la tapisserie au nopces de Peleus et Thetis, continuant la nativité d'Achilles, sa jeunesse descripte par Stace Papinie: ses gestes et faicts d'armes celebrez par Homere: sa mort et exeques descriptz par Ovide, et Quinte Calabrois: finissant en l'apparition de son umbre, et sacrifice de Polyxene descript par Euripides. (541)

But there is clearly more than a strategy of imitation at stake in these tapestries. They also constitute an act of mythic identification and self-creation, an act of "exemplarity." As Timothy Hampton has discussed,[22] it was a common practice in early sixteenth-century France to choose a figure from antiquity as a model on which to fashion the self, and the exemplar was customarily presented as Achilles' life is presented here, as a narrative woven together to form a complete life. But a negativity lurks at the heart of such self-fashioning, a flaw that Pantagruel's choice of the prideful and rebellious Achilles brings forward. Far more than "pseudonymie," the taking of a new name as Jean Starobinski analyzes it, the adoption of a whole new life constitutes an act of protest against one's origins, an act of rebellion against the father and the whole "univers paternel" he represents.[23] Pantagruel "buys" Achilles' life for his own, gives himself a new conception and a new birth, a new father and a new mother, new "gestes et faicts d'armes" (541)–all to replace his life and adventures as Gargantua's son. These tapestries put us in the labyrinth of the family romance as Freud described it[24] and which Bloom feels to be at the heart of the anxiety of influence:[25] the child's need to get free of parents who no longer seem worthy of esteem, and to replace them with others of a higher

---

[22] "Montaigne and the Body of Socrates: Narrative and Exemplarity in the *Essais*," *MLN* 104 (1989): 880-84.

[23] "Stendhal pseudonyme," *L'Oeil vivant* (Paris: Gallimard, 1961) esp. 194-5. Starobinski goes so far as to suggest that "le refus du patronyme tient lieu d'assassinat du père" (194).

[24] "Family Romances," *The Standard Edition of the Complete Psychological Works of Sigmund Freud,* ed. and trans. James Strachey, vol. 9 (London: Hogarth, 1959) 237-38.

[25] The idea of the family romance is central to Bloom's entire argument in *The Anxiety of Influence: A Theory of Poetry* (London: Oxford UP, 1973); but see esp. 62-66.

and more developed type. Here is the deepest significance of Rabelais's situating Medamothi in a market, a place that stands opposed to the field where Gargantua's book was found buried in the first chapter of the 1534 book. Medamothi is above ground, it is a place of choice, not of inheritance. Most important, it is a place of exchange. Rabelais is engaged on this island in an effort he shared with so many of his contemporaries: to exchange one past for another. As the choice of Achilles suggests, this is a deeply flawed and profoundly unsettling design.

Yet, however dramatic this reweaving of Pantagruel's origins, the tapestries alone are not sufficient to accomplish his purposes. He set out on this voyage in quest of originality as well as of origins (Quint) and the tapestries relate to the past only, to his etiological quest. Something more is needed, something alive in the present and oriented toward the future. Thus Pantagruel enters the marketplace again and purchases other things to accompany and supplement the tapestries: "Feist aussi achapter trois beaulx et jeunes Unicornes: un masle, de poil alezan tostade, et deux femelles de poil gris pommelé. Ensemble un Tarande, que luy vendit un Scythien de la contrée des Gelones" (541).

As Thomas Greene points out (19) the modernist itinerary tends to attach itself to literary language. The poetic word needs the tapestry of the past in order to signify, but it must also shape its own emergence from that past. With the unicorns and the tarand, Rabelais plays out the "shaping." These animals have to do with language—they are words, and they are constituted as Plato in the *Phaedrus* (264 b, c) said that all true discourse must be constituted—"as a living creature, with its own body," a *logos-zöon*, which is engendered, born, grows, and belongs to Physis.[26] The concept of the *logos-zöon* is vital to the whole *Quart Livre*, this bestiary of strange creatures, and will be specifically evoked in the episode of the "Parolles dégelées" (chs. 55-56), where Rabelais recalls Aristotle's description of Homer's living words: "voltigeantes, volantes, moventes, et par consequent animées" (668). On Medamothi, we are present at the creation of such living beings.

The unicorns—one male and two females—are the copulative and self-generating power of the word, its promise of fecundity and

---

[26] See Derrida's discussion of the *logos-zöon* in "La Pharmacie de Platon," *La Dissémination* (Paris: Seuil, 1972) 89-90.

proliferation; they are the word in the future. The tarand is the present, the presence of the word, and it is a present that encompasses the past and surpasses it. Rabelais begins by imitating an old text and a deeply loved father–he closely follows Pliny's description of the reindeer in the *Natural History* (8, 52). Like Pliny, Rabelais forges a long chain of metaphors whereby the tarand is anatomized and each of its bodily parts separately compared to a familiar animal or thing:

> Tarande est un animal grand *comme* un jeune taureau, portant teste *comme* est d'un cerf, *peu plus grande*: avecques cornes insignes largement ramées: les piedz forchuz: le poil long *comme* d'un grand Ours: la peau *peu moins dure, qu'*un corps de cuirasse. (541, my italics)

But when Rabelais adds the capacity to change color to the list of the tarand's attributes, he abandons metaphor and moves into another rhetorical domain altogether. He enters the realm of transumption, the trope that "transfers across" and transforms one thing into another, the trope of metamorphosis, and he radically revises Pliny's text in the process. Now the tarand is taken on an extraordinary voyage through color-changing creatures, a voyage that spans the globe and is accomplished by the vast leaps in logic characteristic of transumption. In rapid succession, the northern land animal is associated with sea creatures (the marine polyp and the sea anemone), with mammals of the south (the lynx and the painted wolf of India), and finally transumption reaches its astonishing goal as the large fur-bearing tarand is "carried across" and merged with the chameleon, the small lizard-like creature of Africa and India. Pliny has been left behind;[27] Democritus is quoted in his place because Democritus speaks of magic.[28] Indeed, the transumption has created a magical new *zöon*, a creature which is tarand and

---

[27] Pliny discusses the chameleon and the reindeer in two contiguous paragraphs of the *Natural History* (8, 51 and 52) as animals that change color, but he keeps them in separate categories and on separate continents, for vast logical differences divide the small cold-blooded lizard of Africa and India from the large fur-bearing mammals of the North. It is across such spaces that Rabelais leaps to merge the two creatures.

[28] When he turns to Democritus, Rabelais observes that ". . . le Chaméléon, qui est une espece de Lizart tant admirable que Democritus a faict un livre entier de sa figure, anatomie, vertus, et *proprieté en Magie*" (542, my italics).

chameleon and more–it encompasses all the land and sea animals evoked the trajectory between them. Here is *le Verbe* as Rimbaud envisions it some three hundred years after Rabelais, a word capable of expressing all possible life-forms and of giving color to all unknown landscapes.[29]

Now the narrator intervenes to describe the tarand as he himself has seen it, for the *zöon* is his creation. And, seen through the narrator's eyes, the tarand explodes into a kaleidoscope of color such as we will see again in chapter fifty-six when the frozen words burst and thaw on the deck of the ship: ". . . des motz de gueule, des motz de sinople, des motz de azur, des motz de sable, des motz d'orez" (670). The tarand reflects all of the colors of the external world: "la couleur des herbes, arbres, arbrisseaulx, fleurs, lieux, pastiz, rochiers" (542), and this *logos-zöon* also possesses the power to make visible the colors of its inner self–feelings, fears: "Si est ce que *je l'ay* veu couleur changé . . . de soy mesmes, selon la paour et affections qu'il avoit . . . . (J) e *l'ay veu* certainement verdoyer . . . devenir jaulne, bleu, tanné, violet par succès . . ." (542, my italics). And more, the tarand makes us see, for the first and only time in *Le Quart Livre*, the participants in this voyage, the colors of their clothes which are the colors of the "peurs et affections" they represent:

> Près de Panurge vestu de sa toge bure, le poil luy devenoit gris: près de Pantagruel vestu de sa mante d'escarlate, le poil et peau luy rougissoit: près du pilot vestu à la mode des Isiaces de Anubis en Ægypte, son poil apparut tout blanc. (542)

Quod vidimus testamur (P 215)–We testify to what we have seen. At last, the king of sight returns to his island in the form of the narrator, "Monsieur l'abstracteur," [30] who has always been Philophanes, the king desirous of seeing and being seen. His presence is felt only once before in this chapter and as a voice of nega-

---

[29] "(Le Poète) est chargé de l'humanité, des *animaux* même; il devra faire sentir, palper, écouter ses inventions; si ce qu'il rapporte *de là-bas* a forme, il donne forme: si c'est de l'informe, il donne de l'informe. Trouver une langue . . . ." "Lettre à Paul Demeny," *Oeuvres*, ed. S. Bernard and A. Guyaux (Paris: Garnier, 1981) 347.

[30] The narrator is identified as "Monsieur l'abstracteur" in the tempest episode of both the 1548 and 1552 editions. Panurge pleads with him: "Un petit mot de testament . . . , monsieur l'abstracteur, mon amy, mon Achates . . ." (Huchon 588 and Plattard 99).

tion, telling us what Panurge's tapestry is *not*. Now he intervenes as a voice of affirmation to tell us what the tarand *is*. The writer has forged a new poetic word in this chapter, and defined a mode of imitation, a transumptive mode, that permits him to adopt the ancients as his fathers and then to leap away from them to find his own voice, create his own language, present his own vision. The first chapter which begins in blindness ends with the visionary writer's trumphant shout of vision achieved–*j'ay veu!*

But this is only a provisional affirmation, for the narrator is not through seeing yet, and Pantagruel sees too. While the giant is occupied with the purchase of the tarand and the unicorns, another *zöon* appears on the horizon moving quickly toward Medamothi. It is a boat, "la Chelidoine," carrying the emblem of a bird that is also a flying fish, "une Hirondelle de mer":

> C'est un poisson . . . ayant æsles cartilagineuses (quelles sont es Souriz chaulves) . . . moyenans les quelles *je l'ay souvent veu* voler une toyse au dessus l'eau . . . . Ainsi estoit ce vaisseau legier comme une Hirondelle, de sorte que plus toust sembloit sus mer voler que voguer. (543, my italics)

This winged thing brings Gargantua to Medamothi. The native father hastens to revindicate his rights and assert the primacy of the medieval past that Pantagruel would have traded away in these markets.

Gargantua comes to Medamothi as writing, as a text which Pantagruel says is engraved in his mind: "escripte, voyre certes insculpée et engravée on posterieur ventricule de mon cerveau" (545) (BD: "C'est la memoire") (706). This text is carried by an "engraver" who is a menacing presence, for Malicorne is Gargantua's "meat slicer," his "escuyer tranchant." He brings gifts that seem on the surface to be tokens of Gargantua's affection for Pantagruel: a carrier pigeon (gozal) to be released so that Gargantua can quickly have news of his son (543-4); a letter to Pantagruel "de ta maison paternelle" (544-5); and books, "quelques livres joyeulx" (544). But beneath their surface appearance of affection, these gifts also express antagonism and rivalry–they are "potlatch" offerings that compete with the things Pantagruel has purchased. Indeed, Malicorne himself is just such an offering. He is Gargantua's unicorn, "*ma* -licorne," versus the unicorns that Pantagruel has bought. Like Mercure in the 1552 prologue, Malicorne is the messenger of a god and father who is both *donne-vie* et *donne-mort*. Malicorne's gifts can also kill if the recipient does not acknowledge his true origins. The menace of infanticide hangs over Pantagruel as he steps forward to meet Malicorne. This is the arrow aimed at Achilles' heel. This is Laius and Oedipus come to the crossroads.

The most critical moment of the confrontation between father and son centers on the gozal, "celeste messaigier" (543) and counterpart of the tarand. The gozal is Gargantua's *logos-zöon*, she flies back to "la maison paternelle," to the origins of these books in the spoken word. From the beginning, Rabelais has suggested that his books were dictated and meant to be read aloud,[31] and in the 1548 prologue, he called speech the "father" of his stories, "ma paternité" (716). With the gozal, he also calls the spoken word "mother." She flies back because she has "oeufz et petitz" (543) in her nest. We have seen this imagery before in Rabelais's world, and it was associated with the womb-like mouth of Pantagruel himself whose "mother tongue" covered the soldiers "comme une geline (poule) fait ses poulletz" (P 330).[32] The gozal calls Pantagruel back to this hatching place. She is what Bloom calls a *tessera*,[33] a token of recognition and password between father and son linking them to their common heritage in the telling of tales, their shared way of "giving news" to each other.

But will Pantagruel accept the password and use it correctly, as he and Gargantua have used it in the past? There is a moment of suspense as Pantagruel faces the patricidal temptation, and if he makes the wrong decision, Malicorne stands poised to strike. Now, like Theseus rather than Oedipus, Pantagruel must choose which sign to show to his father: to attach a "bandelette de tafetas blanc" or "jectz noirs" (543) to the gozal's feet. But unlike both Theseus and Oedipus, he resists the patricidal temptation. He shows the white sign to his father and in a flash forward, we see the gozal arriving back in Gargantua's dovecote and observe the fa-

---

[31] In the prologue to *Gargantua*, for example, he speaks of having "dictans" the book (7). See my discussion of the word "lecture" as oral reading in Chapter One (30-1 and n. 11).

[32] See my reading of this episode, "Les 'Mithologies Pantagruelicques': Introduction to a Study of Rabelais's *Quart Livre*," *PMLA* 92 (1977): 473-74.

[33] See *Anxiety*, esp. 66-67. Bloom takes the term from Lacan.

ther's joy.³⁴ The father-son tragedy, so close to the surface of this encounter between Gargantua and Pantagruel, has been averted, but they still have much bargaining to do before a reconciliation and true exchange can occur between them.

The crisis diffused, Pantagruel reads Gargantua's letter and writes back. The episode now becomes focused on their two letters—two texts in juxtaposition representing the two *mundi significantes*³⁵ and rhetorical systems that have always existed in Rabelais's books. Gargantua's letter is a "letre de creance" (543), a message to be credited and believed only when delivered "by word of mouth" (Cotgrave). Pantagruel's letter, to the contrary, is composed in a written style, in a dense and latinate French so convoluted that the text is at times very difficult to follow. In these different styles, both father and son show their vulnerability to each other, both express affection commingled with fear—words such as "paour," "craincte," "anxieté," are repeated with insistence in both texts. But the fears of father and son center on different issues. Gargantua is frightened of the future into which Pantagruel threatens to travel without him, a future that may exclude and annihilate the father. Thus, Gargantua is most concerned with prognostication. He desires to allay his fear of the future by forecasting from the beginning of the voyage that Pantagruel will safely return to the paternal lands.³⁶

Pantagruel's anxieties, by contrast, center on the past and on memory, the inescapable memory of Gargantua that he carries within him, the burden of a past that will not die. As Marcel Tetel³⁷ has pointed out, his letter is a classic expression of the anxiety of influence. Pantagruel reproaches his father for Malicorne's arrival and describes it as an act of aggression against him; such a violent shock

---

³⁴ "... (E)n moins de deux heures il franchit par l'air le long chemin .... Et feut veu entrant dedans le colombier on propre nid de ses petitz. Adoncques entendent le preux Gargantua, qu'il portoit la bandelette blanche resta en joye et sceureté du bon partement de son filz" (543).

³⁵ Greene defines a *mundus significans* as "a signifying universe, which is to say a rhetorical and symbolic vocabulary, a storehouse of signifying capacities potentially available to each member of a given culture" (20).

³⁶ "(J)'ay pour de telle anxieté vuider mon entendement, expressement depesché Malicorne: à ce que par luy je soys acertainé de ton portement sus les premiers jours de ton voyage. Car s'il est prospere, et tel que je le soubhayte, facile me sera preveoir, prognosticquer, et juger du reste" (544).

³⁷ "Carnival and Beyond," *L'Esprit Créateur* 21.1 (1981): 92-3.

and intrusion that he almost died of it.[38] He had hoped, he says, to break away from Gargantua, ". . . je n'esperoys aulcun veoir de vos domesticques, ne de vous nouvelles ouyr avant la fin de cestuy nostre voyage" (545). Now, with the arrival of Gargantua's gifts, he finds himself in "ignominie" and "angustie" (anxiety), "opprimé d'obligations infinies," and threatened with the "crime" of "vivre et mourir ingrat" (546). And more, Pantagruel feels threatened with impotence, a word that he repeats three times in the letter. Gargantua's tenacious life keeps Pantagruel in the intolerable position of being a "perpetual child,"[39] unable to forge his own creativity and move into the freshening he is seeking.

But how to escape from the burden of the past without killing it, a result that, as Malicorne's presence suggests, would mean killing oneself? The answer lies in giving back, in transforming the structure of inheritance into the structure of exchange. The central passage and turning point of Pantagruel's letter expresses this realization: that between the powerful stance of the giver and the passivity of the receiver there lies a third possibility which can make them equal, the element of recompense—of paying for services rendered, remunerating benefits received:

> . . . par la sentence des Stoiciens: lesquelz disoient troys parties estre en benefice. L'une du donnant, l'aultre du recepvant, la tierce du recompensant: et le recepvant tresbien recompenser le donnant quand il accepte voluntiers le bienfaict, et le retient en soubvenance perpetuelle. Comme au rebours le recepvant estre le plus ingrat du monde, qui mespriseroit et oublieroit le benefice. (546)

In this third element of recompense, Pantagruel finds freedom from the weight of his inheritance, for he now has something of his own to give to Gargantua, "les belles et rares choses" he purchased on Medamothi.[40]

---

[38] "Pere tresdebonnaire, comme à tous accidens en ceste vie transitoire non doubtez ne soubsonnez, nos sens et facultez animales patissent plus enormes et impotentes perturbations (*voyre jusques à en estre souvent l'ame desemparée du corps* . . .): ainsi me a grandement esmeu et perturbé l'inopinée venue de vostre escuyer Malicorne" (545, my italics).

[39] Ferguson 282.

[40] For a very different reading of this passage, and of the father-son relationship as it is explored on "l'isle Medamothi," see Duval, *Design* 109-16.

The son begins his legacy to his father with the tarand and the unicorns, and they are sent *cum commento*. Pantagruel describes the nature of these animals to Gargantua and gives instruction on their care and feeding. The dominant theme of this legacy is "taming"–the classical logos must be "domestiqué" and "apprivoisé" by the native father, "nourri" by the fruits of one's own homeland (546). Du Bellay describes a similar process and uses similar imagery in the *Deffence* when he speaks of "cultivating" the French language by "grafting" branches of Latin and Greek onto it,[41] but Rabelais's comparison goes in the other direction. For Rabelais, the native soil is not the desert that it was for Du Bellay nor is French the weaker plant. On the contrary, he criticizes "nos escrivains antiques" for their shortcomings, their failure to understand the nature of these creatures.[42] For Rabelais, the native tradition has the superior vigor; it is the primary source of his creativity. Rather than giving strength, the classical past finds it only when grafted onto this stronger native trunk.

Finally, and for the same reason, the tapestry of Achilles' life is sent back to Gargantua–without explanation, for none is needed. Pantagruel capitulates. The classical fathers he bought in the markets of Medamothi, the "vie et gestes" he assumed for his own, are sent back to decorate the walls of Thelema and to find shelter under Gargantua's roof–where Panurge's tapestries are located. Both pasts nurture Rabelais's book and Pantagruel's gift-giving reconciles them, but in the end, the author chooses between them. In the end, he gives priority to the native father.

This reconciliation receives another and symbolic expression in the banquet that culminates the episode (547). It is a festival where gold and wine are given, symbols of "real money"–this is a festival

---

[41] See especially I. 3. 22-28 where Du Bellay argues that the French must cultivate the neglected "plant" of their language as the Romans did Italian, pruning "useless branches" and grafting on new ones "magistralement tirez de la Langue Greque" (25). "Ainsi puys-je dire de nostre Langue qui . . . n'a point encores fleury, . . . Cela, certainement, non pour le default de la nature d'elle, aussi apte à engendrer que les aultres: mais pour la coulpe de ceux qui l'on euë en garde, & ne l'ont cultivée à suffisance, ains comme une plante sauvaige, en celuy mesmes desert . . . l'ont laissée envieillir & quasi mourir" (24-25). See Ferguson's discussion of Du Bellay's "organic defense" of the French language, 279-80.

[42] "Je m'esbahis comment nos escrivains antiques disent (les unicornes) tant farouches, feroces, et dangereuses, et oncques vives n'avoir esté veues. Si bon vous semble serez espreuve du contraire . . ." (547).

of exchange. Pantagruel covers the tarand and the unicorns with golden embroidery like that in which Achilles' tapestry is woven–a sign of the value that he continues to give to the "knots and plots" of the classical fathers. He also gives gold to Malicorne, but in the form of a golden chain, "une grosse chaine d'Or poisante huyct cens escuz," studded with precious jewels (547). Thus, as Du Bellay ended the *Deffence* with the image of "Hercule Gallique tirant les peuples apres luy par leurs oreilles avecques *une chesne* attachée à sa langue" (197, my italics),[43] Rabelais also evokes a chained figure as he concludes his meditation on origins. This image is deeply ambivalent, for chains are emprisoning–they bind and pull backward. But they also connect and permit communication, and Rabelais makes these links golden. With Malicorne's chain, he acknowledges that he is bound to the native father "by an etiological passage, but the bond does not prove subservience; it proves a concrete relationship."[44]

Having come to terms with the past, the voyage now turns toward the future. Indeed, at the end of the episode, the voyage of *Le Quart Livre* goes in two directions: "Ainsi departirent de Medamothi Malicorne pour retourner vers Gargantua; Pantagruel, pour continuer son naviguage" (547). And at the crossroads of this double intinerary, another exchange occurs–of books. Pantagruel had promised Gargantua a book in the future, a serious book and written record of things seen and discussed on this voyage: "Je ne fauldray à reduire en commentaires et ephemerides tout le discours de nostre naviguaige: affin que à nostre retour vous en ayez lecture veridicque" (546). Gargantua had sent Pantagruel books recovered from the past, joyful stories to "refresh" his seriousness: "J'ay recouvert quelques livres joyeulx.... Tu les liras quand te vouldras refraischir de tes meilleures estudes" (544). These books from the past are finally brought into the future, and the acts of reading, writing, and rewriting merge, for as the voyagers take to the seas again, Pantagruel has Epistemon read Gargantua's book aloud. By this gesture, the writer of the future acknowledges himself to be the reader of the past, "recollecting forward," as Bloom beautifully writes, "into a freshening which yet repeats the precursor's achievements."[45]

---

[43] See Ferguson's reading of this image 286, as well as that of Greene 193-4.
[44] Greene 194.
[45] *Anxiety* 83.

But what of the *reader* of the future? Thus far, the dialectical energy of the episode has been focused on the resolution of Pantagruel's fear, the anxiety that comes to the writer from the past, the anxiety of influence. Gargantua had expressed another anxiety, however, fear of the future, the prospective panic that comes at the thought of being read and revised by his future reader or, worse, of being forgotten and annihilated. In the very last sentence of the Medamothi episode, as the voyagers take to the sea, this anticipatory anxiety[46] bursts forth. It generates a new dialectic and yet another exchange of books: between the narrator and the future reader of this "journal de voyage"–us: "(P)ource que (Pantagruel) trouva (les livres) joyeulx et plaisans, le *transsumpt* volunties vous donneray, si devotement le requerez" (547, my italics).

This final remark puts us back in the domain of transumption where the episode began, but here we see that it contains a dual trajectory and a double-edged sword. Exercised on the past, transumption constitutes a victory for the Rabelais. It empowers him to read and to subsume his precursors, and at the same time, to misread and move away from them into a revisionary space, a space of transformation that he can claim for his own. But the future vistas of transumption are far less appealing, for the chain of filiation and transfer across generations will not stop with the writer. His book must now pass into the hands of readers who possess transumptive powers of their own, the power to misread and revise *him*.

The revisionary powers of the reader have filled Rabelais with anxiety since he first began writing Le *Quart Livre*. Indeed, as discussed in Chapter One, the 1548 prologue is constructed as a defense against his bad readers, "calumniateurs de mes escripts" (718), whose charges of heresy had placed his life in grave peril. It was to forestall such malicious misreadings that Rabelais offered the lesson in good reading contained in the Old Prologue where he called his readers "writers" of the fable of the jays and the magpies and played the role of "reader" of "our" text. Rabelais abandoned the reading lesson in this form when he suppressed the prologue of 1548, but we find its echo in the last sentence of the Medamothi episode–in the image of Pantagruel reading Gargantua, and in the transumption of Pantagruel's reading onto our own. In the end, the

---

[46] Sima Godfrey and her contributors speak of *The Anxiety of Anticipation,* ed. Godfrey, *Yale French Studies* 66 (New Haven: Yale UP, 1984).

writer can only commend his enterprise into the hands of "lecteurs suffisans," in Montaigne's words,[47] whom he must create, in his own image or in the image of his book: "Pantagruélistes" who "jamais en maulvaise partie ne prendront choses quelconques ilz congnoistront sourdre de bon, franc, et loyal couraige" (TL 351).

But it all comes to rest on Rabelais's final "if": "si devotement le requerez"–if we request the book, if we read it, and if we read as "Pantagruélistes." In the end, the writer acknowledges the "otherness" of the "always future reader"[48] whose authority and author-ity remain absolute. Yet, despite the anxiety that the dialogue with this alien creates in him, Rabelais nonetheless consents to give the book, and by this consent he operates the final "pentimento" and repair of the first *Quart Livre*. In the tempest of the 1548 version, "Monsieur l'Abstracteur" had passed over in silence the pleas of Panurge who had urged him to do just this: compose a "testament sur mer," put it in a bottle, and commit it to the risky seas of the future in the blind hope that it will be carried to a benevolent reader on some far shore.[49] In the last sentence of the Medamothi episode of 1552, Rabelais yields to that fearful and hopeful adventure in time. He offers the new *Quart Livre* as a legacy for the future and a "hydrographie" and map for the past. Once again, a manuscript is placed in the bottle-boats and pitched into the violent emptiness of "l'espace littéraire,"[50] the space of Nowhere that by an act of poetic will Rabelais has filled with the echos of his wandering word.[51]

---

[47] *Oeuvres complètes*, ed. Albert Thibaudet and Maurice Rat (Paris: Gallimard, 1962) 126.

[48] Godfrey, "Editor's Preface" vi.

[49] "Quelque bonne vague (respondit Panurge) jectera (le testament) à bort comme feit Ulixes; et quelque fille de Roy . . . le rencontrera, puis le fera tres bien exequuter. Et pres le rivage me fera eriger quelque magnificque cenotaphe . . ." (Plattard 100).

[50] Maurice Blanchot, *L'Espace littéraire* (Paris: Gallimard, 1955).

[51] "Cette parole est essentiellement errante . . . . Elle ressemble à l'écho, quand l'écho ne dit pas seulement tout haut ce qui est d'abord murmuré, mais se confond avec l'immensité chuchotante, est le silence devenu l'espace retentissant, le dehors de toute parole" (Blanchot 46).

Chapter Three

INFERNAL BANQUETS

> Tu ne veids oncques tel apprest de bancquet infernal. Voy tu la fumée des cuisines d'Enfer? . . . Tu ne veids oncques tant d'ames damnées. (698)

1. Points of Departure

THE voyage of *Le Quart Livre* has its origins in a bottle and a pair of glasses, at that moment in *Le Tiers Livre* when the morosophe Triboulet strikes Panurge a blow between the shoulders and places a bottle in his hands:

> (L)'unicque non Lunaticque Triboullet me remect à la Bouteille, et je . . . jure Styx et Acheron en vostre praesence, lunettes au bonnet porter, ne porter braguette à mes chausses, que sus mon entreprinse, je n'aye eu le mot de la Dive Bouteille. (TL, 494)

Faithful to these generating symbols, all the boats of the convoy as they are seen in the port of Thalasse display emblems of light and of wine. There is a lantern to see by and there are drinking mugs, jugs, pitchers, funnels, goblets, toasting glasses, and barrels. Above all, there is the "grande et ample bouteille" (538) of *la Thalamege*, the lead vessel in which Pantagruel and Panurge sail, and this bottle is the symbol of a wine that is double: "à moytié d'argent bien liz et polly: l'autre moytié estoit d'or esmaillé de couleur incarnet. En quoy facile estoit juger, que blanc et claret estoient les couleurs des nobles voyagiers: et qu'ilz alloient pour avoir le mot de la Bouteille" (538).

We have seen the image of "mixed wine" before in Rabelais's books: oil and wine in the Prologue to *Gargantua* (7-8), wine and water in the episode of the "Pantagruelion" at the end of *Le Tiers Livre* (509-10). But *Le Quart Livre* confronts us with a mixture *within* wine: red versus white, dark versus clear, gay wines versus those of more somber tones. Indeed, there are many wines in wine of this book. There is the wine of curiosity, so closely linked to the glasses that Panurge wears on his bonnet, expressing his desire to see and to learn;[1] and the wine of the will[2] which gives to the voyagers the courage needed to embark on the "voyes perilleuses" (537) which lie before them: "(L)'alcool est un thème de vouloir. Il aide à décider. Il donne le courage de partir la nuit seul, sur la mer immense."[3] There are also the shared wines of the humanist banquet as Michel Jeanneret has enumerated them, the wines of conviviality, commensality, and community: "Le banquet est une cérémonie collective, lieu par excellence où l'individu apprend à partager son plaisir, à le rehausser dans l'échange avec la compagnie."[4] Above all, there are the wines of conversation and communication, for food and drink are factors of language, enriching vocabulary, liberating syntax, and freeing the imagination to tell stories. "Les Mets et les Mots" (Jeanneret) are generative of each other. Bacchus and the Muses are conjoined at the banquet table.

But darker reds and somber tones lurk in the depths of these light and gay wines, for wine is also blood, from the torn flesh of victims harvested in the Vineyard of Dionysus,[5] from the innocent body of the passover lamb, the lamb of God. Within the joyful and copious wines of the humanist banquet lies the shadow of the Eucharist, the frugal meal of bread and wine which is the central Christian mystery.[6] As an early Easter hymn (fourth to sixth century) expresses it:

---

[1] On the curiosity *topos*, see Gérard Defaux, *Le curieux, le glorieux et la sagesse du monde dans la première moitié du XVIe siècle: L'exemple de Panurge (Ulysse, Démosthène, Empédocle)* (Lexington, KY: French Forum, 1982).

[2] See Florence Weinberg, *The Wine and the Will: Rabelais's Bacchic Christianity* (Detroit: Wayne State UP, 1972).

[3] Gaston Bachelard, "Les Aventures de Gordon Pym," in *Le droit de rêver* (Paris: PUF, 1970) 136.

[4] *Des Mets et des Mots: Banquets et Propos de Table à la Renaissance* (Paris: Corti, 1987) 28.

[5] A phrase used by Mikhail Bahktin, *Rabelais and His World,* trans. Hélène Iswolsky (Cambridge, MA: MIT, 1968) 209.

[6] A point made by Caroline Walker Bynum, *Holy Feast and Holy Fast: The Religious Significance of Food to Medieval Women* (Berkeley: U of California P, 1987) 48: "But the central Christian meal was not the carnival, not the bacchanal, not an exuberant revel expressing abundance and fertility. The central meal, the central liturgical act, was a frugal repast, evoking less the luxurious, proliferating richness of the natural world than the human life it supported. Indeed, Christ had said it *was* human life, was body and blood."

> We look forward to the supper of the lamb . . . whose sacred body is roasted on the altar of the cross. By drinking his rosy blood, we live with God . . . . Now Christ is our passover, our sacrificial lamb; His flesh, the unleavened bread of sincerity, is offered up.[7]

The dark wine of this liturgical repast is also present in the departure where it is mixed with the clearer tones of an exuberant human meal. After the panoply of the bottle-boats is displayed, an assembly is called on board *la Thalamege* and an evangelical service is conducted. Pantagruel preaches a brief sermon "toute auctorisée de propous extraictz de la saincte escripture, sus l'argument de naviguation" (538) and he offers a prayer, "hault et clair faicte," to God. Then the psalm *Quand Israel hors d'Ægypte sortit* is chanted by the assembly (539). As several critics have argued,[8] this allusion to Exodus recalls the passover lamb slaughtered before the departure from Egypt, which has traditionally been seen as a prefiguration of the Christian Eucharist:

> Le sujet rappelé dans l'hymne . . . n'est donc autre que le grand événement pascal and proto-eucharistique qui est commemoré dans tout repas de communion. . . . Ce psaume est donc le double signe d'une Cène evangélique: d'abord par sa présence même et ensuite par le sujet qu'il rappelle.[9]

After this evangelical service, the tone of the departure changes and modulates into a gay and human feast: "Le pseaulme parachevé feurent sus le tillac les tables dressées, et viandes promptement apportées" (539). The ceremony of communion becomes the celebration of a community which embraces the voyagers together with "les bourgeoys et citadins de Thalasse" (538-9). There has been throughout an insistence on the participation of the citizens, that they see the service, that the prayer be offered "hault et clair" so

---

[7] Quoted and translated by Bynum 49.
[8] See Edwin M. Duval, "La Messe, La Cène, et Le Voyage sans fin du *Quart Livre*," *Rabelais en son demi-millénaire: actes du colloque international de Tours (24-29 septembre 1984), Etudes rabelaisiennes,* 21 (1988): 138-39; Paul J. Smith, *Voyage et écriture: étude sur Le Quart Livre de Rabelais* (Geneva: Droz, 1987) 73-81; V.-L. Saulnier, *Rabelais II. Rabelais dans son enquête. Etude sur Le Quart et le Cinquième Livre* (Paris: CEDES, 1982) 41-43.
[9] E. Duval, "La Messe" 139 n. 19.

that they may hear it, that they join in the singing of the psalm. Now, the Thalassians share in a banquet, and they share not only by feasting, but also by feeding others. They bring food and wine to the communal table: "feirent de leurs maisons force vivres et vinage apporter" (539). The result is a festival of exchange and perfect commensality which is also a principle of healing, a principle of physical and spiritual health: "Tous beurent à eulx. Ilz beurent à tous. Ce feut la cause pourquoy personne de l'assemblée oncques par la marine ne rendit sa guorge, et n'eut perturbation d'estomach, ne de teste" (539).

In the healing power of these shared wines, we see the essential link between the sacred and the secular meals of the departure, for both center on the same principle of giving food, of feeding others—as Christ divided the loaves and the fishes, as he gave his body on the cross. The Eucharist and the human banquet both center on the friendship which Erasmus felt to be the very definition of Christianity,[10] the *caritas* which Rabelais values above all other virtues and which he made Gargantua's motto: Charity seeketh not its own.[11]

By its enactment of *caritas* in both the sacred and the profane registers, the banquet of the departure stands as the prototypical meal of *Le Quart Livre*, the meal against which all others are measured—and found lacking. For when they leave Thalasse, the voyagers sail to islands where the spirit contrary to *caritas* reigns, *philautia*, self-love versus love of others. On these islands there is no giving of food, no feeding of others—eating is a greedy devouring only. Ceremonies are conducted on these islands, but they are perversions of the Eucharist, infernal banquets which profane the sacred meal. The lamb of God is degraded into the pig, the sacrificial animal of *Le Quart Livre*, and the pig is worshiped as the idol of Baal. Conviviality and commensality are banished. Words become lies and empty wind. And in place of laughter there are tears, the tears of Pantagruel, the tears of St. Paul:

---

[10] "Nihil aliud quam vera perfectaque amicitia," "Nothing but true and perfect friendship." *Opus epistolarum Des. Erasmi Roterodami.* Ed. P.S. Allen and H.M. Allen, vol. 1 (Oxford: Oxford UP, 1906) 417.

[11] *Gargantua*, ch. 8. Rabelais quotes in Greek from Paul's First Epistle to the Corinthians 13.5.

(P)roprement . . . avoit le sainct Envoyé escript. *Philippens. 3:* "Plusieurs sont des quelz souvent je vous ay parlé (encores praesentement je le vous diz les larmes à l'oeil) ennemis de la croix du Christ: des quelz Mort sera la consommation: des quelz Ventre est le Dieu." (675)

This "terrible allegory," to use Epistemon's words (578), this recurrent vision of the perversion of the Eucharist, clearly reflects the doctrinaire quarrels that were raging at the time of the composition of *Le Quart Livre* as they had raged throughout the century–among the reformers and the Catholic church and also among the reformers themselves. Caroline Bynum (50-60) describes how, as the Middle Ages progressed, the union of Holy Feast came more and more through the power of the priest, and it was to this power that Luther objected above all. He denied the Catholic doctrine that the mass enacts a sacrifice–the priest does not offer God up on the altar–and he denied the doctrine of transubstantiation which holds that when the priest pronounces the words "This is my body, this is my blood," the bread and wine are transformed into the body of God. But, as Roland H. Bainton clarifies,[12] Luther did not deny the real presence of Christ in the sacrament, for he felt that He is ubiquitous in the material world, and for this belief, Zwingli accused Luther of popery. For Zwingli, the Lord's Supper was only a sign and memorial, the public testimonial of adherence to a religious community.[13] He and Luther met at Marburg in 1529 to try to ressolve this essential difference between them, but their efforts were unsuccessful and the conference ended without agreement.[14] These issues exploded in France in 1534 with the infamous "Affaire des Placards contre la messe," and Calvin's *Petit Traité de la sainte Cène* appeared in 1542. Although, like Luther, Calvin regarded the Eucharist as a channel of spiritual communion with God, like Zwingli, he denied Christ's real presence in the bread and the wine.[15]

---

[12] *The Reformation of the Sixteenth Century* (Boston: Beacon, 1956) 48. The whole of chapter 2, "Luther' s Reform" 36-56, is relevant.
[13] Bainton 89.
[14] Bainton 92-3.
[15] "La Cène de nostre Seigneur est ung signe par lequel soubs le pain et le vin il nous représente la vraye communication spirituelle que nous avons en son corps et son sang." Quoted by Jean Boisset, *Calvin et la souveraineté de Dieu* (Paris: Seghers, 1964) 172. In *Des Sacrements au Concile de Trente* (Paris: Editions Du Cerf, 1985), André Duval explains the complexities of Calvin's position on the

Alarmed at these challenges to its holiest sacrament, the Church convened the Council of Trent in 1545-1549, and again in late 1551 and early 1552 to discuss the mass and the Eucharist and the outcome of all its deliberations was to affirm the Church's traditional beliefs.[16] The composition and publication of Rabelais's *Quart Livres* of 1548 and 1552 are contemporaneous with these sessions, and direct and scathing attacks on the Council of Trent are found throughout the book. The first adventure in 1548, the encounter at sea with Dindenault, begins by alluding to "l'assignation du chapitre general des Lanternes" (548), and during the tempest, Panurge recalls the boatload of "bons et beatz peres Concilipètes" (584) encountered just before the storm en route to the Council: "Jacobins, Jesuites, Capussins, Hermites, Augustins, Bernardins, Celestins, Théatins, Egnatins, Amadeans, Cordeliers, Carmes, Minimes, et aultres saincts religieux" (581). The narrator calls this Council "de Chesil," from the Hebrew word *kessil* meaning "mad" (1525 n. 15), and ridicules its efforts to "grabeler les articles de la foy contre les nouveaulx hoereticques" (581). Off "l'isle Chaneph," Panurge again alludes to the Council as he attacks the island's hypocritical inhabitants: "Il me souvient encores de nos gras Concilipetes de Chesil: que Belzebuz et Astarotz les eussent concilié avecques Proserpine." (690).

But we must be cautious in concluding that Rabelais is condemning as "abominable à tous les egards"[17] the central Catholic beliefs of Christ's sacrifice and his real presence in the bread and the wine. As indicated in Xenomanes' history of the wars between the Catholic Quaresmeprenant and the Swiss Calvinists whom he calls "Andouilles" and "Saulcissons montigenes" (621), Rabelais is above all castigating the Council for its intransigent unwillingness to permit a compromise between the warring factions, thus worsen-

---

Eucharist thus: "A la Cène . . . le chrétien reçoit vraiment le Corps et le Sang du Christ pour ne former avec Lui qu'un seul Corps, Lui habitant en nous et nous en Lui. Seulement, les éléments du pain et du vin demeurent ce qu'ils sont. Ils ne sont pas transformés, comme l'entendent ceux qui parlent de transsubstantiation; ils ne contiennent pas le Christ comme le croit Luther; et cependant, contrairement à la position de Zwingli, ils ne sont pas de purs symboles. C'est par l'oeuvre de l'Esprit-Saint que le communiant entre dans cette union réelle et mystérieuse avec le Christ, qui est l'objet du Testament, dans le Sang de la Nouvelle Alliance . . ." (68).

[16] For a chronology and summary of the Council of Trent's deliberations on the mass, see André Duval 21-59 and 61-150.

[17] E. Duval, "La Messe" 134.

ing the conflict between them.[18] He condemns the Council members and all bad priests, including the Pope, for their evil self-indulgence and for betraying the beliefs they should uphold and protect, and he certainly criticizes many abusive Catholic practices, but it would be difficult at any time to say that the Church's central beliefs are put in question.[19] And the reformers, Calvin in particular, are attacked with equal ferocity.[20] Indeed, Catholics and Protestants are confronted throughout *Le Quart Livre* in a Scylla and Charybdis arrangement of opposites equally to be avoided: Quaresmeprenant and Andouilles, Papimanes and Papefigues, Putherbe and Calvin; these are, as Thomas Greene says, "so many embodiments of polarized passion, so many reefs for the Pantagruelist spirit to avoid."[21]

Between the extremes floats *la Thalamege* and the symbols of mixed wine it carries, the shared wines of communion and community. The Sacrament may mean different things to different Christians, but all belong to "the society of the son of God," as Erasmus said, the body into which "we are ingrafted by faith."[22] Like Eras-

---

[18] "Resterent (Quaresmeprenant et Les Andouilles) toutesfoys moins severes et plus doulx ennemis, que n'estoient par le passé. Mais depuys la denonciation du concile national de Chesil, par laquelle elles (les Andouilles) feurent farfouillés, guodelurées, et intimées: par laquelle aussi feut Quaresmeprenant declairé breneux hallebrené et stocfisé en cas que avecques elles il feit alliance ou appoinctement aulcun, se sont horrificquement aigriz, envenimez, indignez, et obstinez en leurs couraiges . . ." (622).

[19] Like Edwin Duval, Gérard Defaux believes that in *Le Quart Livre*, Rabelais is attacking not only papal and clerical degeneracy and certain Catholic practices, but also basic Catholic dogmas and beliefs. In speaking of "les Papimanes," for example, Defaux suggests that Rabelais is attacking, "de la façon la plus ouverte et la plus mordante" not only "l'abstinence et le jeûne, le culte des images et celui des reliques, le trafic des indulgences, les abus procéduriers du droit canon, les prétentions du pape à la 'plénitude de la puissance'," but also "le scandaleux 'sacrifice' de la messe . . ." *Rabelais Agonistes: Du Rieur au prophète: Etudes sur Pantagruel, Gargantua, le Quart Livre* (Geneva: Droz, 1997) 485.

[20] Pantagruel concludes the myth of Physis and Antiphysie (ch. 32) with this tirade: "Depuys elle (Antiphysie) engendra les Matagoz, Cagotz et Papelars; les Maniacles Pistoletz, *les Demoniacles Calvins imposteurs de Geneve:* les enraigez Putherbes, Briffaulx, Caphars, Chattemites, Canibales: et aultres monstres difformes et contrefaicts en despit de Nature" (615, my italics).

[21] *Rabelais: A Study in Comic Courage* (Englewood Cliffs, NJ: Prentice-Hall, 1970) 88.

[22] David Quint, *Origin and Originality in Renaissance Literature* (New Haven: Yale UP, 1983) 185 quotes this passage from Erasmus' *Lingua* (1525): "If member is torn from member, what will become of the body? If the body is separated from its head, what will happen to its life? This is doubtless what Paul says of us called

mus, Rabelais in *Le Quart Livre* deplores the tearing asunder of the Christian community by doctrinaire disputes; and, with Pantagruel, Panurge, Frère Jean and their companions, puts forth the principle by which the community may be healed and unified again. Despite their different temperaments and often violent disagreements, the voyagers always remain united by bonds of loving friendship. David Quint (195) makes the essential point: "The behavior of the Rabelaisian characters . . . provides a model for one church whose members may disagree but who agree to stay together."

2. DINDENAULT, PANURGE, AND THE DEATH OF THE LAMB

The encounter at sea with Dindenault, present in both the 1548 and 1552 editions of *Le Quart Livre*, is far more complex than it appears on the surface to be. On one level, it is "un tour de vieille guerre" (555) in which we see the return of the old Panurge of the 1532 book, the clever trickster who takes his revenge on the greedy sheep merchant of Taillebourg. But there is more to this story of buying, selling, and killing sheep than first meets the eye. It begins with an allusion to the Council of Trent, ends with a warning of divine vengeance, and in 1548, the episode stands in immediate juxtaposition to the departure with its evocation of Exodus and the passover lamb. In 1552, the link between the two episodes is obscured by the interpolation of the new *escale* on Medamothi, but sheep come to play an important symbolic role later in the new version, on "l'isle des Macraeons," when Pantagruel recounts the death of He who is both shepherd and lamb:

> C'est le bon Pan le grand pasteur qui comme atteste le bergier passionné Corydon, non seulement a en amour et affection ses brebis, mais aussi ses bergiers. (605)[23]

---

together into the society of the Son of God, for we are ingrafted by faith into that body, which is the church: the church really means congregation, not division . . . . What would he say if he heard the confused languages of men in this age: I am a transalpine theologian, I a cisalpine one, I a Scotist, I a Thomist, I an Ockhamist, I a realist, I a nominalist, I of Paris, I of Cologne, I a Lutheran, I a Karlstadtian, I an Evangelical, I a Papist? It makes me ashamed to name them all. O house, how you are dispersed, o community, how you are torn asunder, o body, where is now thy happy . . . (unity), from which whoever is excluded is not in Christ?"

[23] The association of Pan with the shepherd Corydon may reflect the influence

This allusion rebounds back to the Dindenault episode which stands in contrast to the death of Pan as a story about "mauvais pasteurs" of several kinds. The sheep merchant is a bad shepherd in the literal sense, "(le) belinier (berger) de Mahumet" as Panurge calls him (549)–by his greed and self-interest, Dindenault betrays his flock. The allusion to the Council of Trent evokes those who are "mauvais pasteurs" in the figurative sense, bad priests who betray the spirit of the lamb. But Panurge becomes the most guilty of all, for he kills sheep and shepherds, all those who, according to Pan's injunction, should be held "en amour et affection." He is punished for this transgression throughout *Le Quart Livre*.

The episode is highly theatrical, a farce in three acts. It is full of twists and turns, and we are above all surprised by the changes in Panurge's character. Act I begins as Dindenault jeers at Panurge in costume–without codpiece and with glasses attached to his bonnet–and calls him "une belle medaille de Coqu" (548). Panurge responds with insults of his own, and an outbreak of violence ensues. Dindenault goes for his sword, and Panurge reacts with the cowardliness we have come to expect from him–"(il) recourt vers Pantagruel à secours" (549) Act I ends with a false peace imposed upon the two antagonists, and the mercantile comedy of Act II begins. Panurge puts on the mask of an "achapteur de moutons" (550) and invites Dindenault to sell him a sheep.

Now Panurge plays another role entirely. Not only does he suddenly become fearless and in full control of the action, he becomes a *moralisateur* with a lesson to teach. As the bargaining is engaged, Panurge's uncharacteristically laconic replies push Dindenault to ever greater heights of hyperbole. To sell his sheep, the merchant transforms them into mythic creatures like Jason's sheep, cosmic animals whose internal and external parts, even whose waste products, have supernatural powers.[24] The purpose of all his rhetoric is, of course, to extract from Panurge a price five or six times the sheep's worth. As he leads Dindenault to perdition, Panurge warns

---

of *Le Songe de Pantagruel*. See the edition published with an introduction by John Lewis in *Études rabelaisiennes* 18 (1985): 103-62. Gargantua comes to Pantagruel in a dream and advises that the way to true wisdom lies in following the teachings of Pan the Great Shepherd. He exhorts his son to become a "berger" (138-45).

[24] "Par tous les champs es quelz ilz pissent, le bled y provient comme si Dieu y eust pissé . . . . De leur urine les Quintessentiaux tirent le meilleur Salpetre du monde. De leurs crottes (mais qu'il ne vous desplaise) les medicins de nos pays guerissent soixante et dixhuict especes de maladie" (552).

the sheep merchant against the overwhelming greed blinding him to the danger he is in: "Vous n'estez le premier de ma congnoissance, qui trop toust voulent riche devenir et parvenir, est à l'envers tombé en paouvreté: voire quelque foys s'est rompu le coul" (553-54). Re-reading this warning as he wrote it in the 1548 book, Rabelais was inspired to write another fable with the same moral, for Couillatris' imitators in the 1552 prologue make the same fatal misjudgment as Dindenault. "*Sanita et guadain*" (535) are antithetical values. "Opt(ez) et soubhait(ez) mediocrité en matiere de coingnée" (532)–and, we add, "en matière de mouton."

However, as the play moves to Act III, it becomes clear that Panurge is also implicated in this moral. He drops the mask of *moralisateur* and an immoral comedy bursts forth, a comedy of revenge which, as the narrator recounts, comes with shocking swiftness:

> Soudain, je ne sçay comment, le cas fut subit . . . . Panurge, sans aultre chose dire, jette en pleine mer son mouton criant et bellant. Tous les aultres moutons crians et bellans en pareille intonation commencerent soy jecter et saulter en mer après à la file . . . . Comme vous sçavez estre du mouton le naturel, tous jours suyvre le premier, quelque part qu'il aille. (554-5)

With the sheep goes Dindenault in a vain attempt to prevent the catastrophe, and the other "bergiers et moutonniers" go with him.

Now Panurge goes beyond all bounds, transgresses more terribly than Dindenault who only sold the sheep. Panurge slays them, and in a blasphemous way. A shadow story is evoked in this scene, that of Christ casting the swine into the sea (Mark 5 9-13), but Panurge perverts that story. He treats the sheep as if they were swine, and betrays Christ's affection for them. This is a slaughter of the innocents. As sheep and shepherds struggle to save themselves, Panurge pushes them back into the sea with an oar. He drowns them all, while quoting the scriptures and preaching a sermon "comme si feust un petit frere Olivier Maillard, ou un second frere Jan bourgeoys, leurs remonstrant par lieux de Rhetoricque les miseres de ce monde, le bien et l'heur de l'autre vie . . ." (555). And, as he had warned Dindenault, so Frère Jean, in the last sentence of the 1552 episode, warns Panurge that a punishment awaits him: "Tu . . . te damnes comme un vieil diable. Il est escript, *Mihi vindictam, et caetera*. Matiere de breviere" (556).

This warning echoes forward to the tempest, which is linked structurally and thematically to the Dindenault episode. It too begins with an encounter at sea where the Council of Trent is evoked, a meeting with nine boatloads of monks on their way to the "concile de Chesil" (581). Panurge's reaction is highly inappropriate: he enters into an "excès de joye" (581) on seeing the priests and he throws food into their boats. He throws *meat* to them,[25] a gesture not unlike his pitching the sheep into the sea, and immediately thereafter the tempest arrives. On "l'isle des Macraeons" the storm is interpreted as an expression of nature's grief and rage at the death of a hero, the death of Pan, but during the storm, Frère Jean lays the blame on Panurge: "Ce Diable de fol marin est cause de la tempeste, et il seul ne ayde à la chorme" (587). These are parallel explanations which converge on the idea of crimes committed against the spirit of *caritas*, the spirit of the lamb. By his betrayal of the sheep and his slavish affection for the "bad shepherds" on their way to the Council of Trent, Panurge, "Diable tempestatif," as Frère Jean calls him (587), has offended the waters, he has roused the sea to rage, and the waters take their revenge, as Frère Jean foresaw–by threatening Panurge with the same death as that to which he condemned the sheep.

Indeed, there always was a fatal link between Panurge and his victims. Dindenault had persistently associated him to the sheep: "Voyez ce mouton-là, il a nom Robin comme vous. Robin, Robin, Robin,–Bês, Bês, Bês, Bês. O la belle voix" (551). During the tempest, Panurge's cries echo the bleating of the drowning animals, and he also evokes the words of the dying Christ: "Dieu . . . et la benoiste Vierge soient avec nous. Holos, holas, je naye. Bebebebous, bebe, bous, bous. *In manus*" (590). Panurge parodically undergoes Christ's sacrifice, a sacrifice which he, as a comic Judas figure, has caused.[26] Thus, he must replace the sheep as the scapegoated and sacrificial animal of *Le Quart Livre*. "(V)eau co-

---

[25] "Et ayant courtoisement salué les beatz peres and recommendé le salut de son ame à leurs devotes prieres et menuz suffraiges, feist jecter en leurs naufz soixante et dixhuict douzaines de jambons, nombre de Caviatz, dizaines de Cervelatz, centaines de Boutargues, et deux mille beaulx Angelotz pour les ames des trespassez" (581).

[26] Dennis Costa also makes the point that Panurge is a comic Judas, *Irenic Apocalypse: Some Uses of Apocalyptic in Dante, Petrarch and Rabelais* (Stanford: Anma Libri, 1981) 133-34.

quart ... grand veau pleurart ... veau marin" (590) and "boucq estourdy" (697) Panurge is condemned by his transgression to undergo the fate of his victims.

And there is more. The Dindenault episode and the tempest are not only stories of water, they are stories of fire as well–banquet dramas where Panurge, mysteriously, plays all the roles. He is cook as well as killer of the sheep–he conducts their drowning, "a cousté du fougon" (555), near "the cooke roome," in Randle Cotgrave's definition. But Panurge is also meat, as he has been ever since 1532 when we saw him being roasted by the Turks, "en broche tout lardé, comme un connil" (P 263-4). His edible destiny reemerges as a persistent theme in *Le Quart Livre*. During the tempest, Frère Jean tells him that he need not fear drowning, that death by fire, "roasting" is his destiny (113), a message which Pantagruel reiterates during the encounter with the whale.[27] To both, Panurge raises the same objection: "Voire . . . . Mais les cuisiniers des Diables resvent quelque foys, et errent en leur office: et mettent souvent bouillir ce qu'on destinoit pour roustir . . ." (596-7), but he does not deny that he is destined to be devoured as meat. Panurge acknowledges his edible destiny and, in so doing, pulls us into the darkest and most frightening corners of banquet imagery. He evokes the fear that Christ confronted and made sacred when he offered His body as bread and His blood as wine, the darkest truth of the human condition–that we are all made of flesh and all flesh can be consumed.

These banquet and eucharistic fears reach their apex and are dispelled in the last chapter of *Le Quart Livre*. Panurge, we remember, had fled in terror to the hold of the ship, the lowest point of the voyage, which he calls "the kitchens of Hell," and we must pay careful attention to his portrait as he emerges:

> Panurge *comme un boucq estourdy* sort de *la Soutte* en chemise, ayant seulement un demy bas de chausses en jambe: *sa barbe toute mouchetée de miettes de pain* tenent en main un grand chat Soubelin . . . .

---

[27] "Si telle est . . . vostre destinée fatale, comme naguieres exposoit frere Jan, vous doibvez paour avoir de(s) . . . celebres chevaulx du Soleil flammivomes, qui rendent feu par les narines: des Physeteres, qui ne jettent qu'eau par les ouyes et par la gueule, ne doibvez paour aulcune avoir. Jà par leur eau ne serez en dangier de mort. Par cestuy element plus toust serez guaranty et conservé que fasché ne offensé" (617).

> Agua, men emy (disoit il) men frere, men pere spirituel, tous les Diables sont au jourd'huy de nopces. Tu ne veids oncques tel apprest de *bancquet infernal*. Voy tu *la fumée des cuisines d'Enfer?* . . . Tu ne veids oncques tant d'ames damnées. (697-8, my italics)

There is no mistaking the parody of both the Eucharist and the resurrection in this passage. As the scapegoated animal "boucq estourdy (et émissaire)," Panurge has experienced the fate to which he knew he was destined, that of being "roasted" by "les cuisiniers des diables" (596-7) and eaten at an "infernal banquet." He is meat, and he is bread, for according to Cotgrave, "la soutte," the ship's hold, is also "a binne to keep bread in" and we note the breadcrumbs in Panurge's beard. But he emerges whole and entire from this death and this devouring. Dirty and frightened, Panurge is sent to "prendre chemise blanche" (700). The last chapter of *Le Quart Livre* enacts a comic drama of resurrection[28] marked by Pantagruel's laughter, which is Easter laughter, *risus paschilis*,[29] and this drama, too, had been foreseen in the Dindenault episode. Despite the cruelty of his sermon to the drowning shepherds, Panurge had nonetheless held out to them the hope of Jonah's fate–and of Christ's resurrection on the third day:

> (L)eurs optant ce neantmoins, en cas que vivre encores entre les humains ne leurs faschast, et noyer ainsi ne leur vint à propous, bonne adventure, en rencontre de quelque Baleine, laquelle au tiers jour subsequent les rendist sains et saulves en quelque pays de satin, à l'exemple de Jonas. (555)

The three days of darkness have ended. Pan-Christ is disgorged from the jaws of death, as are all the drowned sheep and the one who by mythic necessity was doomed to slay them. Fear is banished. Blood is changed to wine. *Le Quart Livre* and Rabelais's whole odyssey ends with Panurge's final call to drink, his call of triumphant joy and communion. "Beuvons!" is his last word.

Thus, the first encounter with Dindenualt and the last chapter

---

[28] See my reading of the last chapter in *Rabelais: Homo Logos* (Chapel Hill: U of North Carolina P, 1979) 116-21. For a very similar interpretation, see Smith, *Voyage et écriture* 181-191.

[29] On "Easter Laughter," see Bahktin, esp. 78-79.

of the book initiate and complete a sacred parody centering on the Lamb, a cycle which loops through the tempest and the episode on "l'isle des Macraeons." But in the middle, between death and rebirth, *Le Quart Livre* enters the domain of another animal, the pig, whose snout can be discerned in Rouge Museau and the Chiquanous and who is worshipped as a god by the Andouilles and by the Gastrolatres. The Holy Body has been betrayed and communion among humans perverted and destroyed by "les ennemis de la croix du Christ . . . des quelz Ventre est le Dieu" (675). The cycle of the pig stands in dynamic antithesis to the cycle of the lamb throughout *Le Quart Livre*. Eternal emblem of the "low other," of gluttony and greed and the basest forms of carnal self-indulgence,[30] the pig was also a frequent Reformation symbol of moral corruption within Catholic dogma, the corruption of a clergy who betrayed the idea of *caritas* on which Christ's church is founded.[31] At the same time, however, the pig carries positive values equal in weight to the negative ones. Friend to man, pet and "commensal associate,"[32] this animal is also the joyful beast of carnival–symbol of the pleasures of food, giver of succulent and nourishing meat.[33]

---

[30] See the section "Thinking with Pigs" in Peter Stalleybrass and Allon White, *The Politics and Poetics of Transgression* (Ithaca: Cornell UP, 1986) 44-59. The whole chapter, "The Fair, the Pig, Authorship" 27-79 is relevant. See also Edmund Leach's famous article, "Anthropological Aspects of Language: Animal Categories and Verbal Abuse," *New Directions in the Study of Language*, ed. Erich H. Lenneberg (Cambridge, MA: MIT, 1964) esp. 42-50 where Leach argues that pigs transgress the boundaries of all our cultural grids: they are both family and stranger, human and animal, pet and game, friendly and hostile.

[31] Woodcuts of the sixteenth century, for example, show the Pope as a disgusting old sow, or riding on a pig, or copulating with a dog and giving birth to Jesuit swine who were later taught by Pig, professor of Epicurean philosophy, "Pig teaching Minerva," in Rabelais's formulation (162). Such figurations turned the church's own imagery of the pig against itself. The "ungodly beast" cast out by Christ (Mark 5: 9-13) was used by the evangelicals as an emblem of corruption at the top as well as at the bottom of the Church hierarchy. See Bob Scribner, "Reformation, carnival, and the world turned upside down," *Social History* 3 (October, 1978): 303-29.

[32] The phrase comes from Leach, 50. The pig is a "commensal associate" because, in addition to eating garbage and even feces, the animal was also fed with table scraps and kept very close to the farmhouse. See also Stalleybrass and White, 46-47 who describe the many ways that pigs play at the threshold of the human and the animal. Their diet mixes food and feces. Their pink pigmentation and apparent nakedness disturbingly resemble the flesh of human babies and their squeal is uncomfortably close to a baby's cry. In such ways, the pig alarmingly overlaps and debases human habitat, diet, and language.

[33] Claude Gaignebet and Marie-Claude Florentin, in *Le Carnaval: Essais de mythologie populaire* (Paris: Payot, 1974), also describe the ambivalences surround-

With such instabilities and contradictions in mind, we now pass to the perplexities of the stories told on "l'isle Procuration" and to the strange case of Rabelais's Chiquanous.

3. Pigs in High Places: Les Chiquanous

The Chiquanous episode (chs. 12-16) is one of the most complex in the entire *Quart Livre*, because of the labyrinth of its three nested tales. Into the single short chapter of 1548 describing the voyagers' arrival on "l'isle Procuration" and their encounter with the Chiquanous[34] are inserted, in 1552, the Basché story told by Panurge and the tale of the parish priest Etienne Tappecoue told by Basché. Compounding this complex narrative structure is the problematic relationship between the three textual levels. Each takes place in a different place and time, has its own cast of characters and, though all three are stories of crime and punishment, the exact nature of the crime and the identity of the real criminals are far from clear. To use Rabelais's own expression, this episode is constructed "par syncope" (707, see citation below). Much is dropped and left unsaid, leaving gaps that must be recovered by interpretation. There is a dialogue with silence throughout the episode, a tension between what is said and what is not, between what appears onstage and what lurks in the wings. As the proverb suggests, we hear only the sound of one hand clapping.

However, at the end of the 1552 version, we are allowed to hear at least the echo of the other hand. These last paragraphs take the form of a double dialogue between the characters speaking in the text on the one hand, and between the text and messages encoded in the "Briefve Declaration" on the other. The scene begins as the voyagers encounter two old women weeping and lamenting the fate

---

ing the pig at the time of slaughter and at carnival: "(La tuerie du cochon) était l'occasion de réjouissances nettement carnavalesques qui, pourtant, n'allaient pas sans pleurs, le cochon étant un animal familier. Peu d'animaux ont, comme lui, jusqu'à leur mort, partagé la vie de la famille. Jour après jour, il s'est nourri des restes. Très souvent, même, on lui a donné un nom . . . . Quand vient le jour de le tuer, puisqu'il est un animal de consommation, on ne peut oublier le contact quotidien auquel on met ainsi fin" (61).

[34] For the 1548 version, consult Jean Plattard, ed., *Le Quart Livre de Pantagruel (édition dite partielle, Lyon, 1548)* (Paris: Champion, 1909). In contrast to five chapters in 1552, the 1548 episode is comprised of only one short chapter.

of two of the most substantial persons of the land: "... l'on avoit au gibbet *baillé le moine par le coul* aux deux plus gens de bien, qui feussent en tout Chiquanourroys" (578, my italics).[35] Gymnaste responds with perplexity to this turn of phrase,[36] but Frère Jean purports to understand it, using a strange expression of his own: "Voire, voire, ... Vous en parlez comme sainct Jan de la Palisse" (578). Then by this entry in the "Briefve Declaration," Rabelais intervenes to explain Frère Jean's language:

> *Comme Sainct Jan de la Palisse.* Maniere de parler vulgaire par syncope: en lieu de l'Apocalypse: comme Idolatre pour Idolatre. (707)

Important clues are given in this definition. Rabelais evokes divine vengeance in an apocalyptic future and he also evokes the sin that brings down God's wrath, the sin of idolatry which is attacked throughout *Le Quart Livre,* the worship of false gods: "le dieu sur terre" as with the Papimanes, the belly as god as with the Gastrolatres.

And as the dialogue between text and "Briefve Declaration" continues, other sins emerge: "Interrogées sus les causes de cestuy pendaige, (les deux vieilles) respondirent que (les pendus) avoient desrobé les ferremens de la messe et les avoient mussez soubs le manche de la paroece" (578).[37] In the glossary, we are told that "les ferremens" of the mass are its ornaments, "implements, or instruments, belonging to the Mass," in Cotgrave's words, and that the "handle" (Cotgrave) of the parish is the church steeple, "par metaphore assez lourde" (707). The metaphor is indeed "heavy" in every sense of the word. The substance of the mass has been stolen away and perverted by those who should sustain it but who worship other, self-serving gods. The Chiquanous episode is an attack on evil on the inside of the church, from the bottom of the hierarchy with lowly Chiquanous, to its very top, the Pope himself. The

---

[35] The wording is more straightforward in 1548: "l'on avoit mené au gibet les deux plus gens de bien qui fussent en toute l'Isle" (Plattard 91).

[36] "Mes Paiges ... baillent le moine par le pieds à leurs compaignons dormars. (Bailler le moine par le pied = attach a cord to the toe of a sleeping person.) Bailler le moine par le coul, seroit pendre et estrangler la persone" (578).

[37] In 1548, this sentence, the last of the episode, is abbreviated: "... ilz avoient desrobé les ferremens de la Messe" (Plattard 91).

attack is expressed by the Reformation imagery we have discussed, using pigs as emblems of this moral corruption.

From the very outset of the 1548 frame tale, the Chiquanous are presented as piggish creatures and embodiments of the "low other," as indicated by the components of their name (chier/cul/anus) and by the epithet "Red Snout" which describes their physiognomy. Like pigs, the Chiquanous are destined to be cruelly beaten and flayed,[38] a fate which they, with perversity, gladly embrace. Hired to serve slanderous summonses on innocent people who attack them in rage, the Chiquanous earn their living by suing for assault and battery, and they also derive sexual pleasure from the experience as Panurge understands: "C'est . . . comme ceulx, qui, (par le rapport de Cl. Galien), ne peuvent le nerf caverneux vers le cercle equateur dresser, s'ilz ne sont tresbien fouettez" (Plattard 89).

Of course, the Chiquanous are not alone in their perversion. These "low others" have their counterparts at the top, those who send them to be beaten–"un prebstre, un usurier, ou un advocat" (Plattard 89). The motivation of these pigs in high places is more obscure and far more menacing, for their behavior cannot be mitigated by need, as can that of the Chiquanous. Rich and powerful, these enemies initiate the process of beating and suing for purely capricious reasons, because they "veul(ent) mal à quelque gentilhomme" (Plattard 89), and also because they receive pleasure from inflicting hurt or seeing it inflicted, as Pantagruel explains with the anecdote of the Roman gentleman who beat strangers in the street "(par) tyrannicque complexion," "par gayeté de coeur" (Plattard 89) and then paid them to be silent. The Chiquanous and their employers are bound together by a sado-masochistic tie.

More than being linked by corrupt self-interest and sexual perversity, the lowly Chiquanous become, at the end of the 1548 frame story, indistinguishable from those at the top.[39] As they mill around

---

[38] The pig is the only farm animal who lives just to die. "Sheep provide wool, cows provide milk, chickens provide eggs," writes Edmund Leach, "but we rear our pigs for the sole purpose of killing them" (50), and their slaughter has traditionally been very brutal. Pigs were stunned, then stabbed and often left to run wild in agony with the knife in their flesh until they died (Stalleybrass and White 47).

[39] Lawrence Kritzman makes a similar point, saying that "the rabelaisian text blurs the potential identity of the Chiquanous by the to-and-fro movement of mirrored opposites." "Rabelais' comedy of cruelty: the Chiquanous episode," *The Rhetoric of Sexuality and the Literature of the French Renaissance* (Cambridge: Cambridge UP, 1991) 194.

Frère Jean, shouting in Italian, "Io, io, io" and slavishly begging to be beaten, the Chiquanous are no longer the lowly summons-servers they were at the outset of the episode. Red Snout wears a ring on his right hand; another is called "habille homme, bon clerc, et, (comme estoit le bruit commun), honneste homme en court d'Eglise" (Plattard 90). Rabelais has transferred the lowly pigs to the inside of the Church and linked them to the depravity of churchmen.

This link will become far more explicit in 1552, though there are significant differences between the Chiquanous of the 1548 frame story and those of the Basché tale. In contrast to the urban setting of the first version, the action takes place at Basché's country estate, in the green world and the garden, and in this realm, the Chiquanous reacquire the ambivalence that pigs possess in the agricultural setting which is their homeland.[40] In 1548, they inspire only negative emotions, the disgust of Frère Jean and the other voyagers at the Chicquanous' servile eagerness to be beaten. In 1552, they assume the friendly face that pigs also possess and become participants in the festivities. This more positive portrait is possible because, in contrast to the frame tale where corruption in high and low places is merged, the Basché tale makes a clear distinction between the Chiquanous and those responsible for the mischief. These enemies are named at the outset of the 1552 insertion: the piggish Fat Prior, "(le) gras prieur de sainct Louant," who is both the symbol of a corrupt clergy and surrogate for the one responsible for the corruption, the pope, named here as Jules second" (565).[41]

---

[40] The ambivalence of pigs that we have described–objects of disgust and rage, on the one hand, and of affection as providers of food and symbols of the joys of Carnival, on the other–was a rural ambivalence. When herded into cities, they lost their positive values and acquired new negative ones. Because of their dung in the streets, pigs became the sign of "misery from below," the misery of the poor urban slum dweller. Paradoxically, they also became a sign of "misery from above," the cruel repression of the poor by those in power, an attitude reflected in our modern usage of "pig" for policeman (Stalleybrass and White 48-9).

[41] Jules II was pope from 1503 to 1513. He was responsible for the formation of "La Ligue de Cambrai," a coalition of European states originally established to ruin the power of Venice, but which turned against France during the reign of Louis XIII.

The allusion to Jules II also evokes Pope Jules III and the confrontation with Henri II which created the Gallican crisis of 1550-52. The French king, in Defaux's words, desired to "empêcher toute ingérance de la papauté dans les affaires fran-

Panurge tells the Basché story as a "remede tresbon" (565) for the sinister realities evoked in 1548, and it functions as a remedy in many ways, by the festive laughter it evokes—"le tout en riant" is a constant refrain—and by the theatrical illusion which generates this laughter. Like the Dindenault episode, this is a farce and "Tragicque comedie" (566) in three acts, each of which centers on the visit of a Chiquanous sent by the Fat Prior to cite Basché: the first, old, fat, and red; the second, young, tall, and thin; and the third arrives with two "witnesses" who evoke the Chiquanous who have come before. These are the three pigs. All are greeted by a costumed spectacle mounted by Basché, the mock wedding of the baker, Loyre, and his wife, a "service" conducted by the parish priest, Oudart. Basché's people are all given metal gauntlets covered with fur, and the old custom of the "nopces à mitaines," the gauntlet wedding, is enacted.[42] The Chiquanous are soundly thrashed to the rhythm of the drum played by Trudon, in accordance with Basché's instructions:

> Les parolles dictes, et la mariée baisée, au son du tabour vous tous baillerez l'un à l'autre du souvenir des nopces, ce sont petitez coups de poing . . . . Tappez, daubez, frappez . . . . N'ayez peur d'en estre reprins en justice. Je seray guarant pour tous. Telz coups seront donnez en riant, scelon la coustume observée en toutes fiansailles. (566)

This custom permits Basché to gain revenge on the Chiquanous without fear of legal reprisal, but as Basché himself indicates during the beatings, the symbolism of the blows is larger: "Ce sont petites charesses nuptiales" (575). By thus transferring the beatings of 1548 to the marriage bed, the guantlet wedding normalizes the sadomasochism of the frame story and transforms its sterile sexuality into blows that are loving and fertile. Now we are in the garden of Priapus, "gardien des jardins en terre" (530), the sexual garden with its promise of fecundity and renewal.

çaises. Il entend . . . protéger les droits de ses évêques contre l'évidente partialité de la Curie . . . . Il voit de même d'un très mauvais oeil tous les procédés, système de *annates*, ajournements, dispenses, prébendes et bénéfices, procès et autres manoeuvres juridiques, au moyen desquels la 'pompe à phynances' papale tire l'argent de France en Rome." Defaux 481-2. For his discussion of the Gallican Crisis, see 480-6.

[42] This custom and its relevance to the Basché episode are described by Bakhtin 200-207.

Another kind of garden is also evoked in the Basché story, the "Vineyard of Dionysos" with its range of rich associations. As in the "Clos de l'abbaye de Seuillé" where Frère Jean felled 13,622 men "comme porcs" (G, 79), the thrashing of the Chiquanous recalls the festival of the pig slaughter, and it is also a *vendange*, a harvest of bodies as grapes or as grain: "frappez dessus comme sus seigle verde" (566).[43] Above all, the thrashings are a banquet. Each of the three acts begins by offering food and wine to the Chiquanous who, symbolically "harvested" during the cuffings, *become* the banquet—meat to be slaughtered and cooked, grapes to be trampled and drunk. In all of the descriptions, culinary terms are joined with the imagery of anatomizing dismemberment and with the laughter of carnival:[44]

> (I)lz le festoierent à grands coups de guantelez si bien, qu'il resta tout eslourdy et meutry: un oeil poché au beurre noir, huict coustes freussées, le brechet enfondré, les omoplates en quatre quartiers, la maschouere inferieure en trois loppins: et le tout en riant. (567)
> Croyez qu'en Avignon on temps de Carneval, les bacheliers oncques ne jouerent à la Raphe plus melodieusement, que feut joué sus Chiquanous. En fin il tombe par terre. On luy jecta force vin sus la face . . . . (572)

As in the abbey vineyard, blood is changed into wine at Basché's banquet, and the eucharistic associations of this transformation are clear from the outset. Oudart, the good priest who conducts the wedding, is also Basché's "sommeillier," his wine steward, and Oudart marries the baker and his wife who are bread. This is "le service divin, le service du vin" (G 78) and, as Dennis Costa stipulates, there can be no divine service without the service of wine.[45] In the Basché episode, as well as in the scene of Frère Jean in the abby close, eucharistic imagery joins with echos of the apoca-

---

[43] I am following Bahktin in linking the Chiquanous episode to the scene of Friar John's slaughter of 13,622 men in the abby close. See esp. 208-209.

[44] As Bakhtin has argued, "(T)he fighting temperament (war, battles) and the kitchen cross each other at a certain point, and this point is the dismembered, minced flesh" (193). For his reading of the Chiquanous episode where this point is reiterated, see 196-97, 199-207, and 211-13.

[45] Costa makes this point 116. His reading of the Picrocholine Wars is found 115-18.

lypse, that juncture where the enemies of the Lamb are trampled into "the wine of God's wrath."[46] But this winepress of vengeance also has its irenic side, which is present in the Basché episode as well as in the famous scene from *Gargantua*. The punishment of the Chiquanous is at the same time a remedy, for they are gathered into the service of wine and reformed by it. They lose their status as "low others." They become friend and banquet companion.

This transformation and change of attitude are enacted in the last scene. Contrary to their slavish behavior up until this point, the Chiquanous take charge of the ceremony. As will the Andouilles of "l'isle Farouche," they strike the first blow, and they *fight back*, which they have never done before. But rather than generating anger, the carnivalesque *mêlée* is full of friendly feelings: gaity and extraordinary linguistic creativity and, most important, the last battle earns the Chiquanous the pardon of the priest Oudart and of Basché. The fight ends with a toast:

> . . . Oudart renioit and despitoit les nopces, alleguant qu'un des Records luy avoit desincornifistibulé tout l'aultre espaule. Ce non obstant, beuvoit à luy joyeusement . . . .
> La nouvelle mariée pleurante rioyt, riante pleuroit, de ce que Chiquanous . . . d'abondant luy avoit trepignemampenillorifrizonoufressuré les parties honteuses en trahison.
> Le diable, dist Basché, y ayt part! . . . Je ne luy en veulx mal toutesfoys . . . . Je boy à luy de bien bon coeur, et à vous aussi, messieurs les Records. (574-5)

This friendship for the Chiquanous strikes an entirely new note in the 1552 version, and they are excused from culpability by the listeners' commentary after Panurge finishes telling the Basché tale: "En quoy offensoient ces paouvres Diables Chiquanous?" asks Epistemon (576). He rather condemns the sinister personage who is the cause of the harm yet who escapes all punishment: the sadistic gras Prieur:

> Meilleure . . . seroit, si la pluie de ces jeunes guanteletz feust sus le gras Prieur tombée. Il dependoit (dépensait) pour son passetemps argent, part à fascher Basché, part à veoir ses Chiquanous daubbez. (576)

---

[46] *Apoc.* 14.18, quoted by Costa 116.

Though the Fat Prior's name is reiterated throughout the Basché story and the finger of blame repeatedly pointed at him, he is never seen nor heard in the episode, he remains an offstage presence, manipulating the action but removed from it. However, in the third tale, an ecclestiastical surrogate for "le gras Prieur"–himself a surrogate for the Pope–is put on stage, the priest Estienne Tappecoue who receives an extreme punishment at the hands of the poet François Villon. Told by Basché, a character in the story told by Panurge, this anecdote is kept at a safe narrative distance from the fictionally "real" encounter of Pantagruel and his men with the Chiquanous, and at a safe temporal distance too, for it takes place in the fifteenth century. Yet, despite the protective measure of this complex narrative infolding, the story of Tappecoue clearly goes to the heart of the matter. It is a story of crime and punishment directed toward the corrupt clergy who are the true objects of attack in this episode.

The Tappecoue/Villon story (568-70) is made up of many of same elements as the Basché tale. Tappecoue is the negative counterpart of Oudart. He is the bad priest, refuser of festivity and spoiler of the sacraments versus the good priest who is part of the play and sustains its symbolism. Tappecoue withholds, if not "les ferremens de la messe," then the robes necessary to play the role of God the Father in a passion play that Villon is staging. For this crime, like Basché, the poet mounts a "Tragicque comedie" (566), one which plays on the double meaning of the word "passion." Tappecoue mounts a mare to travel to Saint Ligaire, "une jument non encore saillie" (568), a gesture with distinctly sexual overtones, like the gauntlet wedding. When the priest is set upon by Villon's devils who frighten the mare, the second sense of the word *passio,* "suffering," is enacted. Tappecoue falls off the saddle, his foot gets caught in the stirrup, and he is dragged by the horse all over the countryside, leaving parts of his body along the way. When the mare arrives back at the convent, all that is left of the priest is his right foot and shoe, still wedged in the stirrup. Thus the enemy of Dionysus, the enemy of the cross, is punished with flaying and dismemberment, as in the abbey close, as at Basché's banquet.

But this is no vineyard. No renewal is promised for Tappecoue, who disappears piece by piece and dies. Moreover, the joyful regeneration of Basché's Chiquanous is, in the end, erased. Like Tappecoue, they are made to disappear one by one, after the banquet is over: "Depuis n'en fut parlé. La memoire en expira avecques le son des cloches, lesquelles quarrilonnerent à son enterrement" (567). We are disturbed by these deaths and disappearances and we are also troubled by the excessive violence of these tales, as we were with Panurge's punishment of the sheep merchant of Taillebourg.[47] Indeed, as the Dindenault episode ended with Frère Jean's *mihi vindictam* (556), so the story-telling on "l'isle Procuration" ends with Pantagruel's warning about transgressing the limits of human vengeance, and it is a warning which dismisses the gayety of these tales as an illusion: "Ceste narration . . . *sembleroit joyeuse*, ne feust que davant nos oeilz fault la craincte de Dieu continuellement avoir" (576, my italics).

We are also disturbed that the resolutions enacted in the three textual layers of the Chiquanous episode do not carry forth from one level to another, and that the vengeances are not directed to their true object. The punishments of Tappecoue and the Chiquanous do not touch the real enemies, the Fat Prior and the Pope, who always remain beyond the reach of the narrative. And all the remedies offered by the story of Basché are erased by the placement of the tale within the 1548 frame story. The fertile sexuality of the wedding and the garden is defeated by the return to the corrupt city, to Pantagruel's anecdote of the sadistic Roman gentleman who beat strangers in the street "par guayeté de coeur" (576), and to the scene in the court of Rome where Red Snout and the Chiquanous swarm around Frère Jean begging to be beaten (576-7). The sympathy and liking that the Chiquanous acquired at Basché's wedding are lost at the end of the 1552 episode. They revert to their status as "low other" and inspire only disgust.

Most important, the healing laughter fades, as, indeed, the "Briefve Declaration" had warned it would. "Tragicque comedie," a term used to describe the tales of both Basché and Tappecoue, is defined in the "Briefve Declaration" as a "Farce plaisante au commencement, *triste en la fin*" (707, my italics). At the end of the episode, we find ourselves pondering the hanging of the Chi-

---

[47] In the book's last chapter, while speaking of the terror of his experience in the hold of the ship, Panurge evokes Villon, the poet's banishment from France and his death by hanging (699-70). Villon and Panurge's fates are linked and they are punished for the same transgression–exceeding the bounds of human vengeance, meting out punishment which belongs to God, as the *mihi vindictam* of Frère Jean and Pantagruel suggests.

quanous–the punishment of lesser criminals for greater crimes committed against the mass by those who remain beyond the reach of punishment: pigs in high places in the church hierarchy who have corrupted and betrayed the faith. As Pantagruel's *mihi vindictam* and Frère Jean's "syncopated" allusion to "Sainct Jan de la Palisse" (707) indicate, vengeance for these crimes belongs to God and must be deferred to an apocalyptic future. It is this imperative of deferred vengeance that gives the ending of the episode its tonality of tension and dissatisfaction, for in the present, all actions are blocked and all remedies fail. Even fictionally, "les ennemis de la croix du Christ" (675) cannot be defeated. The whole edifice of this complex episode comes to rest on a feeling of despair. As Epistemon's final comment indicates, Rabelais is indeed speaking "en terrible Allegorie" (578).

4. Pigs and Snakes and the Reversible World:
   Les Andouilles of "l'Isle Farouche"

The Chiquanous are not forgotten as the voyage progresses. In the seas between "l'isle Tapinois" and "l'isle Farouche," the voyagers encounter "un grand et monstreux Physetere" (616) which Panurge sends back to them: "Ho Ho Diable Satanas, Leviathan!," he shouts "Vestz (allez) à l'audience, vest aux Chiquanous" (617). By its name and by its essence, "le physetere" evokes Antiphysie, whose story Pantagruel has just told on "'l'isle Tapinois" (614-5), and the upside-down world she and her children incarnate. The spouter, too, inverts nature. This is the monster of the lower depths come to the surface of the world. It blows an upside river from its spout, its maw is the gateway to hell, "(une) grande gueule infernale" (616). But the heroic Pantagruel slays the monster by his mastery of "l'art sagittaire" (618).[48] He deflates the "blower" and windy

---

[48] Duval (*Design* 125-35) finds "le physetère" to be the central episode of *Le Quart Livre*, literally–as the 34th of 67 chapters–as well as symbolically: "(T)he action highlighted at the precise midpoint of the *Quart Livre* appears not only as a heroic exploit performed by a valorous hero, not only as a symbolic victory over the devil, but as a typological act of redemption in which Pantagruel as a figure of Christ fulfills prophecy by destroying a figure of Satan (133).

Michel Jeanneret, to the contrary, in "Rabelais, les monstres et l'interprétation des signes (*Quart Livre* 18-42)," *Writing the Renaissance. Essays on Sixteenth-Century French Literature in Honor of Floyd Gray*, ed. Raymond C. La Charité (Lexing-

beast by throwing arrows and javelins which pierce its skin and, dying, the whale undergoes a metamorphosis. It turns upside down, flattens out, and reveals itself to be a many-legged worm:

> Adoncques mourant le Physetere se renversa ventre sus dours, comme font tous poissons mors: et ainsi renversé les poultres contre bas en mer ressembloit au Scolopendre serpent ayant cent pieds . . . . (620)

The carcass is pulled to the shores of a pleasant island "pour en faire l'anatomie" (620), and we enter the belly of the beast–but what beast? The metamorphoses of the whale continue to multiply on "l'isle Farouche." The animal becomes pig as well as fish, sausage as well as serpent, friend and foe alike. The voyage now enters a world that is not only reversed, but which is also totally reversible, where all creatures and all categories are inextricably merged. The voyage has entered the domain of the Andouilles.

This is a complex and troubling episode, "un poème saugrenu,"[49] and a main focus of its strange poetry is to explore the nether regions of the banquet, the mix of transgression and joy involved in killing, cooking and eating meat–particularly eating pigs, the animal whose slaughter, as we have discussed, arouses so many conflicted feelings (see 80-2 and ns. 30, 32, 33, 38). The poem is played out as an epic battle, a travestied *Iliad*, with the Poet in the Kitchen again, where he was in chapter ten–there cooking up a "fricassé de congres" (563-4), here a "fricassée d'andouilles." The underlying metaphor of the episode is that to cook and eat meat is to "fight" with it, and in this surrealist vision, the meat is reanimated and it fights back. Immediately upon the voyagers' arrival on "l'isle Farouche" (ch. 35), the kitchen tents are set up. The tables are laid, the food is served and it jumps off the plate and attacks. Battalions of sausages invade the banquet site in full battle gear,

---

ton, KY: French Forum, 1992) 65-76 argues that the episode of "le physetère" holds no symbolic significance. "Ce qui aurait pu être un monstre ne montre rien; il n'est qu'un objet insignifiant et passif . . . . Pour sa défense, Pantagruel adopte une stratégie spécifiquement humaine: il compte sur sa force, son adresse et la précision géométrique de ses manoeuvres . . . . L'événement est contingent, immanent et la méthode, résolument profane" (68).

[49] Françoise Charpentier, "La Guerre des Andouilles: *Pantagruel* IV, 35-42," *Etudes Seiziémistes offertes à Monsieur le Professeur V.-L. Saulnier* (Geneva: Droz, 1980) 126.

marching to the sound of bagpipes and flutes, and blowing on pigs' bladders, the origin of our party balloons. This is a poem of carnival, a mock battle of Fat Tuesday where "warriors" fight with sausages and tripes, and pay festive hommage to the slaughtered beast who bestows such plenty. All the action takes place under the sign of the flying pig, Mardigras, who is at once "dieu tutellaire" (637) of the Andouilles and password of the Pantagruelists. Throughout the episode, the distinction between the antagonists is confused by the reiteration of their common allegiance to the god of Carnival: "Vostres, vostres, vostres sommes nous trestous, et à commandement. Tous tenons de Mardigras, vostre antique confoederé" (634).

At the same time, however, this gay confraternity of soldiers and sausages is a source of terror. Like world-upside-down engravings which depict such scenes as an ox flaying a man, or a pig gutting a butcher,[50] the attack of the Andouilles on Pantagruel and his soldiers indicates that they too are meat, equally vulnerable to being slaughtered, disemboweled and devoured. This frightening theme has already emerged in *Le Quart Livre,* but thus far it has been developed only in relation to Panurge, the creature destined to die by fire, roasted and devoured by "les cuisiniers des Diables" (596-7), as Frère Jean had forecast after the tempest, a prognostication repeated by Pantagruel during the encounter with the whale (see n. 27). With the episode of the Andouilles, however, the possibility of this destiny is extended to all the voyagers. The line between *avaleur* and *avalé* is blurred in this episode. Animal and human are intertwined. As Victor Hugo writes, "La pensée se dissout en assouvissement; la consommation charnelle absorbe tout; . . . le ventre mange l'homme."[51]

And more than banquet terrors are at stake in the strange poetry of the Andouilles episode. We are deep in the atmosphere of the belly where the digestive functions loop around the sexual ones, and where birth and death, creation and destruction are inextricably intertwined. Indeed, the great belly itself, with all its ambigui-

---

[50] See the engravings in David Kunzle, "World Upside Down: The Iconography of a European Broadsheet Type," *The Reversible World,* ed. by Barbara A. Babcock (Ithaca: Cornell UP, 1978) 45-47, as well as his text on animal-human inversions, 52-59.

[51] "William Shakespeare," in *Victor Hugo: Oeuvres Complètes,* vol. 12 (Paris: Editions Robert Laffont, 1985) 279.

ties, is wheeled onstage in this episode. Continuing the Homeric travesty and playing on the similarity between "Troye" and "Truye," Rabelais constructs a Trojan Sow (ch. 40). Into its paunch, "comme dedans le cheval de Troye" (631), climb some two hundred soldier-cooks, and the long list of their names includes one "Rabiolas" (633). With this name and by this gesture of entering the sow, the author is rewriting himself as well as Homer, recasting his voyage as a physician into Pantagruel's belly in the 1532 book (ch. 33). There, too, Alcofribas Rabiolas crowded himself with other little men into a copper apple and entered an abdomen, also to "do battle" with intestines–he entered the male abdomen of his own book. At the same time, "La Truye" is a clearly female image which recalls the belly of the pregnant mother Gargamelle, bursting with the battle inside her between the tripes she has eaten and the child in her womb struggling to be born (G ch. 6). As the cooks emerge from the Sow brandishing their frying pans, they enact a process of birth as well as of cooking and chopping. Like the Andouilles, they too are "de Pourceaux extraicts" (637). All of the images and actions of this episode lead us back to a field where the lines between digestion and sexuality, birth and death, male and female are dimmed, if not completely erased.

The fulcrum of these ambiguities is the intestine itself, *la trippe*, which can be linked to both poles of all these antinomies and also to two very different animal worlds. The Andouilles are called "doubles et traistresses" (622) and from the outset they show a double gender and a double derivation. Because they are stuffed and "pregnant," and because they come from the Pig Woman, "La Truye," they are resolutely identified as feminine, "Elles sont, respondit Xenomanes, femelles en sexe, mortelles en condition: aulcunes pucelles, autres non" (607). But the Andouilles also derive from "le physetere" whose "anatomie" began this episode. They are cold-blooded and fishy as well as warm-blooded and pig-like. As Barbara Bowen has argued, "andouilles," sausages, were traditionally conflated with "anguilles," eels,[52] and this association links them with Quaresmeprenant, their supposed enemy and opposite. Above all, whether sausage or eel, the female Andouilles are clearly phallic in form, and male as well as female in nature, an androgyny made explicit by the name of their queen "Niphleseth," glossed in

---

[52] "Lenten Eels and Carnival Sausages," *L'Esprit Créateur* 21.1 (1981): 17-22.

the "Briefve Declaration" as "Membre virile" in Hebrew (709), and by the whole of chapter thirty-eight entitled "Comment Andouilles ne sont à mespriser entre les humains":

> Le serpens qui tenta Eve, estoit andouillicque . . . . Encores maintient on en certaines Academies que ce tentateur estoit l'andouille nommée Ithyphalle, en laquelle feut jadis transformé le bon messer Priapus grand tentateur des femmes par les paradis en Grec, ce sont jardins en François. (628)

The entry of the serpent on the scene also indicates that more than sexual ambiguities are at stake. Moral worlds are also intertwined in the labyrinth of *la trippe:* good and evil, friend and foe, the creative and destructive urges in ourselves and in the world. Pigs and snakes share a common association with the Enemy and Other, "Diable Satanas" as Panurge calls him (617), whom Christ cast into the body of swine (Mark 5: 9-13) and who, as Hugo so eloquently suggests, lurks inside our own bodies as well: "Le serpent est dans l'homme, c'est l'intestin. Il tente, trahit, et punit" (278). It is with such negative associations that chapter thirty-eight begins: by evoking the race of the giants who piled mountain upon mountain "pour combatre les dieux, et du ciel les deniger" (628). But as the above-quoted passage reveals, the carnal aspect of this temptation generates a positive transvaluation of the serpent, for he is also "Great Father Snake,"[33] God of the Garden in both its horticultural and sexual connotations, he who renews the world. Now this chapter, which began by alluding to a race of destroyers, moves on to evoke a race of creators of both sexes who are all "andouillicque" and snake-like: the fairy mother Mellusina and the nymph Ora who both founded great families, and the male builder Erichthonius who invented coaches, litters and chariots for the transportation of his serpentine body. As in the Gaster episode, the serpent in the belly is identified as a "maistre es ars" and is linked positively to human enterprise.

But perhaps the most significant outcome of these transvaluations is to carnivalize the serpent and above all, to make him edible. Great Father Snake is transformed into a stuffed sausage and joins

---

[33] Joseph Campbell uses this expression, *The Hero With a Thousand Faces* (Princeton: Princeton UP, 1949) 155.

with the pig to be celebrated as a carnivalesque emblem of the pleasures of food. As we will argue in Chapter Five, the absorption of the sexual by the digestive principle in *Le Quart Livre* holds negative connotations for the project of paternity, "le projet de génération"[54] which generates the voyage of this book. In the Andouilles episode, however, the banquetization of the serpent constitutes a gay victory over fear. The Devourer can be devoured, the Enemy, too, is meat.

In the episode's final scene, the serpent modulates back into the pig who appears in a startling and miraculous manifestation:

> Du cousté de la Transmontane advola un grand, gras, gros, gris pourceau ayant aesles ... comme sont les aesles d'un moulin à vent. Et estoit le pennaige rouge cramoisy, ... Les oeilz avoit rouges et flamboyans, ... les aureilles verdes comme une esmeraude prassine: les dens jaulnes comme un Topaze: la queue longue noire comme marbre Lucillian .... les pieds blans, diaphanes et transparens, comme un diamant: et estoient largement pattez comme sont les Oyes, et comme jadis à Tholose les portoit la royne Pedaucque. Et avoit un collier d'or au coul, au tour duquel estoient quelques lettres Ionicques ... Pourceau Minerve enseignant. (635-6)

Here is a main image of the reversed and reversible world: the lowest and heaviest creature is taken from the earth and set in the air to fly; the stupidest and most bestial animal teaches wisdom and philosophy; the fleshiest and most carnal of beasts is made hard and bejeweled like an idol–the pig is worshipped as a God. As we have discussed, such imagery was widely used during the Reformation to attack the authority of the Catholic church (see above 80-2 and n. 31), and Edwin Duval develops a similar line of reasoning, interpreting the flying pig as part of a "procès général ... contre l'église romaine."[55] His case centers on the mustard which the pig sprinkles over the wounded Andouilles as it flies away. Queen Niphleseth explains to Pantagruel that mustard is their "Sangreal et Bausme celeste" (637). Duval argues that "Sangreal" is not only a deformation

---

[54] Françoise Charpentier, "Un Royaume qui perdure sans femmes," in Raymond C. La Charité, ed., *Rabelais's Incomparable Book* (Lexington, KY: French Forum, 1986) 195.

[55] "La Messe" 132. His discussion of this episode is found 135-38. See also *Design* 29-32.

of "Saint Graal," the traditional interpretation, but also of "sang réel" or "sang royal." In his view, the flying pig and the Sangreal mustard constitute an attack on the Catholic doctrine of the real presence of Christ at the Eucharist: "(I)l semble assez clair que sous la moutarde eucharistique et régéneratrice des Andouilles, Rabelais attaque le dogme de l'efficacité réelle de l'Eucharistie comme une erreur fondée dans ce qu'Erasme et tant d'autres, suivant saint Paul, appelaient, justement, la *'chair'* " (137).

This reading is supported by many aspects of the episode. In the first chapter (35) of the *escale*, Xenomanes gives a history of the wars between Quaresmeprenant and the Andouilles, a conflict aggravated and extended by "(le) concile national de Chesil" (622), the Council of Trent, which was meeting during 1551-52 to discuss the mass and the Eucharist. Additionally, there is an echo of the theme of "pigs in high places" found in the Chiquanous episode, and an almost word-for-word repetition of the charge of idolatry as it was stated there: one of the soldier-cooks in "La Truye" is named *Guaillardon*, "par syncope" for *Guaillartlardon*, the narrator explains. "Ainsi dictez vous idolatre pour idololatre" (632). Thus is evoked the sin underlying all others in *Le Quart Livre*, the worship of false gods, flying pig or the belly as God, which is the worship of oneself and one's own appetites.

At the same time, however, the Andouilles and "saulcissons montigènes" seem to be associated with the Swiss Calvinists[56] not with the Catholics. Above all, to worship the pig, and "la chair" at carnival time is a festive and not a demonic principle. The tensions and dark corners of the Andouilles episode seem resolved rather than aggravated by the appearance of the flying pig, "dieu tutellaire" (637) of Mardigras, whom the Pantagruelists also worship and whose password they share with the Andouilles. Pantagruel expresses a stubborn faith in the sausages,[57] a faith which culminates in the gay reconciliation and celebration of the end of the episode. Queen Niphleseth swears obeisance and loyalty to the Pantagru-

---

[56] For example: "Les Souisses, peuples maintenant hardy et belliqueux, que sçavons nous si jadis estoient Saulcisses?" (628).

[57] "Pantagruel feist (à deux colonels et leurs soldats) une briefve remonstrance, à ce qu'ilz eussent à soy monstrer vertueux au combat, si par cas estoient contraincts *(car encores ne povoit il croire que les Andouilles feussent si traistresses)* avecques defense de commencer le hourt (combat): et leurs bailla Mardigras pour mot du guet" (627, my italics).

elists and gives them gifts (636-7). The voyagers leave "l'isle Farouche" joyfully and, in the last sentence of the episode, a significant detail is recounted—they take the pig with them. "(Pantagruel) se retira en sa nauf. Aussi feirent tous les bons compaignons avecques leurs armes et *leur Truye*" (637, my italics).

It is rather on "l'isle de Ruach" (chs. 43-44) that a critique of the Andouilles emerges. This episode takes up many of the same themes and images developed positively with the Sausages and gives them a negative outcome. On "l'isle de Ruach," the Belly of the Sow stuffed with tripes and with men becomes Aeolus' bag filled with wind, and the theme of eating wind, and drinking it, inverts and undermines the gay outcome of the preceding episode. "L'isle de Ruach" is "a celebration of emptiness":[58]

> Quant ilz font quelque festin ou banquet, . . . disputent de la bonté, excellence, salubrité, rarité des vens, comme vous, Beuveurs par les banquetz philosophez en matiere de vins. (638)

Though Pantagruel compliments the Ruachians on the ease of their life: "Car vostre vivre qui est de vent, ne vous couste rien ou bien peu: il ne fault que souffler" (640), the darker elements of this imagery prevail. Eating wind is an image of eating nothing, of hunger and starvation, and themes of illness and death dominate on "l'isle de Ruach." Drinking wind in place of wine may be a perversion of the Eucharist,[59] for according to the "Briefve Declaration" (709), "Ruach" means spirit as well as wind, and spirit is brought low in this episode. The soul is degraded to the belly and the anus, and the writer's enterprise is also situated there. There are many references to poets and to poetic creation and Panurge is moved to compose a *dizain*. But his poem is about pissing and passing wind, "le vent punays, qui . . . sortoit (du "fessier" de la femme de Jenin de Quinquenays) comme d'une magistrale Æolipyle" (640, BD: "Porte D'Eole" 710). *Afflatus* becomes *flatus*, and death overwhelms all. On "l'isle de Ruach," one dies of flatulence, amid farts and words: "Ilz meurent tous Hydropicques tympanites. Et meurent les hommes en pedent, les femmes en vesnent. Ainsi leur

---

[58] Terence Cave, *The Cornucopian Text: Problems of Writing in the French Renaissance* (Oxford, Eng.: Oxford UP, 1979) 212.

[59] E. Duval makes this suggestion in "La Messe" 37 and in *Design* 32-4.

sort l'ame par le cul . . . . c'est ce que les Sanctimoniales appellent *sonnet*" (639).

Above all, there is the reiteration of the death of the giant Bringuenarilles, first recounted in chapter seventeen. Like the physeter whose apparition began this sequence of episodes, Bringuenarilles is an *avale-tout* and "(une) grande gueule infernale" (616). The giant is enemy to the Ruachans, for he devours the windmills which provide them with food, and he is also a menace to Rabiolas and the soldier-cooks in the Sow's belly, for he devours the frying pans which are the utensils of their craft. Additionally, the giant swallows things with voices, dogs and chickens which continue to bark and crow inside him[60] and, most relevant to the Andouilles, Bringuenarilles also eats snakes.

With Bringuenarilles, the theme of the serpent in the belly reemerges, but the positive valuation it was given on "l'isle Farouche" is reversed on "l'isle de Ruach" by the important dispute between Frère Jean and Pantagruel which occurs at the end of the episode. The island's potestat had suggested that Bringuenarilles' final convulsion was "as if" he had swallowed a snake: "comme si quelque serpens luy feust par la bouche entré dedans l'estomach" (641). Frère Jean strenuously objects to this comparison and defends the serpent in the belly as harmless, even pleasureful, echoing the double principle of the edible and sexual snake developed in the Andouilles episode:

> Voilà . . . un *comme* mal à propos, et incongru. Car j'ay aultrefoys ouy dire, que le serpens entré dans l'estomach ne faict desplaisir aulcun, et soubdain retourne dehors, si par les pieds on pend le patient, luy praesentant prés la bouche un paeslon plein de laict chauld. (641)

Now Pantagruel intervenes to countermand Frère Jean's defense of the serpent and to condemn the upside-down cure as "ouy dire," and fatally bad medicine.[61] By this judgement, he reverses the

---

[60] This theme of "voices in the belly" will be developed at length on Gaster's island with the Engastrimythes and the devil, Cinncinatule, who speaks from Jacobe Rodogine's abdomen (674-5). See our discussion 103-4.

[61] Pantagruel cites Hippocrates' account of a patient who swallowed a snake and who, when hung upside down, "subit estre mort par spasme et convulsion" (641).

positive transvaluation of the serpent accomplished in the Andouilles episode and reestablishes it as the cold-blooded Other who is untouchable and certainly inedible, the father of lies, the principle of death. In face of the seduction of the inverted world and the seduction, too, of words that create that world, Pantagruel once again intervenes to impose the standard of Nature, of what is upright and good, as he did with the myth of Physis and Antiphysie (614-15) and during the tempest when he held the tree of the mast upright to protect against the upside-down tree seen by Panurge: "l'arbre forchu, les pieds à mont, la teste en bas" (584).[62] Once again, the giant pulls away from the spectacle of antinature and refuses the charms of Bringuenarilles and the Ruachans, and of the Andouilles as well, charms to which he had been susceptible before. In the end, like Kafka's "hunger artist,"[63] Pantagruel repudiates their anti-banquet of wind and of words. This is not the food he seeks.

5. THE HUNGER ARTIST: MESSER GASTER

The Gaster episode is the master text of this series of alimentary episodes, the culminating meditation on the morality of appetite and the proper place of food in human existence, and it is a meditation led by Pantagruel. In the following episode near "l'isle Chaneph" (chs. 63-65), the giant's fellow travelers will turn to him for the resolution of "problemes propousez" (689), but here, Pantagruel confronts his own perplexities. For him, Gaster is "maistre" in the sense of "precepteur" as well as "gouverneur" of the creatural world. Pantagruel studies him: "(il) feut attentif à l'estude de Gaster" (682). The giant's meditation leads back into the labyrinth of *la trippe,* that point where the polar opposites of human

---

[62] The upside-down tree is also seen and condemned in Antiphysie's praise of her children: "Avoir les pieds en l'air, la teste en bas, estoit imitation du createur de l'Univers: veu que les cheveulx sont en l'home comme racines: les jambes comme rameaux. Car les arbres plus commodement sont en terre fichées sus leurs racines, que ne seroient sus leur rameaux. Par ceste demonstration alleguant que trop mieulx et plus aptement estoient ses enfans comme une arbre droicte, que ceulx de Physis: les quelz estoient comme une arbre renversée" (615).

[63] Franz Kafka, "A Hunger Artist" in *Selected Stories of Franz Kafka,* trans. by Willa and Edwin Muir (New York: Random House Modern Library, 1952) 188-201.

life meet and merge: nature versus culture and art; silence versus speech, good versus evil, the spiritual versus the material world. But the episode also leads out of the labyrinth, to Pantagruel's waking up and "raising of the wind" (ch. 63), and to the renewal of joy.

Sir Belly is a profoundly contradictory presence—Gaster *bifrons*, as Michel Jeanneret calls him.[64] The doubleness of his nature is signalled from the outset of the episode by the hieratic figure of "le vieil belier" which Doyac, a soldier of Charles VIII, found at the top of a mountain he thought he was the first to climb (671). The ram is Ares, god of power and potency, king of the hill, but he also carries within him "le jeune Aignelet" he was when transported to the mountain by an eagle or an owl (671). This ram/lamb juxtaposition encapsulates and forecasts many of the contradictions surrounding Gaster that will be developed throughout the episode. Tyrant and peace-maker, god of the city and god of the garden, he is both "imperieux, rigoureux, rond, dur, difficile, inflectible" (672), and "paouvre, vile, chetifve creature" (681).

The belligerant side of Gaster dominates the first chapter (57) of the episode which is marked throughout by patterns of stress and combativeness, and by an "agonistic confrontation of texts."[65] Even the form, "l'assiete," of the island is contradictory. It is a steep on the sides, "scabreuse, pierreuse, montueuse, infertile, mal plaisante à l'oeil, tresdifficile aux pieds" (671), but so pleasant, fertile and "delicious" at the summit that the narrator thinks he has entered the garden of earthly delights, "le vray Jardin et Paradis terrestre" (671). Pantagruel challenges the narrator's biblical identification, affirming that this is, instead, the Rock of Virtue: "le manoir de Areté (c'est Vertus) par Hesiode descript" (671-2). However, Pantagruel's assertion has already been eclipsed by the modern allusion to Doyac's ascent of "le mons de Dauphiné" (671), of equal or more difficult access than Hesiod's.[66] This pattern of subverting an-

---

[64] "Les Paroles dégelées (Rabelais, *Quart Livre*, 48-65)," *Littérature* 17 (1965): 21. In contrast to Jeanneret, Duval reads Gaster as a negative presence only. He calls Sir Belly's island an "anti-paradise in which both Christian and pagan versions of the myth of the Golden Age are deliberately inverted" (*Design* 42, see 39-44 for a discussion of Gaster as an anti-telos); and argues that "the baneful 'premier maistre es arts de ce monde' is in fact anticaritas incarnate" (74-5, see the discussion 74-8).

[65] Terence Cave, "Reading Rabelais: Variations on the Rock of Virtue," *Literary Theory/Renaissance Texts*, ed. Patricia Parker and David Quint (Baltimore: Johns Hopkins UP, 1986) 82.

[66] Cave makes this point, "Rock of Virtue" 83.

cient topoi and texts continues and culminates in the rewriting and appropriation of Plato's *Symposium* (203b) In Rabelais's version, Gaster usurps the marriage bed of Porus, Lord of Abundance, and replaces him as the consort of Penia, "de laquelle . . . nous nasquit Amour le noble enfant mediateur du Ciel et de la Terre . . ." (672). The overriding theme of the first chapter is "Gaster tousjours va devant"–ahead of all earthly authorities, "y feussent Roys, Empereurs, voire certes le Pape" (672-3)–and ahead of all textual authorities, too. The belly, not Love, is the *premium mobile* and "premier maistre es ars du monde" (671).

Among the texts challenged and rewritten is Pantagruel's own story of Physis and Antiphysie (614-15), for Gaster intrudes on the territories of both goddesses. Like Physis, this imperious god is associated with the repudiation of language. He has no ears to hear and no mouth; he speaks with gesture and sign,[67] thus reiterating the theme that Panurge stated when he met Pantagruel in 1532, and that the giant will repeat in the following episode: "L'estomach affamé n'a poinct d'aureilles, il n'oyt goutte. Par signes, gestes et effectz serez satisfaicts. . ." (689). At the same time, however, as "le premier maistre es ars du monde" (671), Gaster acts against Physis. All creatures must labor to serve him and as they do, their natures are deformed. He pulls the birds from the sky, and the fish from the sea; he tames elephants, lions and rhinoceros and makes them danse. He gives them art and technology, and this god of silence also gives them language:

> Mesmes es animans brutaulx il apprent ars desniées de Nature. Les Corbeaulx, les Gays, les Papeguays, les Estourneaux, il rend poëtes. Les pies il faict poëtrides: et leurs aprent languaige humain proferer, parler, chanter. Et tout pour la trippe. (673)

This materialistic litany and copious display of Gaster's power to deform the creatural world create uneasiness in us, and our confusion deepens as we pass to the human sphere in the following chapters (58-60). Suddenly Gaster's dominance wanes and the

---

[67] "Et comme les Ægyptiens disoient Harpocras Dieu de silence, en Grec nommé Sigalion, estre *astomé*, c'est à dire, sans bouche, ainsi Gaster sans oreilles feut crée: comme en Candie le simulachre de Juppiter estoit sans aureilles. Il ne parle que par signes. Mais à ses signes tout le monde obeist plus soubdain que aux edictz des Praeteurs et mandemens des Roys" (672).

weaker "lamb-like" side of his nature emerges. Now he is depicted as vulnerable to the abuse of the Engastrimythes and the Gastrolatres, "deux manieres de gens . . . les quelz (Pantagruel) eut en grande abhomination" (674). However, were it not for this initial judgement to guide our reading, we would be disoriented by the transition to the Engastrimythes and the Gastrolatres, for they share many attributes with the animals described in the preceding chapter to whom no such negativity was attached. Like the poetic birds, the Engastrimythes "parl(ent) du ventre" (674) and like the fish, elephants, camels and lions, the Gastrolatres use art and artifice "tout pour la trippe." Are they the same or different as the animals? Is Gaster innocent or guilty of their abuses? We have again strayed into a field where the opposite categories meet and merge.

The first to be presented are the Engastrimythes who are condemned for their perversion of language, Gaster's gift to the creatural world. They belong to an ancient race of enemies whose slippery natures are expressed by the multiplicity of their names: Plato, Aristophanes and Plutarch called them "Eurycliens"; Hippocrates and the Decretals[68] used the term "Ventriloques," Sophocles called them "Sternomantes" and Rabelais adds the name "Engastrimythes" to the list. However, these multiple appelations are all variations on the same theme of deception and betrayal: "C'estoient divinateurs, enchanteurs, et abuseurs du simple people, semblans non de la bouche, mais du ventre parler et respondre à ceulx qui les interrogeoient" (674).

A double theme of deception is attached to the Engastrimythes. When Plato described the Eurycliens in *The Sophist* (252c), he stressed the notion of self-betrayal as well as betrayal of others: "The foe is in their own household, . . . they carry about with them wherever they go a voice in their own bellies to contradict them."[69] With the anecdote of Jacobe Rodogine, Rabelais develops this idea of the "enemy within," for the Florentine woman is inhabited by a devil who speaks from inside her body:

> Du ventre de laquelle nous avons souvent ouy . . . la voix de l'esprit immonde, certainement basse, foible, et petite: toutesfoys

---

[68] A most dubious authority, after the episode of the Papimanes where the Décrétales are ridiculed at length (656-66).

[69] *The Sophist,* trans. F.M. Cornford, *The Collected Dialogues of Plato,* ed. Edith Hamilton and Huntington Cairns (Princeton: Princeton UP, 1961) 997.

> bien articulée, distincte et intelligible . . . . Cestuy maling esprit se faisoit nommer Crespelu ou Cincinnatule: et sembloit prendre plaisir estant ainsi appellé. (674)

As with the Andouilles, however, the feminization of *engastrimythie* changes everything. The idea of pregnancy evoked by Jacobe's story, the sexual connotations of the serpent "(qui) ne faict desplaisir aulcun" (641), and also the humor of Cincinnatule's speaking from inside Jacobe's belly—all these associations make us smile and mitigate the initial harsh condemnation of the Engastrimythes.

Moreover, this anecdote also undermines the theme of deception it is ostensibly told to support. It is presented as a true story seen by the narrator and other witnesses who took precautions to assure that no fraud was involved.[70] And while Cincinnatule lies about the future, he tells the truth about the present and past, inciting admiration in his auditors: "(D)es cas praesens ou passez, il en respondoit pertinemment, jusques à tirer les auditeurs en admiration" (674-5). The demon is also honest in confessing his ignorance, "faisant un gros pet: ou marmonnant quelques motz non intelligibles, et de barbare termination" (675). Such words recall the "paroles dégleés" which were also unintelligible and also called "motz barbares" (670), and Panurge and the narrator were so fascinated that they wanted to play with the thawed words and pickle them and keep them forever. With Cincinnatule, this same fascination begins to be felt. Unwilling to move farther in this direction, Rabelais abruptly cuts off the anecdote and moves on.

No such ambiguity seems to mark the portrait of the Gastrolatres. They are denounced for their laziness, in contrast to the labor that is associated with Gaster: "tous ocieux, rien ne faisans, poinct ne travaillans, poys et charge inutile de la Terre, comme dict Hesiode: craignans (scelon qu'on povoit juger) le Ventre offenser, et emmaigrir" (675).[71] Above all, the Gastrolatres are condemned for

---

[70] "(Les riches seigneurs et princes de la Guaulle Cisalpine), pour houster tout doubte de fiction et fraulde occulte, la faisoient despouiller toute nue, et luy faisoient clourre la bouche et le nez" (674).

[71] We recall that Pantagruel also used Hesiod's name to praise Gaster's Mount of Virtue (672). The use of the same authority to condemn the lazy Gastrolatres underscores the contrast between them and the hard-working and virtuous followers of Gaster.

their single-minded adoration of the belly. As their name indicates, they represent the culmination of the theme of idolatry that has recurred with insistence throughout *Le Quart Livre*: in the episodes of the Chiquanous who stole "les ferremens de la messe" (578), the Andouilles and their flying pig, and above all, the Papimanes who worshiped the pope as "Dieu en terre" (650).[72] With the Gastrolatres, the narrator goes behind the multiplicity of these icons and idols to identify the single principle that spawns them all—*philautia*, the love of self which leads to the shameless indulgence of one's basest appetites: "Je ne sacrifie que à moy (aux Dieux poinct) et à cestuy mon Ventre le plus grand de tous les Dieux" (675). And as the narrator cites the passage from St. Paul's Epistle to the Philippians (III,18), "unquestionably the most venerable borrowed fragment in the episode,"[73] he also reveals the tears which lie behind the laughter that these episodes have often generated:

> Vous eussiez dict que proprement (des Gastrolatres) avoit le sainct Envoyé escript. *Philippens*. 3. "Plusieurs sont des quelz souvent je vous ay parlé (encores praesentment je le vous diz les larmes à l'oeil) ennemies de la croix du Christ: des quelz Mort sera la consommation: des quelz Ventre est le Dieu. (675)

The Gastrolatres represent the demonization of many themes and images that have heretofore had a positive valorization in this episode and throughout *Le Quart Livre*. Carnival and the artistry associated with "le premier maistre es arts du monde" are demonized. The Gastrolatres use their artistic gifts to construct an idol, Manduce or Maschecroute, a monstrous effigy of the mouth, "avecques amples, larges et horrificques maschoueres bien endentelées... lesquelles, avec l'engin d'une petite chorde... l'on faisait l'une contre l'aultre terrificquement clicquetter" (676), which they carry at the head of a carnivalesque procession. This is *la gueule infernale* which does not speak or laugh, but which only devours, the maw which is the gateway to hell. It turns Carnival into a time of fear and death, not of laughter and renewal.

---

[72] As Michel Jeanneret notes, the Papimanes are Gastrolatres *avant la lettre*: "(L)es Papimanes passent imperceptiblement de l'église au café, de la célébration de la messe à la satisfaction de la panse: leur culte et leurs festins relèvent d'un appétit sensuel unique" ("Les Paroles dégelées" 15).

[73] Cave, "Rock of Virtue" 85.

Above all, the Gastrolatres pervert the banquet in its sacred as well as its secular dimensions. Their ceremony of worship is a parody of the mass and the Eucharist.[74] Manduce, carried on "un long baston bien doré" (676), is clearly an effigy of the crucifix, and the idolaters' first offerings to their "Dieu Ventripotent" (676) are wine, "Hippocras blanc," and bread, "Pain blanc, Choine, ... Pain mollet, Pain bourgeoys..." (676-7). "(P)ain et vin (sont) non seulement parodiés, mais tournés en derision aussi au moyen de plusieurs longues kyrielles qui transforment la communion en grande bouffe...."[75]

However, bread and wine are not the only foods offered to Gaster. A secular banquet emerges from the parody of the Eucharist, and it is an extraordinarily exuberant one. The more than 250 dishes offered by the Gastrolatres to their ventripotent god constitute the longest catalogue of foods in the history of literature,[76] and these foods resume all the banquets of *Le Quart Livre:*

> Salmiguondins .... Andouilles capparassonnées de moustarde fine, Saulcisses, ... Boudins, Cervelatz, Saulcissons, Jambons, ... Coustelletes de porc à l'oignonnade .... Cochons au moust, ... Balaines, ... Congres, ... Anguilles, Anguilletes, ... Serpens, *id est* Anguilles de boys ... (677-81)

As with the Engastrimythes, a countercurrent appears which undermines the perniciousness of the Gastrolatres. At the end, the negative value of idolatry begins to move toward the positive principles always associated with the Rabelais's banquets–the principles of food, drink, laughter, and words.

But what is Gaster's response to the panoply of his worship? He has stood silently and enigmatically behind all of the hullabaloo until at the end, "(il) renvoyait ces Matagotz à sa scelle persée veoir, considerer, philosopher, and contempler quelle divinité ils trouvoient en sa matiere fecale" (682). This is undoubtedly a gesture of derision which reduces the Gastrolatres' banquets and their words to a mound of fecal matter, but it is a positive gesture too. Gaster's affirmation that he is not a god, but a "paouvre, vile, chetifve crea-

---

[74] See E. Duval, "La Messe" 132-35 for a discussion of the elements of the Gastrolatres' ceremony which constitute a deformation of the mass and the Eucharist.
[75] Duval, "La Messe" 132.
[76] Bakhtin makes this point 280.

ture" (681) shatters the grotesque stiffness of the idol the Gastrolatres wanted to make of him and above all, he makes us laugh. This laughter banishes the tensions that have grown up around the Engastrimythes and the Gastrolatres and it also banishes the "abuseurs" from the scene. They are sent away and the episode moves to a new plane–Pantagruel's "attentive" study of Gaster.

The episode's last two chapters (61-62) stand as the giant's meditation on the antinomies that have surrounded Gaster, and these issues are now placed in a context that recalls the "Pantagruélion" described at the end of *Le Tiers Livre* (chs. 49-52). Like that plant, Gaster has his roots in the green world and the garden. His eulogy too rests on the praise of a seed–here the wheat to make bread. Also like the "Pantagruélion," Sir Belly quickly goes beyond nature to *techne*, for the need to cultivate the seed and transform it into bread gives birth to agriculture and to the panoply of arts and inventions of which Gaster is "premier maistre," including the arts of boatmaking and navigation [77] which figure so prominently in the "Pantagruélion." All these technologies culminate in the creation of the city: "Il inventa art de bastir villes, forteresses, et chasteaulx pour reserrer (grain et pain) et en sceureté conserver" (683)–Gaster is a god of Nomos as well as of Physis. He also stands at the juncture of creation and destruction, for the need for bread leads implacably to war and to the invention of gunpowder, the sinister double of grain,[78] the "seed" which destroys the city he created.

The passage, however, does not end on this note. The paradoxical chain of cause and effect continues into the episode's final chapter (62) where the emphasis is on deflecting evil and protecting from harm. In much the same way as the "Pantagruélion asbestin" was invented to protect the Thélèmites from fire (TL, ch. 52), so Gaster "inventa art et moyen de non estre blessé ne touché par coups de Canon" (684)–magnetic stones which suspend gunpowder in the air and even turn it back upon one's enemies (684-85). There follows an enumeration of plants and animals with a similar

---

[77] "(I)l inventa basteaulx, gualeres, et navires (chose de laquelle se sont les Elemens esbahiz) pour oultre mere, oultre fleuve, et rivieres naviger, et de nations barbares, incongneues et loing separées, Grain porter et transporter" (683).

[78] Gunpowder is the double of grain because its constituent elements also come from the ground, from the mining of Mother Earth. See Ulrich Langer, "Gunpowder as Transgressive Invention in Ronsard," *Literary Theory/Renaissance Texts* 98.

power to heal and turn away evil (685-6), but the passage drifts even farther from its starting point to end with this strange discussion of the effects of the cock's crow on the elder tree:

> (L)e Suzeau (sureau) croist, plus canore (sonore) et plus apte au jeu des flustes en pays on quel le chant des Coqs ne seroit ouy: ainsi qu'ont escript les anciens sages, scelon le rapport de Theophraste....
>
> Je sçay que aultres ont ceste sentence entendu du Suzeau saulvaige, provenent en lieux tant esloignez de villes et villages ... sans doubte doist pour flustes et aultres instrumens de Musicque estre esleu et preferé au domestique.... Aultres l'ont entendu plus haultement, non scelon la letre, mais allegoricquement scelon l'usaige des Pythagoriens.... (E)en ceste sentence nous enseignent que les gens saiges et studieux ne se doibvent adonner à la Musique triviale et vulgaire, mais à la celeste, divine, angelique, plus absconse et de plus loing apportée: scavoir est d'une region en laquelle n'est ouy des Coqs le chant. (686-7)

Pantagruel's long meditation thus culminates in a directive on how to read the profound contradictions surrounding Gaster, a "reading lesson" which marks a divergence from the "Pantagruélion" which this eulogy otherwise resembles in so many ways. That episode was brought to a *cul de sac* by the problem of the "mix" of good and evil associated with the plant (see Chapter One 44-5). The Gaster episode, to the contrary, ends by inviting Pantagruel and the reader to go beyond the antinomies, beyond rational understanding and speech, to a region where the opposites meet and merge. This place recalls the Plain of Truth evoked by Pantagruel in the episode of the "Paroles Gelées,"[79] but there the image was of the words' fall from the spiritual to the material world. Here that imagery is reversed. The Gaster episode rather moves upward from the basest materiality to a region beyond the senses "où n'est ouy des Coqs le chant." "Entendu allegoriquement" and pursued to its extreme through a labyrinth of contradictions, physical appetite becomes spiritual appetite and points beyond itself. There is no usurpation of Love by Gaster, no conflict between them, for Sir Belly, too, functions as a "mediateur du Ciel et de la Terre" (672). This insight marks a turning point in the book.

---

[79] "... le manoir de Verité (où habitent) les Parolles, les Idées, les Exemplaires et protraictz de toutes choses passées, et futures..." (668).

6. THE POET IN THE KITCHEN

There is no departure from Gaster's island. The adventure does not end, it drifts off and merges with the following episode which takes place off "l'isle Chaneph" (chs. 63-65). When we see Pantagruel again, he is asleep on the deck of *La Thalamege* and he has fallen asleep over a book:[80] "Telle estoit sa coustume, que trop mieulx par livre dormoit que par coeur" (687). It is as if Pantagruel's meditation on Gaster has carried him to the regions of silence and slumber evoked in the wild elder anecdote, "une region en laquelle n'est ouy des Coqs le chant" (687), and the giant's sleep has menaced the voyage. The wind has fallen and the boats of the convoy are becalmed. All is wrapped in a mantle of silence and Pantagruel's companions have been rendered mute by boredom: "Et restions tous pensifz, matagrabolisez, sesolfiez, et faschez: sans mot dire les uns aux aultres" (687). They engage in inane and petty activities which express their lethargy and which evoke, in miniature, prior episodes: "Panurge avecques la langue parmy un tuyau de *Pantagruelion* faisoit des bulles et guargoulles . . . . Carpalim . . . faisoit un . . . *moulinet* . . . . Xenomanes . . . repetassoit *une vieille lanterne*" (687-8, my italics). As at the end of Rimbaud's *Bateau Ivre*,[81] the grandiose visions of the voyage are shrinking and dissolving; the whole enterprise is in danger of fading away.

But suddenly Pantagruel awakens, and the "tant obstiné silence" (688) is broken as his companions pose a long series of questions asking for remedies to the *acedia* which has overtaken them. These "problemes propousez" (689) take the form of enigmas for Pantagruel to decipher, and are thinly veiled allusions to the voy-

---

[80] The book is "un Heliodore Grec" (687), the *Aethiopica* (see Introduction, n. 19). This romance may have triggered the return of the theme of marriage to *Le Quart Livre,* the discussion of Panurge's future wife which occurs in this episode (693).

[81] The poem's last stanza reads:
>Je ne puis plus, baigné de vos langueurs, ô lames,
>Enlever leur sillage aux porteurs de cotons,
>Ni traverser l'orgueil des drapeaux et des flammes,
>Ni nager sous les yeux horribles des pontons.

Oeuvres de Rimbaud, ed. Suzanne Bernard (Paris: Garnier, 1960) 131

agers' hunger—they are "à jeun," they want to eat.[82] All of these "devinettes" are variations on the "theme" question posed by Frère Jean: "Maniere de haulser le temps en calme?" (688), an expression meaning both "to raise the wind" and "to spend or pass away the time in quaffing, swilling, and carousing" (Cotgrave). The entire episode will be devoted to the interpretation of this expression, but Pantagruel's first response is *not* to answer the question,[83] to remain silent as Gaster dictates. The solution to the problem of hunger lies not in the word, but in the deed—the giant's signal to Frère Jean to let the meal begin: "(il) toucha la chorde de la campanelle frere Jan soubdain courut à la cuisine" (689).

Before this signal, however, even before Pantagruel's awakening, Frère Jean had been in the kitchen consulting "(l')horoscope des fricassées" (687) and preparing the banquet that will "haulser le temps" and solve his own riddle as well as those posed by the other voyagers. The monk is, moreover, preparing words as well as food. Frère Jean has been associated with the dual theme of cooking and verbal creation throughout *Le Quart Livre*: on "l'isle de Cheli" where he fled to the kitchen tent and where Homer's composition of the *Iliad* was compared to frying a "fricassée de congres" (563), and on "l'isle Farouche" where he was packed with the writer "Rabiolas" and the other soldier-cooks inside the Trojan Sow (631-4). That meal of sausages, however, was interrupted and never served.[84] The voyagers left "l'isle Farouche" hungry—but they took the Sow with them (637). It is off "l'isle Chaneph" that Frère Jean finally serves the long-awaited banquet of pork:

> Frère Jean associé des maistres d'hostel, escarques, panetiers, eschansons, escuyers tranchans, couppiers, credentiers, apporta quatre horrificques pastez de jambons si grands qu'il me soubvint des quatre bastions de Turin. Vray Dieu comment il y feut beu et gallé. (691)

---

[82] "Remede contre fascherie?" . . . "Maniere de ne dormir poinct en Chien?" . . . C'est . . . dormir à jeun en hault soleil comme font les Chiens . . . ." "Maniere de æquilibrer et balancer la cornemuse de l'estomach, de mode qu'elle ne panche poinct d'un cousté que d'aultre?" (688).

[83] "Comment, par Pantagruel, ne feut respondu aux problemes proposez" (689).

[84] Cave, *Cornucopian Text*, calls *Le Quart Livre* "the book of the deferred or interrupted feast" (222).

This good meal stands as a remedy and corrective to the bad banquets of the Gastrolatres and of the other *escales* of *Le Quart Livre* in many ways. With four ham pies for ten persons, it is an example of moderate eating, in contrast to the excesses of the Gastrolatres, and the lesson of moderation is elaborated at length by Pantagruel in chapter sixty-five,[85] thus linking the book's ending to the theme of "médiocrité" developed in the 1552 prologue. This meal is correctly tailored to the proportion of the voyagers' hunger, and is eaten at the time hunger is felt: "il n'est horloge plus juste que le ventre" (690). Moreover, it is natural eating, compared to the unnatural meals that have occured in prior escales: eating wind as on "l'isle Ruach," eating windmills and frying pans as did Bringuenarilles, and above all, eating serpents as on "l'isle Farouche." That strange act is recalled by Eusthènes's question: "pourquoy est la sallive de l'home jeun veneneuse à tous Serpens et Animaulx veneneux?" (689) and the problem is solved by the good banquet of pork. As on Ferocious Island, the snake is transformed back into the pig in its positive manifestation as the symbol of succulent nourishment and the pleasures of food (see above 95-6). Unnatural eating has ended and Eusthènes offers a long catalogue of serpents and poisonous beasts (691-2) which are now "en sceureté de (s)a salive" (691).

If the meal off "l'isle Chanelph" stands in opposition to the bad banquets that have preceded it, it also stands in complementary relationship to the feast of the departure. This, too, is both a secular celebration of the friendship and the sense of community that bind the voyagers together, and a meal with eucharistic overtones. Panurge alludes to the Council of Trent as he recalls "nos gras Concilipetes de Chesil" (690) and links them to the clearly Catholic inhabitants of "l'isle Chanelph": "Hypocrites, Hydropicques, Patenostriers, Chattemites, Santorons, Cagotz, Hermites" (689). This banquet defines itself in contrast to their practices as an "Cène évangelique." As in the departure, the voyagers "chanterent divers Cantiques à la louange du treshault Dieu des Cielz" (691) and sev-

---

[85] The giant tells the anecdote of Atlas' and Hercules' "excessif haulsement de temps" (694). Hercules is chastised for drinking as camels do, "pour la soif passée, pour la soif praesente, et pour la soif future" (694), and his excesses cause trepidation in the skies and controversy on earth. The moral of Pantagruel's story is that one must eat and drink moderately to preserve the "occulte sympathie de nature" (694) he has just praised.

eral elements of their banquet recall the Last Supper:[86] the characters grouped around their master expressing their doubts, the echo of Christ's words in Pantagruel's statement: "Ailleurs et en aultre temps nous en dirons d'adventaige, si bon vous semble" (694),[87] and Panurge's reverent postcommunal prayer of thanks for the bread and the wine which comfort both body and spirit:

> Sans poinct de faulte nous doibvons bien louer le bon Dieu nostre createur, servateur, conservateur, qui par ce bon pain, par ce bon vin et frays, par ces bonnes viandes nous guerist de telles perturbations tant du corps comme de l'ame: oultre le plaisir et volupté que nous avons beuvans et mangeans. (694)[88]

In addition to the meal before Christ's crucifiction, this episode evokes the celebration of His resurrection. The feast of ham is also an Easter repast, and it prepares for the comic drama of rebirth enacted by Panurge in the book's last chapter (see above 79-80). Immediately after the voyagers have eaten, the wind rises and fills the sails, marking the renewal of the voyage and the voyagers' joy. It is in this atmosphere of festivity that Pantagruel completes the interpretive task announced at the beginning of the episode, and explicates the expression "maniere de haulser le temps" according to the principles set forth with the anecdote of the wild elder. His reading of the expression is both "scelon la letre" (687) and "allegorical" and he stresses the interconnectedness of the two senses: "Nous haulsans et vuidans les tasses, s'est pareillement le temps haulsé par occulte sympathie de Nature" (694). The literal and the figurative,

---

[86] Saulnier makes this point, 140, as does Smith in the chapter "Au large de Chaneph: eucharistie et interprétation," *Voyage et écriture,* esp. 193-8.

[87] "I have yet many things to say unto you, but ye cannot bear them now. Howbeit when he, the Spirit of truth, is come, he will guide you into all truth . . ." (John 16, 12-13).

[88] Duval argues that this final banquet of the *Quart Livre* stands in place of "la dive Bouteille": "By 'resolving' Panurge's 'doubt' with 'signes, gestes, et effectz' and a non-answer rather than words . . . , as well as 'par l'ayde de Bacchus, c'est le bon vin friant et delicieux' . . . , the hero in effect accomplishes exactly what the Dive Bouteille would have done, if only such a thing as a 'Dive Bouteille' could really exist anywhere outside Panurge's own idle imagination. No more satisfactory telos than this is to be found in the world of the *Quart Livre,* in which baneful Answers abound and all the oracles are mute at best" (*Design* 139). Duval also notes the parallel between the last and the first banquets, and argues that both are eucharistic communions (see 135-41).

the material and the spiritual, are part of the same continuum, and it is a line which leads upward. Pantagruel reiterates the suggestion underlying the Gaster episode that appetite, like love, is a "mediateur du Ciel et de la Terre" (672) when he explains that, while hunger makes us "plus terrestre et poisant" (695), eating and drinking lighten our bodies and elevate our spirits. In elaborating this idea of elevation, Pantagruel not only continues the Gaster episode, he also completes it. The praise of the belly had culminated in a praise of grain and of bread. The episode off "l'isle Chanelph" ends with Pantagruel's eulogy of the grape and of wine, his praise of Bacchus whom he designates as *Psila*, the winged one:

> Car commme les oyzeaulx par ayde de leurs aesles volent hault en l'air legierement: ainsi par l'ayde de Bacchus,c'est le bon vin friant et délicieux, sont hault eslevez les espritz des humains: leurs corps evidentement alaigriz: et assouply ce que en eulx estoit terrestre. (695)

Bread and wine—the good banquet in both its sacred and secular registers has been accomplished. The voyagers' hunger has been assuaged; they have been given food for the body and for the spirit. Their questions have been answered; their doubts washed away. This final meal is a triumph. It banishes the lethargy and tension that had overtaken the voyage: "Le mal temps passe, et retourne le bon,/ Pendant qu'on trinque au tour de gras jambon" (695). Above all, the banquet off "l'isle Chaneph" affirms the friendship and the faith which unite the voyagers. Floating between warring islands embodying the dogmatic and self-interested quarrels of Catholics and reformers, they alone are able to read the bread and the wine of the Eucharist in the proper spirit, the spirit of *caritas*. In the end, we reiterate David Quint's crucial observation (195): "If the Sacrament may mean different things to different Christians, all belong, however, to the same community. The behavior of the Rabelaisian characters . . . provides a model for one church whose members may disagree but who agree to stay together."

CHAPTER FOUR

THE BOOK OF THE DEAD: IMAGES OF READING AND WRITING IN *LE QUART LIVRE*

THE allusion to Exodus in *Le Quart Livre*'s first chapter, the chanting of Psalm 114, *Quand Israel hors d'Egypte sortit*[1] during the festivities of the departure, is one of the book's most important evocations. It gives a sacramental context to the voyage announced at the end of *Le Tiers Livre*, and moves the focus of that voyage from Panurge to Pantagruel. The Exodus theme is sustained throughout *Le Quart Livre* by a thread of allusions to Moses, "chevalereux capitaine," "conducteur du peuple Israelicque" (625), allusions which link Pantagruel and the quest he leads for the word of "la dive Bouteille Bacbuc" (537) to Moses' journey through the wilderness in search of God's Word on which a new city will be founded. The allusion to Exodus announces the drama of exile and the spiritual pilgrimage that will be enacted in *Le Quart Livre* and establishes a hoped-for *transitus* from Egypt to Jerusalem as the underlying figure of the book.[2]

Indeed, many of *Le Quart Livre*'s negative values may be brought to bear on all that "Egypt" signifies. The land of captivity left behind, it is also the desert through which the pilgrims must pass, representing, as for Dante, "the grief and misery of sin.'[3] This

---

[1] "(C)'est la première fois que Rabelais cite un psaume en français (dans le texte de Clément Marot, publié en 1539)." V.-L. Saulnier, *Rabelais II. Rabelais dans son enquête* (Paris: SEDES, 1982) 41.

[2] Saulnier also suggests that Exodus is an underlying figure of *Le Quart Livre*: "Dès la première étape, la navigation . . . se présente comme une manière d'Exode. Rabelais le déclare en fait, ses amis quittent une terre de servitude, pour voguer vers une Terre Promise" (41).

[3] In the letter to Can Grande, Dante says that the *Commedia* is to be read ac-

desert is France become "le pays de la fausse foi,"[4] a land of icons and idols. Much of *Le Quart Livre*'s anti-Catholic satire may be associated with what Egypt represents: the sin of idolatry castigated in so many of the book's episodes as we have discussed in Chapter Three, and also the breakdown of civility caused by the religious quarrels, a breakdown which finds its graphic representation in the warring islands and the images of erosion and decline so often used to describe them. France has become a "città dolente" and a desert where, in Panurge's words, "Les homes (sont) loups es homes" (TL, 363).

To the breakdown of culture corresponds the breakdown of language that Rabelais decries with such passion and such anguish in the 1548 prologue and the "Lettre à Odet." The structure of the lie prevails, and the lie, as Montaigne argues in "Du Dementir," is a betrayal of the public good: "Nostre intelligence se conduisant par la seule voye de la parolle, celuy qui la fauce, trahit la societé publique."[5] The lie is also, in Montaigne's words, "tesmoignage de mespriser Dieu."[6] Rabelais similarly castigates and calls "diabolic"[7] the sins of hypocrisy and calumny which depend on the willful perversion of the meaning of words to misinterpret, mislead, and destroy. To accuse him of heresy, Rabelais's enemies had only to twist his words to use them against him, "... contre tout usaige de raison et de languaige commun, interpretans ce que à poine de mille fois mourir, si autant possible estoit, ne voudrois avoir pensé: comme qui pain, interpretroit pierre: poisson, serpent: oeuf, scorpion" (520).

Moreover, Rabelais goes beyond the lie to envision the possibility of language with no meaning at all. Nature, Physis, is dead in *Le Quart Livre*. The pilot of the voyage is dressed as an Egyptian

---

cording to the figure of Exodus. It signifies, in his words, "the conversion of the soul from the grief and misery of sin to the state of grace." Quoted by John Freccero, "The River of Death: *Inferno* II, 108," *Dante: The Poetics of Conversion*, ed. Rachel Jacoff (Cambridge: Harvard UP, 1986) 56. See also Charles S. Singleton, "In Exitu Israel de Aegypto," *Dante: A Collection of Critical Essays*, ed. John Freccero (Englewood Cliffs, NJ: Prentice Hall, 1965) 102-21.

[4] Saulnier 42.

[5] *Oeuvres Complètes*, ed. Albert Thibaudet and Maurice Rat (Paris: Gallimard, 1962) 650.

[6] Montaigne 649.

[7] "Car en Grec calumnie est dicte diabole. Voyez combien detestable est devant Dieu et les Anges, ce vice dict Calumnie (c'est quand on impugne le bien faict, quand on mesdit des choses bonnes) que par iceluy non par autre, ... sont les Diables d'enfer nommez et appellez" (718).

priest, "vestu à la mode des Isiaces (prêtres) de Anubis en Ægypte" (542), and he leads the pilgrims into the realm of "abios bios" (525), "Vie non vie. Vie non vivable" (BD, 704) and "simulachre de mort" (525). And with the death of nature comes the death of meaning. As Rabelais explains in the 1548 prologue, when the natural referents of words are effaced, they cease to evoke a signifying concept in the mind and thus become incomprehensible inscriptions or sounds. This is fallen language: the language of Egypt as Babel/Babylon:[8]

> . . . Caphards, Cagotz, Matagotz, Botineurs, Papelards, Burgotz, Patespelues, Porteurs de Rogations, Chattemittes. Ce sont noms horrificques seulement oyant leur son . . . . Je n'y ay entendu que le hault Allemant, et ne sçay quelle sorte de bestes comprenez en ces denominations . . . . Je presuppose que c'estoit quelque espece monstreuse de animaulx Barbares ou temps des haultz bonnetz: maintenant est deperie en nature . . . et ne sçavons quelle en soit la diffinition: comme vous sçavez que subject pery, facilement perit sa denomination. (717-18)

This passage from the 1548 prologue disappears from the revised book, but Rabelais's concern with the relationship between words and things does not. These reflections must surely have inspired him to add a glossary of terms, "La Briefve Declaration d'aulcunes dictions plus obscures," to the 1552 book[9] and with it, every episode of *Le Quart Livre* becomes saturated with the con-

---

[8] Margaret Ferguson notes that there was a "longstanding patristic tradition which conflated Babel with Babylon by translating both words as 'confusio.'" "Saint Augustine's Region of Unlikeness: The Crossing of Exile and Language," *Georgia Review* 29.4 (1975): 863.

[9] The glossary was included in some copies of the 1552 edition and in all of those of 1553; that is, it was printed when Rabelais was still alive. For an outline of the quarrels surrounding the authenticity of the "Briefve Declaration," see Mireille Huchon, *Rabelais grammarien: De l'histoire du texte aux problèmes d'authenticité* (Geneva: Droz, 1981) 406-11 and the note in her edition of Rabelais, *Oeuvres Complètes* (Paris: Gallimard, 1994) 1588-1589. It was R. Arveiller, "La Briefve Declaration est-elle de Rabelais?," *Etudes rabelaisiennes* 5 (1964): 9-10, who first questioned some of the definitions, and André Tournon, "La Briefve Declaration n'est pas de Rabelais," *Etudes rabelaisiennes* 13 (1976): 133-38, further elaborated Arveiller's argument. Tournon concluded that there were enough "erroneous or impertinent" definitions (138) to prove that Rabelais could not have been the author of the glossary. However, as Huchon indicates, many of the definitions challenged by Arveiller and Tournon are in fact appropriate, and the style and the tone of the "Briefve Declaration" are consonant with *Le Quart Livre*.

cern for definitions. This concern is also repeatedly expressed within the text–by the recurrent discussions of the names of the islands and their inhabitants and above all by the entire chapter (37) devoted to a "notable discours sus les noms propres des lieux et des persones" (624). To argue that the names of the captains Riflandouille and Tailleboudin forecast victory in the sausage war, Pantagruel alludes to the *Cratylus*, the Platonic dialogue devoted to the relationship between words and things.[10] He also alludes to many passages in the Hebrew Bible, "nous monstrans evidemment en quelle observance et religion leurs estoient les noms propres avecques leurs significations" (627). By such a reiterated concern as well as by the linguistic nature of the quest "pour le Mot," the writer reveals his desire to function as Old Adam dispensing proper names, or as Moses hearing the Word, the Logos that will restore the fundamental relation that language must have with reality and truth, the Word that will heal the world.

Paradoxically, however, such observations lead from an anti-Egyptian into a pro-Egyptian field. Side by side with the negative associations conferred by Exodus, another Renaissance tradition existed which interpreted Egypt positively–as the land of hieroglyphs, the land of good writing.[11] This view is also linked to Plato, to the *Timaeus* (21e-26d) wherein Egypt is described as the land of the oldest wisdom and the oldest writing, preserved by the priests in their temples.[12] The conviction that writing originated in Egypt was elaborated by the thinkers and commentators of the long neo-platonic tradition who felt that hieroglyphs contained the secrets of creation. In order to conceal this divine wisdom from those unworthy to receive it, the Egyptians used whole figures rather than let-

---

[10] "Voyez le *Cratyle* du divin Platon. (Par ma foy, dist Rhizotome, je le veulx lire. Je vous oy souvent le alleguant" (625). For a discussion of the relevance of the *Cratylus* to Rabelais's thinking, see my *Rabelais: Homo Logos* (Chapel Hill: University of North Carolina Press, 1979) 25-30, and François Rigolot, "Cratylisme et pantagruélisme. Rabelais et le statut du signe," *Etudes rabelaisiennes* 13 (1976): 115-32.

[11] My discussion of hieroglyphs is based on Liselotte Dieckmann, *Hieroglyphs: The History of a Literary Symbol* (St Louis: Washington UP, 1970) esp. 1-47.

[12] We recall that in the *Phaedrus*, Plato also designated Egypt as the place where writing originated and described the invention of the alphabet by the god Theuth. However, in this dialogue, Egyptian writing is criticized rather than praised. It is called a "recipe not for memory but for reminder" (275a). Trans. by R. Hackforth in *The Collected Dialogues of Plato,* ed. by Edith Hamilton and Huntington Cairns (Princeton, NJ: Princeton UP, 1961) 520. However, as Dieckmann points out, Plato's warning was forgotten, and both the written word and painting were considered during the Renaissance to contain "truth that one can read" (6).

ters or characters, symbols that "comprehend an entire discourse," in Ficino's words.[13] In this way, only the few who understood the nature of the objects portrayed could comprehend the meaning of the hieroglyphs. First limited to the priests, the wisdom of the Egyptians was subsequently shared with the sages, primarily of Greece, who journeyed there and was thought to have passed through the ages by a chain of ancient wise men which included Zoroaster, Mercury, Orpheus, Pythagoras, Plato, Plotinus and others. Ficino sometimes included Moses in this chain as a prophet equal in age and importance to Zoroaster,[14] but for Pico della Mirandola, Ficino's contemporary and friend, Moses and the Hebrew sources were primary and were privileged over the Egyptian ones as the source of this ancient wisdom. In Pico's view, the first truths were revealed to Abraham who then took them to Egypt where they were reclaimed by Moses.[15] It is perhaps through Pico's influence that Rabelais, in chapter thirty-seven, merges the Platonic with the Hebrew traditions and above all that he gives the Hebrew name of "Bacbuc" to "la dive Bouteille."

In the fifteenth and first half of the sixteenth centuries, these ideas were popularized by three widely disseminated and influential books of emblems and hieroglyphs: the *Horappollo,* a (most certainly inauthentic) encyclopedia of hieroglyphic symbols and their interpretations;[16] Francesco Colonna's *Hypnerotomachia* in which Poliphilo searches for his beloved in a dream where he passes through architectural designs covered with hieroglyphs, and finally, the *Emblemata* of Alciati which contains symbolic pictures, many of them taken from the *Horappollo* and the *Hypnerotomachia,* with explanatory epigrams in Latin.[17]

Rabelais's knowledge of and interest in this tradition go back at least as far as 1534. The first mention of hieroglyphs in his work is

---

[13] Taken from Ficino's introduction and comment on the passage in Plotinus' *Enneads* concerning Egyptian writing. Quoted by Dieckmann 37.

[14] Dieckmann 35. See her discussion of Ficino 34-38.

[15] Dieckmann 38-44.

[16] The full title in English is: *The Hieroglyphics of Horappollo Niliacus, written by him in the Egyptian Tongue and put into Greek by Philip.* Discovered in 1419 on the island of Andros, it was translated from Greek into Latin during the Renaissance. The first Latin version was published by Aldus in 1505. For a discussion of the *Horappollo,* see Dieckmann 27-30.

[17] The *Hypnerotomachia* was published in 1499. The *Emblemata,* circulating since 1521, was first printed in 1531. See Dieckmann's discussions of the two books 44-47.

found in chapter nine of the *Gargantua* as part of a discussion of the baby giant's "couleurs et livrée" (28). The narrator begins by attacking the arbitrary symbolism of *Le blason des couleurs*, a treatise on the significance of colors in royal liveries and devices.[18] He also criticizes the misuse of language by the "transporteurs de noms" (29), punsters whose rebuses play only on phonetic and not on intrinsic similarities, but his enjoyment of such word games is also apparent, for he subsequently offers several puns of his own. Finally, in contrast to these examples of the wrong use of words, the narrator holds up Egyptian hieroglyphs as the model of good writing:

> Bien aultrement faisoient en temps jadis les saiges de Egypte, quand ilz escripvoient par lettres, qu'iz appelloient hieroglyphiques. Lesquelles nul n'entendoit qui n'entendist: et un chascun entendoit qui entendist la vertu, proprieté, et nature des choses par icelles figurées. Desquelles Orus Apollon a en Grec composé deux livres, et Polyphile au *songe d'amours* en a davantaige exposé. En France vous en avez quelque transon en la devise de Monsieur l'Admiral: laquelle premier porta Octavian Auguste. (G 29)[19]

As the citation makes clear, hieroglyphs are the prototypes of good reading as well as of good writing and may thus be linked to the problem of interpretation posed in the *Gargantua* by the two enigmas which encircle the narrative and above all by its famous prologue where an allegorical reading of the book is proposed.[20] Indeed, the concepts of allegory and hieroglyphs seem interwoven in Rabelais's mind and it is a natural alliance, for when emblematic figures are put into motion in a narrative, allegory is the result. The *Tiers Livre*, with its depiction of Panurge's quest for an answer to

---

[18] Composed in 1458 by the herald of Alphonse V of Aragon, *Les blasons* appeared in Paris in 1528 (Huchon 1088 n. 1).

[19] The device is the dolphin-anchor symbol for *festina lente*. Pierre Jourda suggests, *Rabelais: Oeuvres Complètes*, vol. 2 (Paris: Garnier, 1962) 40 n. 5, that the admiral is Guillaume Gouffier, sieur de Bonnivet, but Huchon (1090 n. 21) identifies him as Philippe Chabot, the friend of François I for whom Jean Le Febvre translated Alciati's *Emblemata*.

[20] "(P)ar curieuse leçon, et meditation frequente rompre l'os, et sugcer la sustantificque mouelle. C'est à dire: ce que j'entends par ces symboles Pythagoricques . . . . Car en icelle bien aultre goust trouverez. et doctrine plus absconce, laquelle vous revelera de très haultz sacremens et mysteres horrificques, tant en ce que concerne nostre religion, que aussi l'estat politicq et vie oeconomicque" (G 7).

the problem of marriage as a problem of deciphering enigmas, may also be called a hieroglyphic enterprise.

However, it is not until *Le Quart Livre* that the issues of good reading and good writing are explicitly put back into the Egyptian setting they were given the passage cited above. At the very beginning of the book, in the 1548 prologue, a text is presented, a breviary engraved on the outside with grotesque figures: "(Crocs et Pies) peintes au dessus, et semées en moult belle ordonnance . . . (comme *si fussent lettres hieroglyphiques*). . ." (715, italics mine). The link between writing and reading stressed in chapter nine of the *Gargantua* is here expressed by the strange reversal of fictional roles and relationships that was discussed in our Chapter One (26-31): the writer plays the part of reader as he struggles to penetrate to the interior of a story which is said to be given–and written–by us. The lure of the rebus to which he was so susceptible in 1534 persists as well, for the merging of "crocs" and "pies" forms an expression which also means "to drink": "Doncques vous voulez qu'à prime je boyve vin blanc: à tierce, sexte et nonne, pareillement: à vespres et complies, vin clairet. Cela vous appellez croquer pie. . ." (717).

This prologue disappears from the revised book, but an echo of its perplexities is heard on "l'isle Medamothi," the new *escale* added in first place in 1552. Here, too, books are given, the "livres joyeulx" (544) sent by Gargantua to Pantagruel, and the acts of reading and writing are again merged, for as the voyage begins, Gargantua's books are read aloud at the same time that the writing of Pantagruel's book commences. And, as in the 1548 prologue, the double enterprise of writing and reading is given an Egyptian context, for it is in this episode that the ship's pilot is identified with "les Isiaces (prêtres) de Anubis en Ægypte" (542).

However, the reading/writing process is more complicated on "l'isle Medamothi" than in the 1548 prologue, for it involves not two but three entities: Gargantua, Pantagruel, and the narrator, and the narrator has the last word. In the episode's final line, he too promises a book–a copy of the "livre joyeulx" being read which is also the book being written (see our Chapter Two 65-7). In this way, on "l'isle Medamothi," the narrator appropriates the function of writing, and that appropriation continues throughout *Le Quart Livre*. Omnipresent on the voyage as an eyewitness, often in the foreground of the action, it is the narrator who composes "le discours (du) naviguaige" (546) using hieroglyphic symbols, strange animals and events whose meaning requires great effort to understand. The task of deciphering these enigmas passes to Pantagruel, and the image we are given off "l'isle Chaneph" of the giant asleep over a book (687) is emblematic of his function. Pantagruel is the reader of the *Quart Livre* who strives to resolve the problem of interpretation it poses.

In the following pages, we will study the sites of *Le Quart Livre* where the issues of writing and of reading and interpretation are paramount, and where the two views of Egypt, positive and negative, that we have discussed come into play: the corrupt city, city of false religion and of corrupt language, on the one hand, and the place of sacred writing and of wise readers, on the other. Pantagruel, as Moses, must pass through fearful, barren landscapes, but read hieroglyphically, these places and the creatures who inhabit them have lessons to offer, even truths to tell. Pantagruel leads the interpretive enterprise and is ultimately able to conquer the menace of Babel that has threatened the book.

1. The Land of Death and of Writing

"L'isle des Macraeons" is one of the most important episodes of *Le Quart Livre*. It marks the point where the 1548 book was broken off and taken up again, significantly enough, on the theme of repair.[21] As the first *escale* of the second half of the voyage, it was probably composed at about the same time as "l'isle Medamothi," and both episodes project into the 1552 book the concerns of the suppressed 1548 Prologue. Medamothi restates the reading/writing conundrum and "l'isle des Macraeons" develops the Old Prologue's hieroglyphic theme. From the outset, this place is described as a land of inscriptions to be deciphered:

> Et par la forest umbrageuse et deserte descouvrit plusieurs vieulx temples ruinez, plusieurs obelisces, Pyramides, monu-

---

[21] "Vray est que quia plus n'en dict" was the last sentence of the 1548 *Quart Livre*. See Jean Plattard, ed., *Le Quart Livre de Pantagruel (édition dite partielle, Lyon, 1548)* (Paris: Champion, 1909) 106. In 1552, Rabelais writes: "Vray est que leurs provisions estoient aulcunement endommagées par la tempeste præcedente" (597), and goes on to describe the repair of the boat by the carpenters and artisans of "l'isle des Macraeons."

> mens, et sepulchres antiques, avecques inscriptions et epitaphes divers. Les uns en letres Hieroglyphicques, les aultres en languaige Ionicque, les aultres en langue Arabicque, Agarene, Sclavonicque, et aultres. (598)

Despite the allusion to multiple languages, the predominance of Egyptian elements in this passage is underscored by three entries in the Briefve Declaration: for "obelisces," "Pyramides" and above all for "Hieroglyphicques." This is a long definition which repeats many aspects of the passage from the *Gargantua*—the allusions to the *Horappollo*, the *Hypnerotomachia* and to the dolphin/anchor emblem of *festina lente*, but the definition of hieroglyphs is somewhat different. Here they are called "sacred sculptures":

> *Hieroglyphicques.* Sacres sculptures. Ainsi estoient dictes les letres des antiques saiges Aegyptiens: et estoient faictes des images diverses de arbres, herbes, animaulx, poissons, oiseaulx, instruments: par la nature et office des quelz estoit representé ce qu'ils vouloient désigner. (708)

However, the truths to be read on "l'isle des Macraeons" are not happy ones. Everything has fallen prey to the ravages of time, the island itself, "jadis riche, frequente, opulente, marchande, populeuse.... Maintenant, par laps de temps et sus la declination du monde, paouvre et deserte comme voyez" (599), and its inhabitants too are in decline. This is a country of great men, "Daemons et Heros" (599), but as the name of the island indicates, they have reached the end of their days: "Macraeon en Grec signifie veillart, home qui a des ans beaucoup" (598). The ship's pilot, "priest of Anubis," has lead the voyagers into the land of the dying and of the dead. The whole *escale* is a "meditation de mort."

Three deaths are recounted on "l'isle des Macraeons," and all three are to be read hieroglyphically. The interpretive enterprise is led by Pantagruel and the texts he reads are not only inscribed on paper or etched in stone. One of the dominant convictions expressed in the episode is that nature, too, writes in symbols and ciphers, a conviction derived from the Platonic notion of correspondences which was an intrinsic part of the hieroglyphic tradition.[22]

---

[22] The principle of analogies between the world of the senses and the world of ideas is one of the main themes of the *Timaeus*. (See Dieckman's discussion 5.) The conviction that there exists a correspondence between "that which is above and

THE BOOK OF THE DEAD 123

"Le bon Macrobe" introduces this idea as he interprets the tempest as a sign that one of the island's Heros has died, for such deaths, he explains, are customarily accompanied by natural upheavals.[23] In the long development which follows, Pantagruel argues that these signs announce as well as mourn the deaths of great men. He suggests that comets seen prior to the storm were just such "signification(s) des cieulx" (601) and compares them to the notations used by the Aeropagite judges:

> ... par Ø signifians condemnation à mort: par T absolution; par Λ ampliation: sçavoir, est quand le cas n'estoit encores liquidé.... Ainsi, par telz cometes, comme par notes ætherées disent les cieulx tacitement: Homes mortelz, si de cestes heureuses ames voulez chose aulcune sçavoir, apprandre, entendre, congnoistre, preveoir touchant le bien et utilité publicque ou privée, faictez diligence de vous representer à elles, et d'elles response avoir. Car la fin et catastrophe de la comoedie approche. (602)

These reflections on the cipher-writing of nature are brought from the mythic into the historical realm and are substantiated by Epistemon's account of the second death, that of Guillaume Du Bellay, seigneur de Langey, in 1543. His death too was announced "par prodiges, portentes, monstres, et aultres precedens signes formez contre tout ordre de nature" (602) that were witnessed by sixteen people, including his personal physician "Rabelays."[24] To

---

that which is below" was a basic tenet of the mystical tradition (Dieckman 23), and the same principle was used by Renaissance writers to explain the inner necessity of all hieroglyphic symbolism.

Michel Jeanneret, "Rabelais, les monstres et l'interprétation des signes (*Quart Livre* 18-42)," *Writing the Renaissance. Essays on Sixteenth-Century French Literature in Honor of Floyd Gray*, ed. Raymond C. La Charité (Lexington, KY: French Forum, 1992) also comments on the importance of the idea of correspondences in this episode: "Dans sa réflection sur les signes, l'épisode des Macraeons est donc foncièrement optimiste; de la transcendance à l'immanence, de l'idée cachée à sa manifestation visible, un système de correspondances garantit l'intelligibilité des phénomènes. Dans le monde et dans le livre, des figures nous interpellent, et nous sommes capables de les comprendre" (68).

[23] "(H)ier en soit mort quelqu'un. Au trespas duquel soyt excitée celle horrible tempest que avez pati. Car eulx vivens tout bien abonde en ce lieu et aultres isles voisines: et en mer est bonache (bonace) et serenité continuelle. Au trespas d'un chascun d'iceulx ordinairement oyons nous par la forest grandes et pitoyables lamentations, et voyons en terre pestes, vimeres (désastres naturels) et afflictions, en l'air troublemens et tenebres: en mer tempeste et fortunal" (599).

[24] Rabelais, who had been attached to the Cardinal Jean Du Bellay since 1534,

these eyewitnesses the meaning of the portents was clear. They were signs that France would soon be deprived of the statesman who is described as the very incarnation of civic and political virtue, the true symbol of City Man. The dire omens were fulfilled for, after Du Bellay's death and the death of all the virtues he represented, France fell prey to those with no concern for the common good. It became a woeful city now held "en mespris de tout le monde" (600).

This mourning generates a discussion of the immortality of the soul which is both conclusion to the death of Du Bellay and prelude to the death of Pan, the final tragedy to be recounted and Pantagruel's most significant interpretive act. With it, the focus moves from reading the cipher-writing of nature to "interpretation" in a more conventional sense, the proper reading of a story inscribed in a book. It was Plutarch in *De defectu oraculorum* (419 b-d)[25] who recounted the death of Pan, and the tale was told to support the notion that death quenches the soul, that all souls, even those of demigods, "meurent finablement," in Frère Jean's words (603). The monk attributes this view to the old Macrobe and is very disturbed by it: "(C)es Heroes icy et Semidieux des quelz avez parlé, peuvent ilz par mort finir? Par nettre dene je pensoys en pensaroys qu'ilz feussent immortelz, comme beaulx anges . . ." (603). Pantagruel responds with an unambiguous assertion of Christian orthodoxy:[26] "Je croy . . . que toutes ames intellectives sont exemptes des cizeaulx de Atropos. Toutes sont immortelles: Anges, Dæmons et Humaines. Je vous diray toutes foys une histoire bien estrange . . . à ce propous" (603). He will refute the erroneous notion that souls die by telling the same anecdote that Plutarch had used to promulgate it.

---

also served his brother from 1540 until Langey's death in 1543. The death of this great statesman obviously moved Rabelais deeply, as it is described twice in his books—in chapter twenty-seven of *Le Quart Livre* and in chapter twenty-one of the *Tiers Livre*, the Raminagrobis episode.

[25] *Plutarch's Moralia*, trans. Frank Cole Babbitt, vol. 5 (Cambridge: Harvard UP, 1936) 400-403. Additionally, as noted in Chapter Three, n. 23, Rabelais's interest in the Pan story may also have been generated by *Le Songe de Pantagruel* where Gargangua speaks at length about "Pan le berger."

[26] Screech makes this point 354. As he discusses, Pantagruel has subtly taken issue with the classical notion that souls die by describing death not as an extinction but as a "discession," a separation of body and soul, as Christian belief upholds. *Rabelais* (Ithaca: Cornell UP, 1979) 352-53. Screech's entire discussion of "l'isle des Macraeons" (350-65) is relevant.

Like *Le Quart Livre,* the story of Pan recounted in *De defectu oraculorum* takes place on a boat, this one becalmed in the seas near Paxi off the coast of Greece, and also like Rabelais's adventure, the ship has an Egyptian pilot–with the Greek name of Thamous or Thamoun.[27] Plutarch's story clearly had a great influence on Rabelais and he is faithful to its main outlines. But he also makes significant modifications in the details to prepare for his Christian interpretation. In Pantagruel's version, when a strange voice calls Thamous' name, it orders him to "publier et dire que Pan *le grand Dieu* estoit mort" (604, italics mine). Plutarch had spoken only of "Great Pan"; it is Rabelais who calls him God. His choice of the word "publier" for the Greek "apangeilon," "to announce or report," is also significant, and the word is repeated as Thamous debates whether to "taire ou publier." This phrase might apply to Rabelais's own hesitations about completing and publishing *Le Quart Livre.* But finally, the decision is taken to "publish." Thamous stands at the prow of the ship and announces the death of Pan. As with the other deaths recounted in this episode, nature responds with "grands souspirs, grandes lamentations et effroiz en terre. . ." (604-5).

The point of greatest divergence between Rabelais and Plutarch, however, is the all-important issue of the god's identity. The classical author had been content to accept the conjectures of Tiberius' scholars that Pan was "the son born of Hermes and Penelopê" (403), an opinion which Pantagruel refutes. He rather thinks of Another, also the son of a god and a mortal woman, who was crucified in Jerusalem during the reign of Tiberius Cesar:

> Toutes foys je le interpreteroys de celluy grand Servateur des fideles, qui feut en Judée ignominieusement occis par l'envie et iniquité des Pontifes, docteurs, prebstres de la loy Mosaicque.[28] Et ne me semble l'interpretation abhorrente. Car à bon droict peut il estre en languaige Gregoys dict Pan. Veu que il est le nostre Tout, tout ce que sommes, tout ce que vivons, tout ce que avons, tout ce que esperons est luy, en luy, de luy, par luy.[29] (605)

---

[27] These are the nominative and accusative forms of the name. Rabelais uses both, depending on the case in the Greek text.

[28] This is the only allusion to Moses in *Le Quart Livre* which could be construed as negative. However, the emphasis is less on the prophet himself than on the iniquitious priests who corrupted the old law and their successors who continue this corruption under the new law of Christ.

[29] For the predecessors and sources of Rabelais's interpretation, see Screech 257-63.

Thus, Pantagruel invites us to a somber allegorical interpretation of *Le Quart Livre*. It is as if Christ is being crucified again by iniquitious pontifs, priests and monks who betray His sacrifice, and by the religious quarrels in France which are tearing the body politic and His body asunder once again. With the death of Pan-Christ, the book passes into the Lenten days of sorrow and mourning, and there is no mention of resurrection. The story of Pan ends in grief as Pantagruel falls silent and weeps.

But the episode does not end with this story. In the last few lines, the voice of the *escale*'s final eyewitness is heard, that of Alcofribas, anagram and projection of the "Rabelays" who witnessed Du Bellay's death (602), and with his intervention, the tone and point of view change radically. Now the weeping giant is seen through the eyes of Alcofribas who describes his tears as "grosses comme oeufz de Austruche" (605), an observation which seems flippant in view of Pantagruel's grief and the sacredness of the story he has just told. Then, in the episode's last line, Alcofribas co-opts the entire narration by asserting that *he* has not lied, that this is *his* story: "Je me donne à Dieu si j'en mens d'un seul mot" (605).[30] Thus, as on "l'isle Medamothi," the narrator intervenes to appropriate the function of writing. He had remained in the background throughout the episode and let others speak for him, but in the end, Alcofribas is compelled to assert that he has stood behind their words, that the events on "l'isle des Macraeons" are ultimately of his making.

2. The Land of False Faith

Papimania is one of the most Egyptian sites of *Le Quart Livre* in the negative sense: a corrupt city, a place of cruel repression and, above all, a land of idolatry and of perverted faith. This episode contains the book's most overt and fiercest anti-Catholic satire.[31]

---

[30] The formula is surprising. We would expect him to say, "je me donne au diable," as he had done so often before when protesting the "truth" of his outrageous fictions. But here, doubtless because of the sacredness of the story of Pan, Alcofribas "gives himself to God."

[31] The satire is directed against the pretensions of the papal curia and papist lawyers that the pope was *quasi Deus in terris*, "as though God on earth," a claim that shocked not only protestants but many Catholics as well (Screech 404). It was

The pope is worshipped as "God on earth"; he is called "L'unicque" (649), "celluy qui est" (649), and "Messyas" (651). In place of this god whom they have never seen, the Papimanes worship his portrait, kept under lock and key near the altar of the church and shown only on feast days. This icon forecasts Manduce, "une effigie monstrueuse, ridicule, hydeuse" (676) fashioned by the Gastrolatres which also appears on feast days and at Carnival time. The episode in Papimania quickly passes from the church to the cabaret and to a copious banquet for which the citizens are forced to pay (656), and in the café, the Papimanes worship their true god. They are Gastrolatres *avant la lettre:* "ennemis de la croix du Christ . . . desquelz Ventre est le Dieu" (675).[32]

Another powerful icon is worshipped in Papimania, the Decretals,[33] a book of papal ordinances which are a similacrum of the Holy Scriptures. Kept in the temple near the papal portrait, the Decretals are bejeweled, "un gros livre d'oré, tout couvert de fines et precieuses pierres, Balais, Esmeraulaes, Diamans et Unions" (652) and, like the Andouilles' flying pig, the book hangs in the air. These are Decret-*ales,* in Frère Jean's words, decrees which have wings,[34] and Bishop Homenaz makes extravagant claims for their

---

the climate of the Gallican crisis of 1550-51 which gave Rabelais the freedom to "faire la figue au Pape" without fear of retribution because the attack served the interests of the crown. In 1551, when the episode was probably composed, Henri II was planning a war on the Pope who, in his turn, was considering the King's excommunication. However, by 1552 when *Le Quart Livre* was published, the antagonisms had calmed (Huchon 1465-7. See also Gérard Defaux, *Rabelais Agonistes: Du Rieur au prophète: Etudes sur Pantagruel, Gargantua, le Quart Livre* (Geneva: Droz, 1997) 480-86.

[32] Jeanneret makes a similar point: "Fidèles à ces valeurs, les Papimanes passent imperceptiblement de l'église au café, de la célébration de la messe à la satisfaction de la panse. . . . Les avatars tangibles du surnaturel et l'abondance des aliments assurent les mêmes satisfactions et aboutissent à la fusion abjecte de l'idolâtrie et de la gastrolâtrie. . ." "Les Paroles Dégelées (Rabelais, *Quart Livre* 48-65)," *Littérature* 17 (1965): 15.

[33] According to Mireille Huchon (1564), Rabelais's satire is directed toward the Decretals posterior to the Decret of Gratien which was accepted by the Gallicans. The texts under attack are those which affirmed the temporal power of the popes: the Decretals composed in 1234 during the reign of Pope Gregory IX; "the Sixth" (1298) written under Boniface VIII, "the Clementines" (1313) under Clement V, and "the Extravagants," a collection of earlier texts published in 1500.

[34] See Frère Jean's *dicton,* cited below. Screech (404) also stresses the importance of "decrees which took on wings," as does Lawrence Kritzman, "Rabelais in Papimania: power and the rule of law," *The Rhetoric of Sexuality and the Literature of the French Renaissance* (Cambridge: Cambridge UP, 1991) 202-3.

divinity. He calls them "uranopetes" (651) and likens them to other heaven-sent words, including the law given to Moses, "escripte des doigts propres de Dieu," and the inscription on the temple of the oracle at Delphi also "divinement escripte et transmise des Cieulx" (652). However, the epithet "urano-*pete*" contains a *double entendre* which undermines Homenaz's claims of the Decretals' glory. These are the "farts of heaven." As on "l'isle de Ruach," spirit is brought low in Papimania and degraded to the anus. The Decretals have their origins in the all-too-human, and the "god" who wrote them, "dieu en terre," may also be called Satan, "prince de ce monde."

Papimania stands in direct contrast to "l'isle des Macraeons" as the land of perverted Christianity and of bad writing and reading. This episode is about "abus de parolles" in Pantagruel's words: "User ainsi du sacre nom de Dieu en choses tant hordes (sales) et abhominables. Fy, j'en diz fy!" (655).[35] And Bishop Homenaz, in contrast to Pantagruel, is the quintessential bad reader of *Le Quart Livre*. Like those whom Rabelais castigates in the "Lettre à Odet," Homenaz interprets the Decretals "perversement et contre tout usaige de raison et de languaige commun" (520), using them to justify the cruelty of the the papal wars[36] and offering a lyrical vision of a new paradise under their rule: "O lors abondance de tous biens en terre! O lors paix obstinée infringible en l'Univers" (657). However, we need only to invert Homenaz's eulogy to arrive at the truth: "The Bible is being perverted and driven out by decretaline law; kings and princes are being held subject to papal authority; monasteries flourish; torturing and killing heretics is all the rage . . . ."[37] Frère Jean's *dicton* sums up these realities:

> Depuis que Decretz eurent ales,
> Et gensdarmes porterent males (malles),
> Moines allerent à cheval,
> En ce monde abonda tout mal
>
> (662)

---

[35] Pantagruel is reproaching Frère Jean for his anecdote about the beggar who has "une jambe de Dieu," a diseased leg which earns him generous alms (654-5), but the reproach is certainly also applicable to Homenaz's praise of the Decretals.

[36] "Cela . . . est commendé par les sacres Decretales: et doibt à feu incontinent Empereurs, Roys, Ducz, Princes, Republiques et à sang mettre, qu'ilz trangresseront un iota de ses mandemens " (655).

[37] Screech 404.

The catalogue of the deleterious effects of the Decretals goes beyond the social and political realm into a domain which strikes at the heart of Rabelais's own enterprise. From the prologue to the *Pantagruel* in 1532, Rabelais has argued that his books have medicinal powers, that they are a remedy to heal the body as well as the mind of his readers, and this claim is made with special insistence for *Le Quart Livre* in the 1548 Prologue and in the "Lettre à Odet" (see Chapter One 32-41). At the same time however, he has always understood that words can be a poison as well as a remedy when used by persons motivated by self-interest and self-love, and in Papimania, the poisonous power of bad words is copiously displayed. The Decretals are imbued with a black magic that tempts even Pantagruel to violence,[38] and his companions offer many other examples of the decrees' negative alchemy (658-62). They cause constipation in Panurge and hemorrhoids in Frère Jean. They turn remedies into poison in an apothecary. Masks made from the Decretals stick to the skin, raising boils and pistules and pox. They spoil a tailor's patterns, and cause arrows to deflect from a target. Gold beaten between leaves of Decretals is left torn and full of holes, and the guimples of Rhizotome's two sisters turn from white to black. This last example has particular relevance for Homenaz's rhetoric which operates the same transformation in reverse. He turns black into white as he interprets every aberration as a miracle or as divine punishment for the "blasphemous" uses to which the Decretals have been put: "Abuser en choses prophanes de ces tant sacres escriptures." (659).

However, the writer-physician surmounts the decrees' negative magic with the transformative powers of his own writing. As in the other episodes we have discussed, the "je" intervenes to assert his primacy, and he does so as the action moves from the church to the cabaret and the banquet begins. Alcofribas notes "deux choses memorables": "l'une, que viande ne feut apportée, quelle que feust ... en laquelle n'y eust abondance de farce magistrale" (656). With this intervention, the tone of the episode is altered, for farce with its double link to food and theatricality generates laughter which is open-hearted and gay, in contrast to the attack and derision of

---

[38] "Et (Pantagruel) nous affermoit que au touchement (des Décrétales) il sentoit un doulx prurit des ongles et desgourdissement de bras: ensemble temptation vehemente en son esprit de battre un sergent ou deux ..." (652).

satire which dominates the episode's first chapters. There is, moreover, a corresponding change in attitude toward Homenaz. At the banquet, the repressive bishop becomes a clown "tout joyeulx et esbaudy" (657), coughing, sputtering, and laughing: "Vous me doibvez ceste là! Ha, ha, ha, ha, ha!' Icy commença Homenaz rocter, peter, rire, baver et suer" (664). And the voyagers enter into the spirit of the farce: "(ils) commencerent au couvert de leurs serviettes crier, 'Myault, myault, myault,' faignans ce pendent s'essuer les oeilz, comme s'ilz eussent ploré" (665). This is a "Tragicque comedie" (566) which bears many resemblances to those staged by Basché, and here too the play has transformative powers. Like the Chiquanous, Homenaz who began as enemy is in the end accepted as a banquet companion: "*Vivat* (s'escria Epistemon) *uivat, fifat, pipat, bibat.* O secret Apocalyptique" (665).

The change in attitude toward Homenaz is also linked to the second characteristic of the banquet noted by the narrator: "l'aultre (chose memorable), que tout le sert et dessert feut porté par les filles pucelles mariables du lieu, belles, je vous affie . . ." (656). These young women light up the banquet with wine and with their presence, as Homenaz expresses with his often-repeated cry, "*Clerice,* esclaire icy." They are the only women of marriageable age presented positively in all of Rabelais's four books, and with them, as in the land of the Chiquanous, the themes of marriage and fertility are introduced into Papimania. The "pucelles mariables" represent the green world and the sexual garden, an association which Homenaz brings forth with his other refrain: "au fruict, pucelles," an injunction to bring–and to bear–fruit. Their potential fertility links them to the future, in contrast to Homenaz who represents the past and, astonishingly, the past accedes to the future in Papimania. The bishop passes his hat to the young women in a gesture of submission, a voluntary "uncrowning." The repressive old male world gives way to the young women and to the births that they promise:

> . . . et (Homenaz) bailla son gros, gras bonnet à quatre braguettes (cornes) à une des filles: laquelle le posa sus son beau chef en grande alaigresse, après l'avoir amoureusement baisé, comme guaige et asceurance qu'elle seroit premiere mariée. (664)

It is in the context of Homenaz's uncrowning that we must read the episode's last chapter which contains Pantagruel's praise of the

Papimanes and of the fruit which he calls "poires de bon Christian": "Car oncques ne veiz Christians meilleurs que ces bons Papimanes" (666). There are undoubtedly irony and derision in this praise, and a *double entendre* resembling the play on the word "urano*pete*," for "poire" in old French meant "to fart." [39] Like the inhabitants of "l'isle de Ruach," these "poires de bon Christian" are nothing but broken wind.

At the same time, however, Pantagruel's praise of the pears seems genuine and may be explained by the new direction the episode has taken. It ends in the garden–the young women are the "poires de bon Christian." Pantagruel speaks of the planting he will undertake when he returns home: "(Q)uand je seray en mon mesnaige (ce sera, si Dieu plaist, bient tost) j'en affieray et hanteray en mon jardin de Touraine sus la rive de Loyre" (666). And Frère Jean, who has coveted the young women since the moment he saw them "comme un chien qui emporte un plumail" (656-7) underscores the sexual connotations of the "planting." To renew the race of his country, he wants to take the women home: "(p)our les saigner . . . droict entre les deux gros horteilz . . . . En ce faisant sus elles nous hanterions (grefferions) des enfants de bon Christian, et la race en nos pays multiplierioit" (666). Homenaz refuses the request, but Pantagruel intervenes to assure that such a "planting" will occur. His last gesture before departing from the island is to leave dowry money to support the young women's marriages "en temps oportun" (667).

It is a fact of no little irony that the hope for regeneration and renewal lies on the Catholic island of Papimania rather in the land of those who "font la figue au Pape" (chs. 45-47). In contrast to the Papimanes' young "poires de bon Christian," the Pape*figues* are associated with a wrinkled and dessicated fruit and, despite their efforts to cultivate their garden, it remains barren, for no child can be

---

[39] Screech offers this reading 408-9. Kritzman also suggests that the text "ironically undercuts the notions of *vray Christian* and *bon Catholicque*" (206). Jeanneret pauses over the naming of the pears, noting that it is Pantagruel who confers the designation "poires *de bon Christian*" (my italics)–Homenaz simply calls them "pears": "Nous sommes simples gens . . . . Et appelons les figues, figues: les prunes, prunes: et les poires, poires" (666). According to Jeanneret, "Homenaz est un nominaliste: il ne connaît d'autre réalité que celle désignée préalablement par un signe; sa saisie est circonscrite au phénomènes nommés clairement par les mots. La position de Pantagruel est inverse. Il façonne le signe à sa volonté et transforme la donnée évidente . . ." ("Les Paroles dégelées" 16).

born to the old. This failed hope of regeneration is graphically represented by the image of the old man in place of a baby in the baptismal font (643). Do these contrasting outcomes signify that, despite Rabelais's anger at current Catholic practices, he remains attached to the church and is still hopeful that the traditional faith can be restored and rejuvenated? The final chapter of the episode in Papimania could lead to that conclusion.

3. Frozen Versus Thawed Words

The Papimanes' contention that the Decretals are heaven-sent, "uranopetes" and "angeliquement transmises," leads to the episode of the "Parolles gelées" (chs. 55-56). This new adventure also centers on the idea of "words in the air" and it explores the two contradictory values that this image has held, not only in Papimania but in other episodes of Le Quart Livre as well. "Voices in the air" are, first, a metaphor for divinely-inspired language, words from heaven like those given to Moses on the mountain, or like the voice heard on "l'isle des Macraeons" announcing the death of Pan. But this image has also been the figuration of language without meaning in Le Quart Livre, *flatus voci* like the speech of the Ruachans or the language condemned in the 1548 prologue and in Papimania. Rabelais may have derived this negative meaning of "speaking in the air" from St Paul who used the expression to castigate incomprehensible speech (I Corinthians 14:9).[40]

The Papimanes clearly mistake the second kind of "words in the air" for the first as they praise the divinity of the Decretals. However, their ability to make this substitution holds troubling implications for the Pantagruelists who share the faith that some words are god-given and that a new city can be founded on the law which these divine words express. Can they be similarly deceived? The episode in Papimania has thrown into question the very premise of the quest "pour le Mot," and this doubt generates the adventure of the "Parolles gelées." This episode begins the meditation on the

---

[40] Paul Smith makes this suggestion, *Voyage et écriture: Etudes sur Le Quart Livre de Rabelais* (Geneva: Droz, 1987) 13. The biblical passage reads: "So likewise ye, except ye utter by the tongue words easy to be understood, how shall it be known what is spoken? for ye shall speak into the air."

origins and nature of language which dominates the final chapters of the book.

The travellers have unwittingly strayed into the edges of "la mer Glaciale," marked from the beginning of the voyage as a place to be avoided and feared,[41] and strange murmurings, "voix diverses en l'air, tant de homes comme de femmes" (667), are heard, first by Pantagruel and then by his companions. The sounds are initially assumed to be the hostile voices of an attacking enemy force, an idea which frightens all the voyagers, but especially Panurge who explodes in terror. However, Pantagruel, the wise reader and interpreter of *Le Quart Livre*, abruptly changes the tenor and tone of these speculations as he puts forth the first and sacred interpretation of "voices in the air." In his mind, these sounds are emanations from heaven.[42] To explain their divine nature, the giant offers four hypotheses which are all rooted in the Platonic tradition. He is, in many ways, continuing and deepening the discussion begun on "l'isle des Macraeons."

Indeed, like the story of Pan's death, the giant's first speculation is also taken from Plutarch's *De defectu oraculorum* (XXII). It is a Platonic fable attributed to a philosopher named Petron who imagined hundreds of worlds arranged in an equilateral triangle around a central field which Plutarch called "the Plain of Truth" and which Pantagruel renames "le manoir de Verité":[43]

---

[41] In chapter one, when describing the route the voyage will follow, the danger of travelling too far to the north is stressed. The ships will stay at the latitude of the port of Olone, "de paour d'entrer et estre retenuz en la mer Glaciale" (539).

[42] In Jeanneret's words: "Ces voix qui émanent du ciel et animent la nature témoignent pour lui des fondements sacrés du langage; elles signifient que les mots plongent leurs racines dans la transcendance" ("Les Paroles dégelées" 18).

Duval, to the contrary, asserts that Pantagruel does not believe his own speculations about the origin and nature of the words, that he offers these theories merely to assuage the fears of Panurge and the crew. "His four tentative and highly improbable conjectures are not offered as serious explanations but as calming reassurances designed to suggest that such inexplicable and terrifying phenomena as these *could* be harmless, and *might* even be pleasant and beneficial" (*Design* 37). These theories are debunked by the meaninglessness of the thawed words, Duval argues, indicating that the episode is intended as a "brutal satire of the notions of Platonic idealism or transcendent Truth..." (39).

[43] The transformation of "the Plain of Truth" to "le manoir de Verité" links this episode to "l'isle des Macraeons" and its "manoir... des Heros" (116). Additionally, the phrase forecasts Gaster's "manoir de Areté (c'est vertu)" (209). Screech also makes this point 421-22.

> ... et là habiter les Parolles, les Idées, les Exemplaires et portraiz de toutes choses passées et futures: au tour d'icelles estre le Siecle. Et en certaines anneés par longs intervalles, part d'icelles tomber sus les humains comme catarrhes, et comme tomba la rousée sus la toizon de Gedeon: part là rester reservée pour l'advenir, jusques à la consommation du Siecle. (668)

As with the story of Pan's death, Pantagruel modifies and reinterprets the fable in several ways. Most significantly, he translates the word *logoi* as "parolles," whereas in Plutarch, the word would have meant "reasons" or "accounts."[44] It is of capital importance to the quest of *Le Quart Livre* that Pantagruel conceptualizes the *logoi* as supernal Words, that he identifies these Words with Ideas and Examplars and makes them equal as the objects of knowledge. It is equally important that, in contrast to Plutarch where the *logoi* remain immutable in the Plain of Truth, Pantagruel envisions their fall into the human realm on certain privileged occasions. Such are the time and place that Pantagruel hopes they have entered in the Frozen Sea and such are the words he hopes they will encounter, words falling from the world of Ideas which when thawed will bring truth.

Having identified the divine origins of the "Parolles," Pantagruel is now concerned with their flow into the human realm and who receives them. In the first degree of proximity to the "manoir de Verité" are the elect upon whom the words fall as the dew on Gideon's fleece–the writer-philosophers who are the protagonists of the following three anecdotes: Aristotle, Homer, Plato, and Orpheus. With them, "words in the air" are the image of inspiration and also express the nature of the language created by the divinely-inspired poet-philosophers. Touched by the dew falling from the Plain of Truth "comme catarrhes," their words are like the winged souls described in the *Phaedrus* (246a-249d). Gifted with life, "voligeantes, volantes, moventes, et par consequent animées" (668), the words soar back their place of origin in heaven.

The second degree of proximity to the divine "Parolles"–the relationship of the writer-philosopher and his readers–is more problematic and is the subject of the anecdote which gives this episode its name, Plato's doctrine of the Frozen Words. The dichotomy of

---

[44] See Screech's discussion of this word, 422; and my own, *Homo Logos*, 105.

frozen versus thawed words re-states the double problem of expression and communication that Rabelais has always associated with the hieroglyphic tradition (see above 118-21). Because the sacred nature of the intuitions does not lend itself to straightforword discourse, the poet must use veiled language, and the wisdom contained in his words will remain "frozen" and inaccessible to those who have no affinity with it or who are too young to understand. At the same time, the image also suggests the resolution of the interpretive dilemma, for with time and study, the words may be "thawed" and understood by those who seek the wisdom they contain:

> D'adventaige Antiphanes disoit la doctrine de Platon es parolles estre semblable lesquelles en quelque contrée on temps du fort hyver lors que sont proferées, gelent et glassent à la froydeur de l'air, et ne sont ouyes. Semblablement ce que Platon enseignoyt es jeunes enfans, à peine estre d'iceulx entendu, lors que estoient vieulx devenuz. (668-9)

The allusion to Orpheus which concludes chapter fifty-five continues the speculations related to Plato's doctrine of Frozen Words, for it was felt by the Renaissance that Orpheus was the parent of such writing and that Plato learned it from him.[45] But what is stressed now is rather the price paid for the unveiling. Orpheus is the dark side of Homer, the dark side of Plato. With him, inspiration is represented as a fall into the underworld, a fall into fear, and the thawing of the Frozen Words becomes a terrifying image of dissolution and dismemberment, of liquification and of death. Orpheus' words do not fly through the air, they issue from his decapitated head as it floats on the sea and they lament his death in a "chant lugubre" (669). With this image, Pantagruel, who spurned the fear of the others at the outset of the episode, is himself afraid.[46]

But fear is banished in chapter fifty-six as an entirely different

---

[45] "... Orpheus interwove the mysteries of his doctrines with the texture of fables and covered them with a poetic veil, in order that anyone reading his hymns would think them to contain nothing but the sheerest tales and trifles." Edgar Wind, *Pagan Mysteries in the Renaissance* (Harmondsworth, Eng.: Penguin Books, 1967) 18. He showed only the "crust of the mysteries to the vulgar, while reserving the marrow of the true sense for higher and more perfect spirits" (17).

[46] The first words spoken in chapter 56 are those of the pilot to Pantagruel: "Seigneur, de rien ne vous effrayez" (669).

explanation of "les parolles gelées" is offered by the ship's pilot. These words prove not to have their origins in the Plain of Truth, but in the all-too-human and in destruction rather than in creation. As had first been speculated, they are indeed words of war but they do not announce an impending attack. They are rather echos of the past, of a battle fought the preceeding winter between the Arismapiens and the Nephelibates, "the cloud walkers." The warriors are vanished or dead. All that remain are their shouts and cries which froze in the cold air and are now beginning to thaw. With these sounds, the second and negative value of "words in the air" is developed: *flatus voci* and *baragouin*. Far from being the place of sacred writing and wise readers that Pantagruel had envisioned, the Frozen Sea proves rather to be the place of Babel.

Chapter fifty-six plays on many contrasts to chapter fifty-five: the human versus the divine origin of the words, their thawed versus their frozen state, and the responses of the voyagers also change dramatically. Panurge, who fell into hysterical terror when the sounds were first heard, is now fascinated by the words and wants to see and touch them. The pilot's explanation has clearly calmed his fears, but Pantagruel's speculations have also had their effect, for Panurge evokes Moses as the giant has so often done in the past. However, Panurge holds a very different view of the prophet. Pantagruel imagined Moses on the mountain in pure and unmediated communication with the divine source of truth, and the words the giant envisioned remained "frozen" abstractions; they were never seen nor heard. Panurge, to the contrary, considers the prophet in communication with the people below–and the writing of the laws. To speak of voices from heaven as Pantagruel has done, even to hear them, is all very well, but Panurge insists that the Word be made Flesh:

> Mais en pourrions nous veoir quelqu'une? Me soubvient avoir leu que l'orée de la montaigne en laquelle Moses receut la loy des Juifz le people voyoit les voix sensiblement. (669)

And Pantagruel, with the gesture of a king, throws them down on the deck.

"Voix sensibles" is the key to the nature of the "parolles dégelées" and they betray all of Pantagruel's hopes for them. These words have no link with transcendence; they belong to the domain of pure materiality. As they rain down still in a frozen state, the words are things, marvelous toys that can be seen and touched and played with: "(E)t sembloient dragée perlée de diverses couleurs. Nous y veismes des motz de gueule, des motz de sinople, des motz de azur, des motz de sable, des motz d'orez" (670). When the words thaw, they burst into a cacophony of sound which is devoid of intelligible meaning but which nonetheless carries a tremendous expressive power: "Et y veids des parolles bien picquantes, des parolles sanglantes . . . , des parolles horrificques . . ." (670). It is also significant that the cries of horses and the sounds of trumpets commingle with human voices in the *tintamarre*. The thawed words reveal the origins of speech to be in the animal. This is food and beast language. These are the "words" of Messer Gaster.

We have seen such primitive anti-language before in *Le Quart Livre*, and it has always been associated with Panurge. His inarticulate shrieks and moans during the tempest, in the Frozen Sea, and at so many other junctures of the book both forecast and echo the noise of the thawed words. Such language has also been associated with Alcofribas who faithfully recorded Panurge's nonsensical language as well as Pantagruel's allegories, and who so persistently proclaimed himself to be the writer of this book. The first-person narrator is omnipresent throughout chapter fifty-six and his frequent use of the pronoun "nous" allies him to Panurge above all. Alcofribas speaks for both of them as he expresses the pleasure taken in the spectacle of the thawing words: "Croyez que nous y eusmez du passetemps beaucoup" (670). Unlike Pantagruel who seeks truth in language, Panurge and Alcofribas enjoy it as pure *baragouin*.

But the giant's opprobium comes to mitigate their joy. For him, the thawed words represent the kind of language that has been repudiated from the 1548 prologue throughout all of *Le Quart Livre*: words whose speakers and whose referents are "deperie(s) en nature" (718), words which tell of war and of the breakdown of culture and meaning. The fascination of the thawed words is, moreover, dangerous to the quest for the Word, for Panurge and Alcofribas would linger in the Frozen Sea and play with the "parolles dégelées" forever. Thus, Pantagruel rebukes them one by one. To Panurge who wants more and more words, he admonishes:

> . . . donner parolles (est) acte des amoureux. "Vendez m'en doncques, disoit Panurge.
> —C'est acte de advocatz, respondit Pantagruel, vendre parolles. Je vous vendroys plustost silence et plus cherement . . . . (670)

And Pantagruel has this exchange with Alcofribas:

> Je vouloys quelques motz de gueule mettre en reserve dedans de l'huille comme l'on guarde la neige et la glace, et entre du feurre (paille) bien nect. Mais Pantagruel ne le voulut: disant estre follie faire reserve de ce dont jamais l'on n'a faulte, et que tous jours on a en main, comme sont motz de gueule entre tous bons et joyeulx Pantagruelists. (670-1)

The instinct to preserve these "motz de gueule" is the desire to write and print them, and this desire has always before been victorious in *Le Quart Livre*. Always before, as on "l'isle Medamothi" and on "l'isle des Macraeons," Alcofribas has asserted his primacy over Pantagruel as the writer of the voyage, his power to take the story in the direction he wants it to go. But here, Pantagruel dominates—and silences—the writer. He also dominates Panurge, so linked in nature and spirit to Alcofribas, he who had wanted Moses' words to be made flesh. After a bitter and confusing argument with Frère Jean,[47] he is suddenly persuaded to the giant's point of view. The entire edifice of this chapter comes to rest on Panurge's rejection of the thawed words which had so fascinated him. Suddenly he desires what Pantagruel desires, the Word which when thawed will bring truth: "Pleust à Dieu que icy, sans plus avant proceder, j'eusse le mot de la dive Bouteille." (671).

But what is the nature of this word? The episode in the Frozen Sea has set forth two opposing views of language without indicating a middle ground between them. And Pantagruel's victory over Panurge and Alcofribas, his preference for silence over "fallen" human language, threatens to end the voyage and thus to end the quest for the Word. Pantagruel has deviated from the hieroglyphic tradition which, as explained on "l'isle des Macraeons," advocates the clothing of transcendent truths in the very food and beast lan-

---

[47] "Là, Panurge fascha quelque peu frere Jan, et le feist entrer en resverie, car il le vous print au mot, sus l'instant qu'il ne s'en doubtoit mie, et frere Jan menassa de l'en faire repentir . . ." (671).

guage he disdains: "(L)es letres des antiques saiges Aegyptiens . . . estoient faictes des images diverses de arbres, herbes, animaulx, poissons, oiseaulx, instrumens . . ." (708). An important focus of the final chapters of the book is to reiterate that lesson and to find a compromise between "frozen" and "thawed" words.

4. "Le Mot de la Dive Bouteille"

As we have seen in Chapter Three (110-13), the issues of writing and interpretation are intertwined with banquet imagery at the end of *Le Quart Livre,* and that commingling begins with the *escale* on the island of Messer Gaster (chs. 57-62). This creature encompasses in his nature the contradictions explored in the Frozen Sea; he is Pantagruel's "maistre" in matters of language as well as of food. With the refrain, "tout pour la trippe" (673), Gaster confirms the message of "les parolles dégelées"–that the origins of speech are in the beast, that words are vulnerable to meaninglessness and to the self-interested deceptiveness which so severely threatens the city. Sir Belly teaches Pantagruel that all Jerusalems contain within themselves the seeds of Egypt and that all words are subject to the demonic perversion of the Engastrimythes, the Gastrolatres, and the Papimanes.

But the anecdote of the "sureau sauvage" (686-7) teaches another lesson. It shows that imperfect creatural words, so prone to deception and betrayal, can also be used to point beyond themselves to transcendent truths apprehended in the silence that both Gaster and Pantagruel cherish, and the giant applies this "reading lesson" in the seas off "l'isle Chaneph" (chs. 63-65). Like Oedipus facing the Sphinx, he must answer the enigmatic question posed by Frère Jean: "Maniere de haulser le temps en calme?" (688). Pantagruel solves the riddle following the principles set forth in the wild elder anecdote, explicating it both "scelon la letre" and "allegoricquement scelon l'usaige des Pythagoriens" (687). In its literal meaning, the expression is tied to the creatural needs that Gaster governs, for "haulser le temps" means both "to raise the wind" and "to spend or pass away the time in quaffing, swilling, and carousing" (Cotgrave). But the expression's allegorical sense takes the reading to a higher level–the wind to be raised is also the breath of spirit and of the inspiration needed to banish the silence which has captured the voyage. The banquet called forth by Pantagruel regenerates the joyous table talk that had been silenced in the Frozen Sea and he concludes the meal with his final explication, of the nature of the god of wine in his spiritual as well as material manifestation:

> Ne sçavez vous que jadis les Amycleens sus tous Dieux reveroient et adoroient le noble pere Bacchus, et le nommoient *Psila* en propre et convenente denomination? *Psila*, en langue Doricque, signifie æsles. Car comme les oyzeaulx par ayde de leurs æsles volent hault en l'air legierement: ainsi par l'ayde de Bacchus, c'est le bon vin friant et delicieux, sont hault eslevez les espritz des humains: leurs corps evidentement alaigriz: et assouply ce que en eulx estoit terrestre. (695)

Pantagruel's explication of "maniere de haulser le temps" thus resolves the tension between the two kinds of "words in the air" displayed throughout *Le Quart Livre* and reveals the dual nature of "le mot de la dive Bouteille." It is both a "mot de gueule" rooted in creatural pleasure and a "parole voligeante, volante" (668) like the words the giant envisioned in the Frozen Sea, a word which points the way to high truths apprehended in silence. In the end, the book affirms the hieroglyphic view of language set forth on "l'isle des Macraeons" and in the Prologue to *Gargantua*. Here, too, we are urged to accept and enjoy the appeal of words to the senses, savour the flavour of the bone, at the same time as we are told that these words may contain a "marrow" of deep and serious meaning. The duplicity of wine, its association both to drunkenness and to divine inspiration, reflects that silenic message and *Le Quart Livre* ends with Bacchus' injunction. "Beuvons" is the book's last word (248).

The menace of Babel is not dispelled, however. It still exists on Chaneph, the island off the coast of which the triumphant banquet occurs, the island rejected by the voyagers as a land of hypocrisy and lies. They also pass by Ganabin (ch. 66), another place of false faith and "abus de parolles" (655),[48] but this island is more difficult

---

[48] In contrast to V.-L. Saulnier, "Pantagruel au large de Ganabin ou la peur de Panurge," *BHR* 16 (1954): 58-81, who identified Ganabin as Paris, Gérard Defaux sees Rome: "Rome symbolisée dans le texte par les 'deux crouppes' du Capitole, Rome assimilée par Rabelais à la *spelunca latronum* de l'Ecriture, à la 'caverne des brigands' dont parlent Jérémie (7.11) et Matthieu (21.13)." *Rabelais Agonistes* 541. See the discussion 541-559 and his article, "Rabelais au large de Ganabin: de la 'fiction en archipel' au 'symbolisme polémique,'" *Rabelais pour le XXIe siècle: Actes du Colloque du Centre d'Etudes Supérieures de la Renaissance (Chinon-Tours, 1994)*, ed. Michel Simonin (Geneva: Droz, 1998) 213-39.

for Rabelais's characters to reject. Despite their opprobium of Ganabin and its inhabitants, Pantagruel's men are nonetheless greatly tempted to stop there because it contains "la plus belle fontaine du monde" (696), a spring which recalls the "fontaine Caballine" that Rabelais called his "unicque Enthusiasme" in the prologue to the *Tiers Livre* (349). His old fascination with word-play of all sorts, bad as well as good, still exerts its pull in the seas off Ganabin.

The debate about visiting Ganabin is settled by an inner voice "comme le Dæmon de Socrates" (697) urging Pantagruel to pass by the island which is finally condemned as a place of negative inspiration, a "mons Antiparnasse" (697). However, this is only a provisional solution, for bad words and bad writing continue to surround the imaginative world of *Le Quart Livre*. The pilgrims have not yet passed out of Egypt; their drama of exile has not ended. "Le mot de la dive Bouteille Bacbuc" still floats at sea among enemy lands, and the new city to be founded on that word is not attained at the end of Rabelais's odyssey.

CHAPTER FIVE

DARK BIRTHS: RABELAIS'S ENACTMENT
OF MALE MATERNITY

WE have thus far discussed the voyage of *Le Quart Livre* as a quest for renewal and for *renaissance*. To place this desire on the Christian calendar, we can say that Pantagruel and Panurge are seeking the spring miracle of Easter, of resurrection and renewal, in this book. However, another quest also underlies *Le Quart Livre*, the project of marriage and paternity, "le projet de génération"[1] carried over from *Le Tiers Livre*. This is the desire for *naissance*, and the birth of a child is associated with a different miracle and a different season—Advent which occurs in deepest winter. Though submerged and overwhelmed by the search for *renaissance*, the lure of *naissance* continues to exert its pull, and it deeply affects the quest for rebirth. We will now explore the interplay between these two quests as they are enacted in *Le Quart Livre*.

The two miracles are urgently desired, for this book depicts a world sorely in need of both Easter and Advent. The universe of *Le Quart Livre* lies in thrall to the dark principle that Rabelais calls *philautia* and it has left the garden barren and the city in ruins. On "l'isle des Macraeons" (chs. 25-28), we mourn with "Dr. Rabelays" who witnessed it, the death of the great statesman Guillaume Du Bellay who incarnates the virtue of *urbanitas*–this is the death of city man. We also mourn the death of Pan, the pagan god of

---

[1] See Françoise Charpentier, "Un Royaume qui perdure sans femmes," *Rabelais's Incomparable Book*, ed. Raymond C. La Charité (Lexington, KY: French Forum, 1986) 195: "La narration du *Pantagruel* peut être envisagé sous l'angle d'un projet de mariage, ou plus exactement, d'un projet de génération. Plus voilé aux deux premiers livres, ce projet devient à partir du *Tiers Livre*, la véritable dynamique du monde pantagruélien."

nature, a death interpreted by Pantagruel as an allegory for the crucifixion of Christ (see Chapter Four 121-6). And spring is left in jeopardy on "l'isle des Macraeons" for, though the immortality of the soul is affirmed,[2] the resurrection of the body is *not*. Therefore, like all redeemers, Pantagruel must descend to the underworld in quest of the renewing secret, the word and the wine of "la dive Bouteille."

This is the cycle of renaissance and we must pause to reflect that the spring miracle of resurrection is largely an affair among men: between the King and the Prince and especially, in the Christian tradition, between the Father and the Son. It is the Father who commands that his Son must die, condemns Him to spend three days in the tomb, and who resurrects Him again to assure the salvation of the world. The Mother plays only a peripheral role in the sacrament. We must further reflect that, however triumphant, the miracle of resurrection is inadequate to fulfill the year, for it involves the rebirth of the already formed, of the adult man—Christ, or Lazarus, or Jonah.[3] To complete the year and assure that the future will not be only a recurrence of the past, a child must be born. And for a child to be born, there must be a mother. Advent is needed to complete the cycle of Easter, and Advent is the domain of the maternal principle.

Herein lies the rub in Rabelais's odyssey. These books are marked by the suppression of the Mother and without Her, the future stands in peril. The first mother in the order of composition, Badebec, died when Pantagruel was born in 1532, and the first mother in the order of the genealogy, Gargamelle, disappears from the story after giving birth to Gargantua. After 1534, the woman becomes literally and figuratively *un trou à remplir* in Rabelais's books. What urges Panurge forward in *Le Tiers Livre*, despite his fear of being cuckolded, beaten, and robbed, is his desire to find a wife, a mother for his children so that he can become the "batisseur de pierres vives" that he desires to be.[4] Pantagruel stands apart and

---

[2] "Je croy (dist Pantagruel) que toutes ames intellectives sont exemptes des cizeaulx de Atropos. Toutes sont immortelles: Anges, Dæmons et Humaines" (603).

[3] We recall that Christ compares himself to Jonah as He promises His resurrection: "For as Jonas was three days and three nights in the whale's belly; so shall the Son of man be three days and three nights in the heart of the earth" (Matthew 12: 40. See also Luke 11: 29-32).

[4] "Je ne bastis que pierres vives, ce sont homes" (TL 370).

as an observer of Panurge's quest in *Le Tiers Livre*; but his own marriage and his own paternity have been equally at stake from 1532 onward.[5] Indeed, Pantagruel's marriage is the more pressing issue, for he bears the responsibility of perpetuating his lineage, of assuring that the genealogy of the giants will not end with him. To fulfill this responsibility, Pantagruel must step away from the sidelines and follow Panurge's example. He must engage in the quest for a wife–something he is deeply disinclined to do. So detached has Pantagruel become from the physical and passionate side of life[6] that a supernatural intervention is required to engage him again. Gargantua must be resurrected from the dead to command his austere son to marry:[7]

> (F)ils trescher . . . . je vouldrois que pareillement vous vint en vouloir et desire vous marier. Me semble que dorenavant venez en aage à ce competent. Panurge s'est assez efforcé rompre les difficultez, qui luy pouvoient estre en empeschement. *Parlez pour vous.* (TL 496-7 my italics)

Always the dutiful son, Pantagruel accedes to his father's will and, at the end of the *Tiers Livre*, important promises and prognostications are made. Gargantua plans for a wedding to be celebrated upon his son's return from the voyage,[8] and in the episode of the "Pantagruélion," the gods look even farther into the future and

---

[5] In chapter 34, the last chapter of the *Pantagruel*, a sea voyage and two marriages are promised: that of Panurge "coqu dés le premier moys de ses nopces," and of Pantagruel, "(qui) espousa la fille du roy de Inde" (P 336).

[6] Consider this statement of Pantagruel's detachment: "Car tous les biens que le Ciel couvre: et que la Terre contient en toutes ses dimensions: haulteur, profondité, longitude, et latitude, ne sont dignes d'esmouvoir nos affections, et troubler nos sens et espritz" (TL 357).

[7] Of Gargantua's return from the dead and his injunction to his son to marry, Carla Freccero remarks: "Once again, as in chapter 15 of *Pantagruel*, it is as if the issue of the hero's marriage cannot be avoided, though there is an effort to displace it. And it seems important, in the case of both marriage and the quest, that the hero's father be there to sanction and to determine the actions of his son." *Father Figures: Genealogy and Narrative Structure in Rabelais* (Ithaca: Cornell UP, 1991) 163.

Pantagruel's resistance to marriage, she feels, is caused partially by the issues raised by the debates of the *Tiers Livre*, anxieties about cuckoldry and castration, but primarily by his desire to "avoid the oedipal problem of succession to the king" (165).

[8] "Pendant vostre absence, je feray les appretz et d'une femme vostre, et d'un festin, que je veulx à vos nopces faire celebre, si oncques en feut" (TL 500).

foresee that this marriage will indeed come to pass and that children will be born of it: "Il sera de brief marié, de sa femme aura enfans" (TL 509).

These same prognostications are reiterated at the outset of *Le Quart Livre*. All of the calendrical indications at the beginning of the book situate the voyage under the sign of the quest for the Mother. In the first sentence of chapter one, we are told that the voyage begins "On moys de Juin, au jour des festes Vestales. . ." (537), and the June date is reiterated in the letters on "l'isle Medamothi" (545, 547). As Ovid recounts in the *Fasti*, June is the month of Juno,[9] the mother goddess, and the day of the departure celebrates the feast of the virgin Vesta, goddess of the hearth and keeper of the flame. We are also told that the voyage will last for four months (540), from June to September; that is, that it will move toward the end of the year, the time of marriage and birth foreseen in the *Tiers Livre*. And the goal and desired outcome of the quest is the word of a female oracle, "le mot de la dive Bouteille Bacbuc." This name, conferred on the oracle in 1552, echos the name of the first mother, Badebec, Pantagruel's mother, who died the day he was born thirty years earlier.

But the voyage does not follow this seasonal itinerary; it does not move forward from June toward the end of the year. There is rather a retrograde movement back to spring, the paternal season. Pantagruel's tears for the death of Pan-Christ on "l'isle des Macraeons" mark the calendar clearly–this is Ash Wednesday, we are at the beginning of Lent. On "l'isle Tapinois" which follows, we are thrown back one day earlier, to Shrove Tuesday, Mardi Gras. Many critics: Marcel Tetel, Samuel Kinser, Claude Gaignebet, and, of course, Mikhail Bakhtin,[10] have argued that carnival imagery

---

[9] In the first verses of Book Six, the goddess says to the poet: "(J)une, I tell thee, derives its name from mine." Ovid, *The Fasti, Tristia, Pontic Epistles, Ibis, and Halieuticon*, trans. Henry T. Riley (London: G. Bell, 1915) 211-12. Ovid discusses the nature of Vesta in verses 249-318 (222-25). The Vestalia was celebrated on June 9 and not on June 7 as Rabelais suggests in "La Briefve Declaration" (251).

[10] Marcel Tetel, "Carnival and Beyond," *L'Esprit Créateur* 21.1 (1981): 88-104; Samuel Kinser, *Rabelais's Carnival: Text, Context, Metatext* (Berkeley: U of California P, 1990); Claude Gaignebet, *A plus hault sens: l'ésotérisme spirituel et charnel de Rabelais*, 2 vols. (Paris: Maisonneuve et Larose, 1986); Claude Gaignebet and Marie-Claude Florentin, *Le Carnaval: essais de mythologie populaire* (Paris: Payot, 1974); Mikhail Bakhtin, *Rabelais and His World*, trans. Hélène Iswolsky (Cambridge: MIT, 1965).

dominates *Le Quart Livre*, but only Gaignebet notes, and only briefly, that these images are out of season: "Carême en juin!," he exclaims (*Hault sens* xxii). But this unseasonality changes everything! It casts a new light on "the Old Plot of Carnival" (Kinser 56), brings to the foreground an antagonism that always lurked in the festivities: a war on women, a war on the maternal principle. The struggle between Carnival and Lent was characteristically depicted as a battle between a man and a woman,[11] but another recurrent Carnival performance holds our attention above all: the spectacle of male pregnancy and parturition such as Goethe witnessed it in Rome on his *Italian Journey*:

> A group of men . . . stroll back and forth with youths who have disguised themselves as women. One of the latter looks highly pregnant . . . . Suddenly the men fall out . . . , the quarrel intensifies, finally the combatants draw large knives of silvered cardboard, and attack each other. The women scream horribly . . . . Meanwhile, the highly pregnant woman becomes ill with fright; a chair is brought up, the other women assist her, she acts miserable, and in the twinkling of an eye, to the great amusement of the spectators, she gives birth to some grotesque shape or other.[12]

As Gaignebet argues–and Roberto Zapperi in *L'Homme Enceint* would agree[13]–such performances stem from a deep male envy of the one biological experience that men cannot have: "Par et à travers de tels fantasmes, les hommes vont pouvoir s'approprier symboliquement le grand privilège des femmes, celui d'avoir des enfants" (*Carnaval* 150).

---

[11] See Kinser 46-60 and Barbara Bowen, "Lenten Eels and Carnival Sausages," *L'Esprit Créateur* 21.1 (1981): 12-16.

[12] Johann Wolfgang von Goethe, *Italian Journey*, ed. Thomas P. Saine and Jeffrey L. Sammons, trans. Robert R. Heitner (New York: Suhrkamp, 1989) 405.

[13] *L'Homme Enceint: l'homme, la femme et le pouvoir*, trans. Marie-Ange Maire Vigueur (Paris: PUF, 1983). Zapperi discusses images of male pregnancy as they appear in cathedral sculptures and paintings of sacred subjects, and is particularly interested in the image of Adam pregnant with Eve. As his subtitle indicates, Zapperi sees power and dominance as the motives for this male usurpation of maternity: "Toute société fondée sur les valeurs masculines ressent le besoin de renverser les données biologiques de la génération . . . pour revendiquer la primauté naturelle de la paternité" (29). Thus in Christianity, the creation of the world is accomplished by God the Father without the aid of the Mother, and thus She is systematically deprived of the divinity accorded to Her by other religions. Mary appears as a simple woman, excluded from the Divine Trinity. Her natural place has been usurped by that ambiguous but distinctly male entity called the Holy Ghost (80-81).

This same carnivalesque fantasy of male maternity is enacted throughout *Le Quart Livre,* and it explains the seasonal confusion underlying the book. Rabelais could not overcome the compulsive misogyny of his imagination, he could not to allow the quest for the mother to move forward from June toward its fulfillment at the end of the year as he intended to do. Instead, the voyage reverts back to the spring season, to the time of the year when paternity was free to take on the characteristics of maternity. Easter strives to *replace* Advent in this book, Renaissance attempts to *become* naissance. This fantasy cannot, of course, truly come to pass and, if images of male pregnancy in *Le Quart Livre* generate laughter, they also generate repugnance and despair.

1. Eating Wind: "l'Isle Ennasin," "l'Isle de Ruach" and Bringuenarilles

At the outset, there is this fascinating question: How did men get pregnant in the carnivalesque imagination? Sometimes anally, but most often gastrically. Men got pregnant by "eating wind," or to be more precise, by eating windy foods, foods which provoked flatulence and the pregnant-seeming distention of the belly (Gaignebet, *Carnaval* 51-54). Among windy foods, the broad bean called "la fève" was preeminent for, according to Pythagorian doctrine, "la fève" could develop into an embryo in forty days (*Carnaval* 53, 149). So sacred was the fava bean that its eating was restricted to members of special male *confréries*, one of whom ate "la fève" at Epiphany and was given the title of "King." It was he who, forty days later went into labor and gave anal birth to the child of Carnival (*Carnaval* 148-50). And, if we judge from a very similar scene of parturition recounted by Rabelais in chapter twenty-seven of the *Pantagruel*, a large dose of distaste mitigated the gaity of such spectacles. Like the race of pygmies engendered by Pantagruel's farts and poops, babies born to men are "nains et contrefaitcz" (P 310)–monstrous forms of *abios bios*, the negative principle that Rabelais condemns so strongly in the 1552 prologue (525). For these creatures are made of intestinal wind and excrement. Male maternity is a bathroom activity.

However, men do have a more elevated form of birthing available to them. They can also be inspired by the divine breath and then give birth to words. Story telling and story writing have traditionally been compared to pregnancy and birth, and the image of the book as child has a long and distinguished history going back to Plato.[14] But, as Bakhtin has stressed, Rabelais always moves toward degradation and materialization of the high and spiritual,[15] and thus, like all male pregnancy, literary creation is a gastric activity in his books. It begins by eating wind–eating *words*–or giving words to eat. Rabelais often situates the poet in the kitchen. He situates *himself* there on "l'isle Farouche," as Rabiolas, one of the warrior-cooks doing battle with the sausages (633) and Antagoras and Homer are pictured in the kitchen tent in chapter eleven, cooking up a "fricassée de congres" (563-4). This windy banquet leads to the inevitable excremental birth and to the image of the poet in the bathroom, where François Villon is found in chapter sixty-seven, the last chapter of the book.[16]

The digestive odyssey of male pregnancy is repeatedly played out in *Le Quart Livre* where images of eating wind, flatulence, and the anal birth of books and other monstrous babies are everywhere present. There are, first, the Ennasins (ch. 9) who, in an *ajout* of 1552, are specifically tied to the windy carnival bean which makes men pregnant–their race is said to spring from the family Fabian, a name derived from *faba*, "la fève" (Gaignebet, *Carnaval* 21-22). This family, "trois cens six hommes de guerre tous parens" (557), was killed and their bodily parts scattered. The Fabians are resurrected on "l'isle Ennasin," but their "members" are put together wrongly, an arm where an ear should be, a tongue for a nose, for they are put together by words only. The Ennasins are puffs of wind "belonging to the nose" (Cotgrave), but they also belong to the anus. Like the

---

[14] For a discussion of the book as child, see Ernst Robert Curtius, *European Literature and the Latin Middle Ages* (London: Routledge and Kegan Paul, 1953) 132-34.

[15] This idea runs throughout *Rabelais and His World*, but see especially his chapter on "Images of the Material Bodily Lower Stratum" 368-436.

[16] The narrator tells the anecdote of Villon attending Edward the Fifth of England who taunts the poet with the disrespect he shows the kings of France by having their coat of arms near his "scelle persée." Villon replies that this placement rather shows the wisdom of Edward's doctors, for the painting will surely cure the king's constipation: "seulement voyant (les armes de France) vous avez telle vezarde, et paour si horrificque, que soubdain vous fiantez comme dixhuyct Bonases de Paeonie" (699), animals whose excremental feats are described in the "Briefve Declaration" (712).

pygmies engendered by Pantagruel, they are born in the male way; "(C)e Ped et ceste Vesse . . . sortirent invisiblement tous deux ensemble d'un trou en un instant" (559).

There are also the "mangeurs de vent" who inhabit "l'isle de Ruach" (chs. 43-44), the island of wind and of spirit (BD 709). On the one hand, this is a gay place, a place of "Volupté . . . facile et non penible," as Pantagruel calls it, "Car vostre vivre qui est de vent, ne vous couste rien ou bien peu, il ne fault que souffler" (640). Gardens of wind are cultivated, wind is eaten and drunk like wine and thus the elements of a banquet are always at the ready.[17] The wind of inspiration also blows on "l'isle de Ruach." Panurge is moved to compose a poem on this island, and there are many references to poets and to poetic creation, above all to Homer's *Odyssey* and to "le bon ronfleur Æolus" (639), "Dieu des vents, selon les Poëtes" (BD 710).

But Panurge's dizain is about farting[18] and the gayety of the banquet on "l'isle de Ruach" is darkened by the fact that "eating wind" is also an image of eating nothing, of fasting and starvation. The "mangeurs de vent" live in constant menace of death, and death and poetic creation are linked on "l'isle de Ruach." Both are degraded as bathroom activities. When the "mangeurs de vent" die, they give anal birth to their souls—and to poetry: "Il meurent tous Hydropicques tympanites. Et meurent les hommes en pedent, les femmes en vesnent. Ainsi leur sort l'ame par le cul . . . . c'est ce que les Sanctimoniales appellent sonnet" (639).

Above all, there is Bringuenarilles, a creature so important to *Le Quart Livre* that his story is told twice, on Thohu Bohu (ch. 17) and again on "l'isle de Ruach" (ch. 44). Bringuenarilles is the great enemy of the "mangeurs de vent," for while he will eat almost anything—hens and roosters and foxes and dogs which bark and sing and crow inside his belly (640-41)—he prefers windy foods: whistles and, especially, windmills which he swallows "comme pillules" (641)

---

[17] "Quand ilz font quelque festin ou banquet . . . disputent de la bonté, excellence, salubrité, rarité des vens, comme vous Beuveurs par les banquetz philosophez en matiere de vins" (638).

[18] Panurge offers this summary of his poem: "(J)enin de Quinquenays pissant sus le fessier de sa femme Quelot abatit le vent punays qui en sortoit comme d'une magistrale Æolipyle" (640). In the "Briefve Declaration," Rabelais explains the Greek word thus: "Porte d'Æolus . . . . Ainsi sont engendrez les vents en l'air, et les ventositez es corps humains . . ." (710).

Bringuenarilles is very close to the archetypal myth of the male made pregnant by what he eats–Jonah swallowed by the whale–and in the book from which Rabelais borrowed Bringuenarilles, *Le Voyage et Navigation que fist Panurge, Disciple de Pantagruel*,[19] the link with the Jonah story is quite clear. Encountered at sea in the *Disciple*, Bringuenarilles is something of a cross between a giant and a sailing vessel and a whale who swallows everything in his path, including whole boatloads of men.[20] The intertextuality becomes even more complex when we remember that this anonymous author originally borrowed Bringuenarilles from Rabelais. As we have argued (Introduction 18-20), the giant as he appears in the *Disciple* was clearly inspired by Pantagruel at the end of the 1532 book; *l'avale-tout* who in chapter thirty-two first swallowed a Jonah called Alcofribas into his mouth and then in chapter thirty-three swallowed him again, this time into his belly, and he swallowed him, if not in a bean, then inside a copper apple: "ainsi l'avalla Pantagruel comme une petite pillule" (P 335). Bringuenarilles, like Pantagruel, often suffered from olympian cases of indigestion; his belly, too, frequently needed to be "ramonné" by physicians; and he too was made pregnant by what he ate: eggs which hatched inside him, and above all, a windmill containing a miller who continued to grind wheat inside his belly. And both abdominal odysseys culminate in strange and windy births. Alcofribas and his *confrères* emerge from Pantagruel's mouth as he belches them back into the world and, in the *Disciple*, the miller lights a fire in Bringuenarilles' belly and is reborn in a sneeze from his nose.[21]

However, unlike Pantagruel, Bringuenarilles dies of his adventure and his death has great and terrible implications for Rabelais's giant. As V.-L. Saulnier persuasively argued,[22] the death of Bringuenarilles as it is recounted on Thohu Bohu foreshadows the death of

---

[19] Ed. Guy Demerson and Christiane Lauvergnat-Gagnière (Paris: Nizet, 1982). See our discussion 14-5, 18-9.

[20] "Il y eut quelque foys ung navire de portugaloys qui deslachèrent leur grosse artillerie contre luy . . . . (P)ar despit il print leur navire à belle dens & l'avala tout entier sans mascher avec tout ce qui estoit dedans, dont il se trouva fort mal car audict navire y avoit bien cinq cens marmotz & autant de cinges qui luy saultoient dedans le ventre incessamment. . ." (*Le Disciple* 17-8).

[21] The story of the "ramonneur" is found in the *Disciple* 12-13; of the eggs which hatched chicks, 16-17; and of the miller and his rebirth, 19-21.

[22] *Rabelais II: Rabelais dans son enquête. Etude sur le Quart et le Cinquième Livre* (Paris: SEDES, 1982) 70-71.

Pan on "l'isle des Macraeons." I would add that both deaths foreshadow the death of Pantagruel; he is linked to Bringuenarilles by his origins and to Pan by his name. An even more fearful augury is the fact that there is no miller in Rabelais's version of Bringuenarilles, no Jonah figure, no image of rebirth, and this omission turns back upon Alcofribas himself, the Jonah reborn from Pantagruel in 1532. The specter of the writer's death as well as that of his creation haunts these episodes. On Thohu-Bohu he is evoked as a chronicler of strange deaths named "Bacabery l'aisné" (581). During the tempest, he is present as a writer of testaments called "monsieur l'abstracteur" (588). On "l'isle Farouche," "Rabiolas" is one of the soldier cooks inside the Trojan Sow (633), and on "l'isle des Macraeons," he appears as a physician, but here the real name is revealed: Rabelays (602). Have *pneuma* and *ruach*, the wind of *his* spirit and of *his* inspiration, been irrevocably swallowed? Can the wind be raised again? Or will the writer and all his world die with a fart and a belch as the wind-eaters and Bringuenarilles die? It is not until the end of the book that these fearful questions are answered.

2. QUARESMEPRENANT, ANTIPHYSIE, AND "LES ANDOUILLES"

The whale is always a windy beast, but what is its gender? It appears off "l'isle Farouche" in a resolutely masculine form, as "*le physetere*" (chs. 33-34), "the blower." However, in chapter eight, when Panurge is preaching a sermon to the drowning Dindenault, he holds out the hope of Jonah's fate to him, and in so doing, calls the whale by its feminine name: "la baleine,"[23] *ballæna,* from the Greek root designating "puffed up" and "swollen." As Bakhtin and Gaston Bachelard have explored,[24] the belly is the bodily zone where the most radical and unsettling contradictions of corporeal life meet—refuge and womb, serpent and tomb, repository of new life and engenderer of death—how can female and male elements be separated in this confusion? It is precisely this confusion of gender

---

[23] ". . .optant (aux moutonniers) . . . bonne adventure, et rencontre de quelque Baleine, laquelle au tiers jour subsequent les rendist sains et saulves en quelque pays de satin, à l'exemple de Jonas" (555).

[24] Gaston Bachelard, *La Terre et les rêveries du repos* (Paris: Corti, 1948). The whole of the chapter on Jonah (128-82) is relevant, but see especially 146-50. In Bakhtin, see especially "The Material Bodily Lower Stratum" 368-436.

which plagues the episodes of Quaresmeprenant (chs. 29-32) and the Andouilles (chs. 35-42).

At first, the battle lines between them seem clearly drawn. Quaresmeprenant, who inhabits "l'isle Tapinois," is Lenten, Catholic and very much a man: "(U)n grand avalleur de poys gris . . . confalonnier des Ichthyophages . . . calcineur de cendres: père et nourrison des medicins: foisonnant en pardons, indulgences et stations: home de bien: bon catholic, et de grande devotion" (606). His mortal enemies, the Andouilles of "l'isle Farouche," are to the contrary, fat, female and carnivalesque: "femelles en sexe, mortelles en condition: aulcunes pucelles et aultres non" (607), and are under the protection of their good neighbor, "le noble Mardigras" (607).

However, as Kinser has so persuasively argued (83-84), the terms of this battle are not as clear-cut as they would seem, for Quaresmeprenant, this seemingly Lenten creature, bears one of the names of Carnival. Quaresme-*prenant* too designates Shrove Tuesday, the day that "takes hold of" (*prehendere*) Lent. Nor is he totally masculine for, as Leo Spitzer suggested long ago, -*prenant* may also be derived from the Latin *praegnans*, "to be full of something imminent."[25] Carnival pregnant with Lent—in this image of male maternity, Kinser finds the key to the ambivalence of Quaresmeprenant and the day for which he stands: a day filled with both joy and dread, pregnant with the last great feast of the season but which also says farewell to meat,[26] is also pregnant with the fasting to come, the season of sorrow and of death.

Indeed, Quaresmeprenant is pregnant in just the same way as the other male mothers we have discussed. Like the "mangeurs de vent," he is associated with the Lenten banquet: "Rien ne mangeoit jeusnant: jeusnoit rien ne mangeant. Grignotoit par soubson: beuvoit par imagination" (614). Like Bringuenarilles, he is associated with the illness that results from this windy diet and with bad medicine. Quaresmeprenant breeds doctors and is bred by them: he is "père et nourrison des medicins" (606). He is also child and father of words. Quaresmeprenant *writes*: "Escrivoit sus parchemin

---

[25] In "Zu *carnaval* im Französischen," *Wörter und Sachen* 5 (1914): 19, n. 2. Quoted by Kinser 84.

[26] On the etymology of the word "carnival," Gaignebet suggests: "Dès le IXè siècle, les auteurs ecclésiastiques croient y reconnaître . . . *carnestollendas* («tollere»), *carnevale* («carne levare»), l'adieu à la chair, adieu logiquement marqué par les abus carnés qui précèdent le carême" (*Carnaval* 147).

velu avecques son gros gallimart Prognostications et Almanachz" (614), and he *is written*. Like Bringuenarilles, he is never seen, he is only recounted; his substance is purely verbal.

Of all, however, Quaresmeprenant most resembles the Ennasins. He too is created by a series of "alliances," a long chain of metaphors which are really "mésalliances," "(des) *comme(s)* mal à propous et incongru(s)," to use Frère Jean's expression (641). Both episodes illustrate the principle of *prosthesis* whereby the body is first anatomized, cut apart, and then put back together again, piece by artificial piece.[27] But the body is put together wrongly, for it is reassembled by words and by wind. There is only emptiness and erasure at the heart of this monster. No sense of a whole creature is possible nor is there any generic term to describe what Quaresmeprenant is, and Pantagruel points to the linguistic failure he embodies, the failure of the name: "Voylà . . . une estrange et monstreuse membreure d'home: *si home le doibs nommer*" (614, my italics). He can only be called *abios bios* (525), "Vie non vie" (BD 704), or he can be called Amodunt and Discordance, for Quaresmeprenant, too, is an offspring of Antiphysie.

It is no mistake that the presentation of Quaresmeprenant, pregnant with sterility and with his own monstrousness, ends on a discussion of maternity, the myth of Physie and Antiphysie (614-15). When the maternal principle is represented positively in *Le Quart Livre*, it is as Physis is represented in this myth: as a Virgin Mother like Vesta,[28] an absence like Bacbuc, and as a silence, for Physis does not speak and is spoken about only very briefly. Language is rather the domain of Antiphysie who is not an entirely feminine entity. Her children, Amodunt and Discordance, are engendered by copulation with Tel-

---

[27] Michel Jeanneret, additionally, stresses the dehumanizing effect of comparing the parts of Quaresmeprenant to objects: "L'unité de la personne se désagrège en une poussière de parties disjointes. Mais l'effect de déshumanisation, dans le portrait du monstre, tient encore à une autre aberration. Chacun des membres de l'anatomie est comparé à un object–un ustensile, un appareil. Le mariage troublant de l'animé et de l'inerte, l'invasion saugrenue du règne des choses vivantes par des matières dures et hostiles, tout cela évoque le spectre de la machine qui prend le contrôle de l'homme." "Rabelais, les monstres et l'interprétation des signes" (*Quart Livre* 18-42)," *Writing the Renaissance. Essays on Sixteenth-Century French Literature in Honor of Floyd Gray*, ed. Raymond C. La Charité (Lexington, KY: French Forum, 1992) 71-2.

[28] "Physis (c'est nature) en sa première portée enfanta Beauté et Harmonie sans copulation charnelle: comme de soy mesmes est grandement feconde et fertile" (614).

lumon, a goddess whom Rabelais makes masculine.[29] A *male* god of the primordially *female* earth? Then who infecondates whom? Who is the mother and who is the father in this myth? There is a conflation of the maternal and the paternal principles here, a disturbing bisexuality which is carried over into Antiphysie's offspring. With their round heads, round feet and strange method of locomotion, "faisans la roue, cul sus teste, les pieds contrement" (615), they clearly recall the Androgyna in Plato's *Symposium*. But the paternal elements are dominant in the sexual mix, for Antiphysie gives birth in the male way. Her children enter the world as the Ennasins and the wind-eaters are born: as puffs of wind, as lying words–bad gas:

> Depuys elle engendra les Matagotz, Cagotz, et Papelars: les Maniacles Pistoletz: les Demoniacles Calvins imposteurs de Geneva: les enraigez Putherbes, Briffaulx, Caphars, Chattemittes, Canibales: et aultres monstres difformes et contrefaicts en despit de Nature. (615)

Yet the female belly does seem to make its appearance in *Le Quart Livre* on "l'isle Farouche" (chs. 35-42). Here is a fertile island which stands opposed to Quaresmeprenant's barren place. Here the other name of Carnival, Mardi Gras, is sounded. This is the kingdom of *Ste. Cochonne*–flying pig and Trojan sow–and of the sausages that are born from her belly. Indeed, the main images of this episode recall the mothers of Rabelais' giants: Badebec and her cornucopian belly (P, ch. 2); Gargamelle, pregnant with the tripe she has eaten and with the child Gargantua (G, ch. 6), and it is above all "La grande Truye" (chs. 40-41) who recalls them. This creature too combines banquet and birthing principles; she is pregnant with little men who are *cooks* (including one called Rabiolas) and who are "born" from her belly brandishing their kitchen utensils and shouting an invitation to the banquet table, the name of the general-cook *Nabuzardan!* (635). Like Gargamelle, the Trojan sow is a principle of "succulent nourishment" and of fecundity, "womb-rich and man-sheltering" (Kinser 103).

However, as Xenomanes warns: "Andouilles sont andouilles, tous jours doubles et traistresses" (622). Like Quaresmeprenant

---

[29] As Huchon notes, Tellumon was "(l)a déese romaine qui présidait aux forces génératrices de la terre; Rabelais la considère par erreur comme une divinité masculine" (1545).

and Antiphysie, they contain elements of their opposite and enemy. "L'isle Farouche" is not the place of feasting it seems to be. A banquet begun by the voyagers when they arrive on the island is disrupted by the attacking Andouilles (621),[30] and no sausages are subsequently consumed. Feasting is only talked about. We eat wind on this island, we eat *words* as we did on "l'isle Tapinois," as do the "mangeurs de vent" on "l'isle de Ruach"–on "l'isle Farouche," too, the whole issue of language, the relation of the name to the thing, is intensely problematized.[31] Moreover, there is a fishy side to the supposedly carnivalesque Andouilles who, as Bowen has argued ("Lenten Eels" 17-22), were traditionally conflated with eels, "anguilles," a Lenten food. And whether sausage or eel, both had the connotation that "a nasty modern mind would expect" (Bowen 19). As anyone can plainly see, the Andouilles have a most masculine contour and their Priapic associations are insistently developed throughout the episode: by glosing, in the "Briefve Declaration," the name of their queen, Niphleseth, as "Membre viril" (709), and by the whole long development of chapter thirty-eight, "Comment Andouilles ne sont à mespriser entre les humains":

> Le serpens qui tenta Eve, estoit andouillicque .... Encores maintient on en certaines Academies que ce tentateur estoit l'andouille nommée Ithyphalle, en laquelle feut jadis transformé le bon messer Priapus grand tentateur des femmes par les paradis en Grec, ce sont Jardins en François. (628)

As on "l'isle Tapinois," we have on "l'isle Farouche" again strayed into a field where the opposing sides are blurred: Carnival and Lent, male and female, paternity and maternity, penis and womb. Yet as always, the blurring and bisexuality are slanted toward the male principle. Indeed, Priapus, "Great Father Snake" as Joseph Campbell calls him,[32] undergoes a most astonishing experi-

---

[30] Terence Cave calls *Le Quart Livre* "the book of the deferred or the interrupted feast." *The Cornucopian Text: Problems of Writing in the French Renaissance* (London: Oxford UP, 1979) 222.

[31] The whole of chapter 37 is devoted to the issue of language: "Comment Pantagruel manda querir les capitaines Riflandouille et Tailleboudin: avecques un notable discours sur les noms propres des lieux et des persones." See Françoise Charpentier's discussion of the language problem in this episode: "La Guerre des Andouilles: *Pantagruel* IV, 35-42," *Etudes seiziémistes offertes à V.-L. Saulnier par plusieurs de ses anciens doctorants* (Geneva: Droz, 1980) 121-26.

[32] *The Hero with a Thousand Faces* (Princeton: Princeton UP, 1949) 155.

ence in this episode. As a gesture of peace, the queenly "membre viril" sends several bushels of Andouilles back to Gargantua, "soubs la conduicte de la jeune Niphleseth Infante de l'isle." Most do not survive the transit, "par faulte de moustarde," but one among them "Nipleseth la jeune," not only survives, s/he survives to marry and bear children: "Depuys feut mariée en bon et riche lieu, et feist plusieurs beaulx enfans, dont loué soit Dieu" (637). We are thus confronted, on "l'isle Farouche," with the image of a pregnant penus, a penus become mother!

We must not forget, however, that this is an edible pregnancy. If Great Father Snake has gained maternity on "l'isle Farouche," he has lost his sexual identity in the process. Priapus, "gardian des jardins en terre" (530), whom we saw lifting his red head and speaking with assurance in the Prologue (527), that proud fellow has been reduced to a sausage, *a god who can be eaten*, and we remember that, near "l'isle Chaneph," the voyagers discuss eating the serpent.[33] And the garden overseen by Messer Priapus is no longer a garden of sexual delight. It is a locus of digestion only, a gastric paradise, the domain of his brother and alter-ego, Messer Gaster (chs. 57-62), *the god who eats*. Sexuality is done away with on Gaster's island, Eve is banished from his garden, and she is defeated in a way that we have seen before. As on "l'isle Tapinois," a myth of maternity is evoked, the story of Penie (672) who is very like Physie. Penie, too, is a holy mother of illustrious maternities. The wife of Porus, the lord of Abundance, according to Plato in the *Symposium* (203 B), she gave birth to the God of Love, and Rabelais amplifies her glory. He also designates Penie as "mère des neuf Muses" (672).[34] But Gaster usurps all her maternities.[35] On his island, the principle of stomachic necessity replaces love as the *pri-*

---

[33] The issue of eating the serpent is the "problem" posed to Pantagruel by Eusthènes (689). It is solved by the voyagers' good banquet, and the serpents who "escaped his saliva," as Eusthènes puts it, are praised in a long catalogue (691-2).

[34] "Avec (Gaster) pacifiquement residoit la bonne dame Penie, aultrement dict Souffreté, mere des neuf Muses: de laquelle jadis en compagnie de Porus seigneur d'Abondance, nous nasquit Amour le noble enfant mediateur du Ciel et de la Terre, comme atteste Platon *in Symposio*" (672).

[35] Cave also speaks of a drama of usurpation when he discusses this myth, but feels that Gaster usurps Porus, not Penie as I am arguing here. See *Cornucopian Text*, 214, 219 and also "Reading Rabelais: Variations on the Rock of Virtue," *Literary Theory/Renaissance Texts*, ed. Patricia Parker and David Quint (Baltimore: Johns Hopkins UP, 1986) 80.

mum mobile, and in place of a mother, the muses are given a father. Gaster is "le premier maistre es ars du monde" (671): "Les Corbeaulx, les Gays, les Papeguays, les Estourneaulx, il rend poëtes. Les Pies il faict poëtrides: et leurs aprent languaige humain proferer, parler, chanter. Et tout pour la trippe" (673).

However, it is a dark victory for both Messer Gaster and Messer Priapus because, as Françoise Charpentier put it so delicately, "la nourriture finit mal" ("Andouilles" 132).[36] The god who can be eaten is consumed by the god who eats. "Andouilles. . . Sauscisses. . . Boudins . . . Cervelatz . . . Saulcissons . . . Cochons . . . Purées de poys . . . Saulgrenées de febves . . . Anguilletes sallés . . . Balaines . . . Congres . . . Anguilles . . . Serpens . . ." (677-81)–all of the foods that have been talked and written in *Le Quart Livre* are stuffed into the gaping maw of Manduce (676) and into the belly of Gaster–puffs of wind that make him pregnant. And he responds by the typical gesture of male maternity: he sits on his "scelle persée" and gives birth to a mound of fecal matter (681-82). "(U)n monde qui mange sans générer s'arrêtera bien un jour" (Charpentier, "Andouilles" 133). Gaster without Penie, father without mother, digestion without sexuality, can only give birth to death.

3. LES PAPEFIGUES

Of all the episodes of *Le Quart Livre*, the one most explicitly concerned with birth and rebirth occurs on "l'isle des Papefigues" (chs. 45-47). This island stands as the infertile garden in juxtaposition to the corrupt city of the Papimanes, and the garden was made barren by religious enmity. The episode begins with the sad tale of how the Papefigues acquired their name and their fate. In a prosperous past, they were called "Guaillardetz" (642) but seeing the papal portrait carried through the streets of Papimania, one Guaillard "luy feist la figue. Qui est en icelluy pays signe de contempnement et derision manifeste" (642). The Papimanes immediately attacked in retaliation, subjected the Guaillardetz to cruel and igno-

---

[36] Michel Jeanneret makes a similar juxtaposition of the sexual and the digestive principles in the Andouilles episode: "Phalliques et fécales, elles n'en demeurent pas moins des saucisses, conjuguant ainsi les jouissances de la bouche, celle du sexe et celles de l'excrétion. En elles se cristallisent deux solidarités d'ordinaire inavouées: la parenté secrète des activités orales et anales" ("Les Monstres" 72).

minious punishment,[37] and changed their name. Since that time, "avoit en l'isle regné une pestilence tant horrible que pour la moitié et plus, le pays estoit resté desert, et les terres sans possesseurs" (643)

The Papefigues' island is barren sexually as well as agriculturally; like "l'isle des Macraeons," this is a land of the old. The episode centers on the story of an aging "Laboureur" and his wife, "une Vieille de Papefiguiere," who try to cultivate the garden in the figurative as well as in the literal sense. On both levels, their old age is played off against the youth of a devil "bien jeune au mestier" (645) who comes to claim his share of the revenues from their farm, and the confrontation between youth and old age leads to contradictory outcomes. The Laborer faces the devil first and, with the wisdom of age, is able to outwit him. Unlike the youth, the old man understands the cycle of planting: "Le grain que voyez en terre, est mort et corrumpu, la corruption d'icelluy a esté generation de l'aultre. . ." (645). He therefore plants wheat when the Diableteau demands the half of the harvest that lies below ground, and beets when the Devil's share is to be what grows above. However, if the "Laboureur" wins the battle, he loses the war. Impotent to renew the garden in the sexual sense, he is the "old seed" that by his own account must give way to the new, and the young devil now asserts his superior power. Angered by the deception, he proposes a scratching contest to see who will control the field. The Laborer knows he is defeated: "je me rendray au premier coup et lui quitteray (céderai) le champ" (647), and now the old woman comes to the forefront of the action. She sends her husband to hide in the church's "benoistier" where we find him when the story begins (643).[38] She will conduct the scratching contest with the young devil.

---

[37] The mature men, "portant barbe" (171) were killed. The women and young men were submitted to the punishment of Federic Barbarousse of Milan; i.e., pulling a fig from the hind quarters of a mule without their hands (642-3).

[38] This episode shows a narrative complexity comparable to that of the three-tiered story of the Chiquanous (see Chapter Three, 82-91). After the introductory description of how the Papefigues got their name, the voyagers enter a chapel near the port "(pour prendre) de l'eaue beniste" (643). There they see the old man in the baptismal font. Pantagruel asks for an explanation of this strange sight, and an unspecified narrator tells the tale of the old man's encounter with the young devil. This brings the episode into the narrative present, and we realize that the scratching contest between the old woman and the young devil had been occurring while we were hearing the Laborer's story: "Sus l'instant qu'on nous racontoit cette histoire, eusmez advertissement que la vieille avoit trompé le Diable, et guaigné le champ" (648).

With "la Vieille de Papefiguiere," we see Rabelais's characteristic degradation of women as old, ugly, and sexually repugnant. Like "la Sibylle de Panzoust" (TL chs. 16-18), she shows a superior wit and intelligence, but she does so by displaying her sex as a terrible wound made by her husband, a scenario similar to that of the fable of the lion, the fox, and the old woman recounted in the *Pantagruel* (269-71). This is "le trou de la Sybille," this is the gateway to Proserpine's underworld, and the sight of it frightens the young devil away. However, neither he nor the "Vieux Laboureur" could have renewed the garden that "La Vieille de Papefiguiere" represents for, like the fig evoked in the name of this island, she is an old and desiccated "fruit." As suggested in Chapter Four (130-31), her infertility stands in contrast to the young women, "poires de bon Christian," of "l'isle des Papimanes" (ch. 54) with their promise of future fecundity. The sexual garden of the Papefigues remains sterile and barren.

However, if female birthing fails in this episode, two scenes of masculine pregnancy are enacted. There is, first, the portrait of Lucifer's belly stuffed with the souls of "escholiers . . . advocatz . . . vinerons . . . chambrieres . . . Farfadetz . . . Caphards . . . marchans usuriers, apothecaires, faulsaires, billoneurs, adulterateurs de marchandises" and many more (646-7). He became pregnant in the male way, by eating too many of these souls which were prepared by his "Diables souillars de cuisine" (646). As in the case of Bringuenarilles, Lucifer now suffers from a "forte colicque" which may be linked to the pains of childbirth. He too is a "Laboureur" and the young devil's injunction to the old man also applies to him: "Travaille, villain, travaille" (647).

Above all, there is the vignette of the old man immersed in the "benoistier," "tout dedans l'eaue caché, comme un Canart au plonge, excepté un peu du nez pour respirer" (643) and he is there in place of the babe who should be born and baptized. This is a very archaic image of male birthing, one that suppresses the female principle altogether. Like the myth of the Phoenix, it is a dream of being born from the "egg" of one's own death, of giving birth to oneself. This fantasy, like so many others in *Le Quart Livre,* came to Rabelais from *Le Disciple* (64-68) where a very similar image of self-creation is presented. The narrator recounts a visit to an island where there are no women because there is no need to bear children. When the men are old, they are put into "ung grand tonneau plain de malvaisie doulce comme seucre, & là meurent bien doulcement" (64). Their bodies are subsequently dried and burned, and the ashes, mixed with egg, are put into molds "semblables que ont aultresfoys esté iceulx deffunctz avant leur mort" (65-66). To animate them, "leur souffle l'on au cul" (66) and they are reborn with a sneeze as the young men they used to be.

The old man in the baptismal font on "l'isle des Papefigues" recalls the "tonneau de Malvesie" from *Le Disciple*, which also makes its appearance in chapter thirty-three of *Le Quart Livre* (617).[39] With this image, the fantasies of birth and rebirth collapse into one another: to be simultaneously "pere et nourrison" (606) like Quaresmeprenant, to enter the barrel/*bénitier* as an old man and emerge as a child ready to start life anew. The quest for the wine of the "dive Bouteille" holds many values, but it also incorporates this dream of double rejuvenation.

4. THE CARNIVAL CHILD

Le Quart Livre does not, however, end on the somber note sounded on "l'isle des Papefigues" and on the other *escales* we have discussed. The wind swallowed into the belly of the whale, the male belly of Bringuenarilles and the Devil, does not die there. *Ruach* and *pneuma* are raised again, "le temps est haulsé" off "l'isle Chanelph" (chs. 53-55) and this wind blows through the end of the book. The main images of the last episodes of *Le Quart Livre* are images of resurrection: waking from an extraordinary sleep, a "good" banquet which renews and raises the spirits of the voyagers,[40] the evocation of the winged Bacchus, *Psila*, who is

---

[39] During the physeter episode, Panurge deplores that the whale throws salty water. If this were wine, he says he would not be afraid to drown and recalls the death of Edward IV of England's brother who "esleut mourir nayé dedans un tonneau de Malvesie" (617). This story is recounted by Commynes, *Mémoires*, I, vii. Cited by Huchon 1547.

[40] Paul J. Smith, *Voyage et écriture: étude sur Le Quart Livre de Rabelais* (Geneva: Droz, 1987) 193-206, reads the episode near "l'isle Chanelph" as a reenactment of the Eucharist, an interpretation with which I fully agree and have set forth in Chapter Three above. See also Edwin M. Duval, "La Messe, la Cène, et le Voyage sans fin du *Quart Livre*, *Rabelais en son demi-millénaire: actes du Colloque internation de Tour (24-29 septembre 1984), Etudes rabelaisiennes*, vol. 21 (Geneva: Droz, 1988) 130-40.

Dionysos and Dithyrambos, the twice-born God, "him of the double door."[41] But above all, the images of resurrection center on Panurge in chapter sixty-seven. He had, we remember, fled in terror to the hold of the ship, the lowest point of the voyage. When the guns of the convoy are sounded, he bursts out in a terrible state: he has lost one legging of his breeches and there is a cat hanging onto the other; he has lost control of his anal sphincter and "par male paour, (Panurge) se conchia" (697). But, despite its vulgarity, a sacrament is being enacted here.[42] This is a drama of purification and a parable of regeneration. Panurge is sent to put on a white shirt as a sign of his cleansing and above all, there is the laughter of Pantagruel. This is pascal laughter, *risus paschalis*[43] and it overcomes and banishes the Lenten tears that he shed on "l'isle des Macraeons." Pan is reborn at the end of *Le Quart Livre* in his manifestation as *Pan-ourgos*, the irrepressible life force. Spring is found. The quest for renaissance is achieved.

But the shadow of another and failed sacrament also lurks in this episode, the sacrament of Advent, and its failure darkens and undermines the triumph of Easter. Panurge is not only a Jonah being reborn, he is also a male mother giving anal birth–to excrement and to poetry like Villon, but above all, to that cat, Rodilardus, hanging onto his breeches. This is a carnivalesque spectacle. This is the monstrous baby born anally to the King in the streets midst the laughter of the spectators. And this is a demonic usurpation of Advent, for the cat is associated by Panurge himself to the devil:

---

[41] Campbell 142-43. Dionysus' double-gendered birth, from the womb of Semele and the thigh of Zeus, brings forth another variant of the myth of male pregnancy: the hermaphroditic man who completes gestation in a part of the body other than the belly. Lucian, in *The True History* recounts seeing a similar phenomenon on the moon where there are no women: "Up until the age of 25, each man is a wife, and thereafter a husband. They carry their children in the calf of the leg instead of in the belly. When conception takes place the calf begins to swell. In course of time they cut it open and deliver the child dead, and then they bring it to life by putting it in the wind with its mouth open." *Lucian*, trans. A.M. Harmon, vol. 1 (Cambridge: Harvard UP, 1913) 275. Lucian also describes the Arboreals who plant the right genital gland in the ground. It produces a tree with huge fruit. "When these ripen, they harvest them and shell out the men" (275-77).

[42] See our discussion in Chapter 3, esp. 79-80 and in *Rabelais: Homo Logos* (Chapel Hill: U of North Carolina P, 1979) 116-18, 120. Smith (193-213) reads the last chapter similarly, as a ritual of baptism.

[43] On Easter laughter, see Bakhtin 78-79.

> (J)e me donne au Diable, si je ne pensoys que feust un Diableteau à poil follet, lequel nagueres j'avois cappiettement happé en Tapinois à belles mouffles d'un bas de chausse, dedans la grande husche d'Enfer". (700)

To use Yeats' imagery, the ceremony of innocence is drowned at the end of *Le Quart Livre*, a rough beast is born in usurpation of Penie-Physie's Child, the Mother's Son who is the object of the world's need and desire. Because Rabelais could not conceptualize the mother positively, admit her as a generative force into his imagination, the future stands in jeopardy at the end of *Le Quart Livre*. No child is born and the genealogy of the giants comes to an end with this book.

Conclusion

THE CHARM OF CATASTROPHE

LIKE the poet in Dante's *Inferno*, Rabelais's characters descend into a broken world in *Le Quart Livre* and wander in search of all that is lost. In our study, we have explored the catastrophes enacted in this book, and the many values of the quest for "le mot de la dive Bouteille." It is the hero's voyage into the underworld in search of the secret that will make life bloom again and, at the same time, it is the physician's descent into the sick body in order to restore health and harmony to the self and to the world. This is Jonah's passage into the belly of the whale, that ambiguous zone of death and of rebirth, and the voyage has social and linguistic as well as sacramental implications. It also enacts Moses' pilgrimage out of Egypt, land of false faith and of the lie, in quest of the *logos* on which the new city can be founded, the word that will restore truth to words. In *Le Quart Livre,* the word sought is that of a woman, the wife and mother who will give birth to a child and thus fulfill the quest for paternity also enacted in this book.

Now we must return to the question posed at the beginning of our study: Does this polyvalent quest succeed? As we have seen, some of the answers are negative. The joyful return home promised at the outset of *Le Quart Livre* is not accomplished,[1] and from this nonfulfillment stem other disappointments. Like Moses, Pantagruel never sees the new Jerusalem he had hoped to establish. The healing of the sick city is not accomplished–as we know, the religious strife in France continued to worsen and soon degenerated into civ-

---

[1] In the departure, we are told that the voyage "tant de l'aller que *du retour*" will be conducted in high spirits and good health (538, my italics).

il war. Nor is the quest for birth achieved. Pantagruel never returns to celebrate the festival of marriage that Gargantua had planned for him at the end of *Le Tiers Livre* (601), and the gods' prognostication of his paternity (TL 613-4) is not fulfilled. The race of the giants ends with him.

These problems, however, all derive from the fact that Rabelais did not complete the voyage.[2] He died in 1553,[3] leaving his characters at sea, still *en route* to the oracle of the divine bottle. As we know, two books attributed to him appeared nine and eleven years after his death: *L'Isle Sonante* in 1562 and a *Cinquiesme Livre* in 1564,[4] but their authenticity has been in dispute almost since their publication. Mireille Huchon has proposed the most satisfactory solution to date of the problem, suggesting that these books are a compilation by editors and copyists of early drafts of episodes originally intended to be included in the *Tiers* and *Quart Livres*. "Mais il n'en reste pas moins que le Ve livre n'a jamais existé tant que tel dans l'esprit de l'auteur: ce n'est qu'un montage et l'une des plus extraordinaires supercheries de l'histoire littéraire."[5]

And, as Huchon also suggests, we do not need to rely on this montage created by editors, for if the temple of "la dive Bouteille" is not reached in *Le Quart Livre,* her word is certainly found.[6] The

---

[2] Edwin Duval, in *The Design of Rabelais's Quart Livre de Pantagruel* (Geneva: Droz, 1998) argues to the contrary that this is a completed and finished work. The book's "design," he feels, consists of a long series of utopias unmasked or debunked, and the quest for the word proves to be a telos just as false as the others. The *Quart Livre* is "a complete epic account of a potentially endless voyage that is littered with the debris of would-be ends—utopias, Golden Ages, absolutes, *mots*—all of which prove to be false at best, oppressive and even fatal at worst" (47). "The last word of the *Quart Livre* is that there can be—indeed that there *must* be—no 'last word' for the Pantagruelians, because last words and final solutions are never the answer, they are always the problem" (48). See the entire Chapter 1, "The Quest for the Holy Word," 25-46.

[3] See Mireille Huchon's "Chronologie," *Rabelais, Oeuvres Complètes* (Paris: Gallimard, 1994) lxxxi. A legal paper naming his brother as legatee is dated March 14, 1553, but an epitaph at the church of St. Paul in Paris where he was buried cites April 9.

[4] *L'Isle Sonante* comprises 16 chapters. *Le Cinquiesme Livre* includes 15 of these, and adds a prologue and 32 new chapters for a total of 47.

[5] *Rabelais grammarien* (Geneva: Droz, 1981) 489. See the discussion of "Le Prétendu Ve Livre" 412-89 and her "Notice" to *Le Cinquiesme livre* in *Oeuvres Complètes* 1595-1607.

[6] "Toutefois, si le mot de la fin de la geste pantagruéline devait être ce *trinch*, mot panomphée, entendu de toutes les nations, propre à combler l'attente du public qui a réservé un succès à la publication du *Cinquiesme livre,* il était déjà inscrit, beaucoup plus subtilement, en fin du *Quart livre* dans le *Sela, Beuvons*" ("Notice" 1607).

"Sela, Beuvons" which ends this book is just as fully as "le mot de la dive Bouteille" as *Le Cinquiesme Livre*'s "Trinch," and Rabelais's word turns all the negative outcomes we have enumerated into positive ones. His "Beuvons" banishes the terrors and disappointments that Pantagruel and Panurge have faced and opens onto a hopeful future. It also praises the past, for it incites Rabelais's characters to pursue with new vigor and confidence the endeavors they have always pursued: the quests for renewal and for birth, for creation and creativity of all sorts. In the end, Pantagruel and Panurge stand eternally poised to begin again, in the spirit of the bottle they have always carried with them. Optimism, joy of life, and *caritas*, faith in one's fellow creatures–these are the values affirmed by *Le Quart Livre*'s final "Beuvons."

Moreover, as Rabelais tells us in the prologues, these are the same values which inspired him to write this book. *The Fourth Book*'s strivings have been his quests too, and he undertook them in face of the fear that his readers might harm or repudiate him and in the very likely knowledge that he would be unable to bring the voyage to completion. He nonetheless pitched his bottle-book into the seas of time in the hope that it would find, on the other shore, "beuveurs" and "pantagruélistes" who would drink of it in the same generous spirit in which it was composed. This faith is expressed in *Le Quart Livre*'s final word which, unlike *Le Cinquiesme Livre*'s "Trinch," unites reader and writer in the second-person plural, in an "us" that triumphs over time and despair. Across more than four hundred years, Rabelais's voice still urges us to overcome fear with the vibrant optimism he embodies, and to join with him in his eternal "yes!"

BIBLIOGRAPHY

Aristophanes. *Comedies*. Trans. W.J. Hickie. London: George Bell, 1893.
Bachelard, Gaston. *Le droit de rêver*. Paris: PUF, 1970.
———. *La Terre et les rêveries du repos*. Paris: Corti, 1948.
Bainton, Roland H. *The Reformation of the Sixteenth Century*. Boston: Beacon, 1956.
Bakhtin, Mikhail. *Rabelais and His World*. Trans. Hélène Iswolsky. Cambridge: MIT, 1968.
Barkan, Leonard. *The Gods Made Flesh: Metamorphosis and the Pursuit of Paganism*. New Haven: Yale UP, 1986.
———. *Transuming Passion: Ganymede and the Erotics of Humanism*. Stanford: Stanford UP, 1991.
Berry, Alice F. "Les 'Mithologies Pantagruelicques': Introduction to a Study of Rabelais's *Quart Livre*." *PMLA* 92 (1977): 471-80.
———. *Rabelais: Homo Logos*. Chapel Hill: U of North Carolina P, 1979.
Blanchot, Maurice. *L'espace littéraire*. Paris: Gallimard, 1955.
Bloom, Harold. *The Anxiety of Influence: A Theory of Poetry*. London: Oxford UP, 1973.
———. *A Map of Misreading*. Oxford: Oxford UP, 1975.
Boisset, Jean. *Calvin et la souveraineté de Dieu*. Paris: Seghers, 1964.
Bowen, Barbara C. *Enter Rabelais, Laughing*. Nashville: Vanderbilt UP, 1998.
———. "Lenten Eels and Carnival Sausages." *L'Esprit Créateur* 21.1 (1981): 12-25.
Bynum, Caroline Walker. *Holy Feast and Holy Fast: The Religious Significance of Food to Medieval Women*. Berkeley: U of California P, 1987.
Campbell, Joseph. *The Hero with a Thousand Faces*. Princeton: Princeton UP, 1949.
Carron, Jean-Claude, ed. *François Rabelais: Critical Assessments*. Baltimore: Johns Hopkins UP, 1995.
Cave, Terence. *The Cornucopian Text: Problems of Writing in the French Renaissance*. London: Oxford UP, 1979.
———. "Reading Rabelais: Variations on the Rock of Virtue." *Literary Theory/Renaissance Texts*. Ed. Patricia Parker and David Quint. Baltimore: Johns Hopkins UP, 1986. 78-95.
Céard, Jean and Jean-Claude Margolin, eds. *Rabelais en son demi-millénaire. Actes du colloque international de Tours (24-29 septembre, 1984)*. Geneva: Droz, 1988.
Charpentier, Françoise. "La Guerre des Andouilles: *Pantagruel* IV, 35-42." *Etudes seiziémistes offertes à Monsieur le Professeur V.-L Saulnier*. Geneva: Droz, 1980. 119-35.
———. "Un Royaume qui perdure sans femmes." *Rabelais's Incomparable Book*. Ed. Raymond C. La Charité. Lexington, KY: French Forum, 1986. 195-209.

Clement, Nemours H. *The Influence of the Arthurian Romances on the Five Books of Rabelais.* New York: Phaeton, 1970.
Costa, Dennis. *Irenic Apocalypse. Some Uses of Apocalyptic in Dante, Petrarch and Rabelais.* Stanford: Anma Libri, 1981.
Cotgrave, Randle. *A Dictionarie of the French and English Tongues.* London, 1611. Columbia: South Carolina UP, 1950.
Curtius, Ernst Robert. *European Literature and the Latin Middle Ages.* London: Routledge and Kegan Paul, 1953.
Defaux, Gérard. *Le curieux, le glorieux et la sagesse du monde dans la première moitié du XVIe siècle: l'Exemple de Panurge (Ulysse, Démosthène, Empédocle).* Lexington, KY: French Forum, 1982.
———. "Rabelais au large de Ganabin: de la «fiction en archipel» au «symbolisme polémique»." *Rabelais pour le XXIe siècle: Actes du Colloque du Centre d'Etudes Supérieures de la Renaissance (Chinon-Tours, 1994).* Ed. Michel Simonin. Geneva: Droz, 1998. 213-39.
———, ed. *Le Quart Livre.* Paris: Livre de Poche, 1994.
———. *Rabelais Agonistes: Du Rieur au prophète: Etudes sur Pantagruel, Gargantua, Le Quart Livre.* Geneva: Droz, 1997.
Derrida, Jacques. "La Pharmacie de Platon." *La Dissémination.* Paris: Seuil, 1972. 69-197.
Dieckmann, Liselotte. *Hieroglyphs: The History of a Literary Symbol.* St. Louis: Washington UP, 1970.
Le Disciple de Pantagruel (Les Navigations de Panurge). Ed. Guy Demerson and Christiane Lauvergnat-Gagnière. Paris: Nizet, 1982.
Duval, André. *Des Sacrements au Concile de Trente.* Paris: Editions du Cerf, 1985.
Duval, Edwin M. *The Design of Rabelais's Quart Livre de Pantagruel.* Geneva: Droz, 1998.
———. "La Messe, La Cène, et Le Voyage sans fin du *Quart Livre.*" *Rabelais en son demi-millénaire: Actes du colloque international de Tours (24-29 septembre 1984). Etudes rabelaisiennes* 21 (1988): 130-40.
Erasmus. *Opus epistolarum Des. Erasmi Roterodami.* Ed. P.S. Allen and H.M. Allen. Vol. 1. Oxford: Oxford UP, 1906.
Ferguson Margaret W. "The Exile's Defense: Du Bellay's *La deffence et illustration de la langue françoyse.*" *PMLA* 93 (1978): 275-89.
———. "Saint Augustine's Region of Unlikeness: The Crossing of Exile and Language." *Georgia Review* 29.4 (1975): 842-64.
Fletcher, Angus. *Allegory: The Theory of a Symbolic Mode.* Ithaca: Cornell UP, 1964.
Foucault, Michel. *The Order of Things.* New York: Pantheon Books, 1970.
Freccero, Carla. *Father Figures: Genealogy and Narrative Structure in Rabelais.* Ithaca: Cornell UP, 1991.
Freccero, John. "The River of Death: *Inferno* II,108." *Dante: The Poetics of Conversion.* Ed. Rachel Jacoff. Cambridge: Harvard UP, 1986. 55-69.
Freud, Sigmund. "Family Romances." *The Standard Edition of the Complete Psychological Works of Sigmund Freud.* Ed. and trans. James Strachey. Vol. 9. London: Hogarth, 1959. 237-41.
Gaignebet, Claude. *A plus hault sens: l'ésotérisme spirituel et charnel de Rabelais.* Paris: Maisonneuve et Larose, 1986. 2 vols.
Gaignebet, Claude and Marie-Claude Florentin. *Le Carnaval: Essais de mythologie populaire.* Paris: Payot, 1974.
Gauna, Max. *The Rabelaisian Mythologies.* Madison: Fairleigh Dickinson UP, 1996.
Godfrey, Sima. "Editor's Preface: The Anxiety of Anticipation." *The Anxiety of Anticipation.* Ed. Godfrey. Yale French Studies 66. New Haven: Yale UP, 1984. iii-ix.

Goethe, Johann Wolfgang von. *Italian Journey*. Trans. Robert R. Heitner. Ed. Thomas P. Saine and Jeffrey L Sammons. Vol. 6. New York: Suhrkamp, 1989.

Greene, Thomas M. *The Light in Troy: Imitation and Discovery in Renaissance Poetry*. New Haven: Yale UP, 1982.

——. *Rabelais: A Study in Comic Courage*. Englewood Cliffs: Prentice Hall, 1970.

Habert, François. *Le Songe de Pantagruel*. Ed. John Lewis. *Etudes rabelaisiennes* 18 (1985): 103-62.

Hampton, Timothy. "Montaigne and the Body of Socrates: Narrative and Exemplarity in the *Essais*." *MLN* 104 (1989): 880-98.

Hippocrates. *Oeuvres complètes*. Ed. E. Littré. Vol. 6. Paris: Baillière, 1849.

Hollander, John. *The Figure of Echo: A Mode of Allusion in Milton and After*. Berkeley: U of California P, 1981.

Huchon, Mireille. "Archéologie du Ve Livre." *Rabelais en son demi-millénaire. Actes du colloque international de Tours (24-29 septembre 1984)*. Ed. Jean Céard and Jean-Claude Margolin. Geneva: Droz, 1988.

——. *Rabelais grammarien: De l'histoire du texte aux problèmes d'authenticité*. Geneva: Droz, 1981.

——, ed. *Rabelais, Oeuvres complètes*. Paris: Gallimard, 1994.

Hugo, Victor. "William Shakespeare." *Oeuvres Complètes*. Vol. 12. Paris: Editions Robert Laffont, 1985. 278-80.

Jeanneret, Michel. *Le Défi des signes: Rabelais et la crise de l'interprétation à la Renaissance*. Orléans: Paradigme, 1994.

——. *Des Mets et des Mots: Banquets et Propos de Table à la Renaissance*. Paris: Corti, 1987.

——. "Les Paroles dégelées (Rabelais, *Quart Livre* 48-65)." *Littérature* 17 (1965): 14-30.

——. "Rabelais, les monstres et l'interprétation des signes (*Quart Livre* 18-42)." *Writing the Renaissance. Essays on Sixteenth-Century French Literature in Honor of Floyd Gray*. Ed. Raymond C. La Charité. Lexington, KY: French Forum, 1992.

Kafka, Franz. "A Hunger Artist." *Selected Stories of Franz Kafka*. Trans. Willa and Edwin Muir. New York: Random House Modern Library, 1952. 188-201.

Kinser, Samuel. *Rabelais's Carnival: Text, Context, Metatext*. Berkeley: U of California P, 1990.

Klibansky, Raymond. *The Continuity of the Platonic Tradition*. London: The Warburg Institute, 1939.

Kritzman, Lawrence. *The Rhetoric of Sexuality and the Literature of the French Renaissance*. Cambridge: Cambridge UP, 1991.

Kunzle, David. "World Upside Down: The Iconography of a European Broadsheet Type." *The Reversible World*. Ed. Barbara A. Babcock. Ithaca: Cornell UP, 1978.

La Charité, Raymond, ed. *Rabelais's Incomparable Book. Essays on His Art*. Lexington, KY: French Forum Monographs, 1986.

Laín Entralgo, Pedro. *The Therapy of the Word in Classical Antiquity*. Trans. J. Rather and J.M. Sharp. New Haven: Yale UP, 1970.

Langer, Ulrich. "Gunpowder as Transgressive Invention in Ronsard." *Literary Theory/Renaissance Texts*. Ed. Patricia Parker and David Quint. Baltimore: Johns Hopkins UP, 1986. 96-114.

Leach, Edmund. "Anthropological Aspects of Language: Animal Categories and Verbal Abuse." *New Directions in the Study of Language*. Ed. Erich H. Lenneberg. Cambridge, MA: MIT, 1964.

LeFranc, Abel. "Le Platon de Rabelais." *Bibliothèque du Bibliophile et du Bibliothécaire* (1901) 104-14, 169-81.

Lestringant, Frank. "La famille des 'tempêtes en mer': essai de généalogie (Rabelais, Thevet et quelques autres)." *Etudes de Lettres* 2 (1984): 45-62.

———. "L'Insulaire de Rabelais ou la fiction en archipel (pour une lecture topographique du *Quart Livre*." *Rabelais en son demi-millénaire. Actes du colloque international de Tours (24-29 septembre 1984)*. Ed. Jean Céard et Jean-Claude Margolin. Geneva: Droz, 1988. 249-74.

———. "Rabelais et le récit toponymique." *Poétique* 50 (1982): 207-25.

Lucian. *A True Story*. Trans. A.M. Harmon. *Lucian*. Vol. 1. Cambridge: Harvard UP, 1913. 247-357.

Marichal, Robert. "L'Attitude de Rabelais devant le Néo-platonisme et l'italianisme (*Quart Livre*, Ch. ix-xi)." *François Rabelais: Ouvrage publié pour le quatrième centenaire de sa mort*. Geneva: Droz, 1953. 181-209.

———. "Quart Livre: Commentaires." *Etudes rabelaisiennes* 5 (1964): 100-46.

———, ed. *Le Quart Livre*. Geneva: Droz, 1947.

Marot, Clément. *Oeuvres*. Ed. Georges Guiffrey and Jean Plattard. Paris: Schmeit, 1931.

Montaigne, Michel de. *Oeuvres complètes*. Ed. Albert Thibaudet and Maurice Rat. Paris: Gallimard, 1962.

Ong, Walter J. "The Writer's Audience is Always a Fiction." *PMLA* 90 (1975): 9-21.

Ovid. *The Fasti, Tristia, Pontic Epistles, Ibis, and Halieuticon*. Trans. Henry T. Riley. London: G. Bell, 1915.

Plato. *Collected Dialogues*. Ed. Edith Hamilton and Huntington Cairns. Princeton: Princeton UP, 1973.

Plattard, Jean. *François Rabelais*. Paris: Boivin, 1932.

———, ed. *Le Quart Livre de Pantagruel (edition dite partielle, Lyon, 1548)*. Paris: Champion, 1909.

Pliny. *Natural History*. Trans. H. Rackham. Vol. 3. Cambridge: Harvard UP, 1940.

Plutarch. *Moralia*. Trans. Frank Cole Babbit. Vol. 5. Cambridge: Harvard UP, 1936.

Quint, David. *Origin and Originality in Renaissance Literature: Versions of the Source*. New Haven: Yale UP, 1983.

Rabelais, François. *Oeuvres Complètes*. Ed. Mireille Huchon. Paris: Gallimard, 1994.

———. *Oeuvres Complètes*. Ed. Pierre Jourda. 2 vols. Paris: Garnier, 1962.

———. *Le Quart Livre*. Ed. Gérard Defaux. Paris: Livre de Poche, 1994.

———. *Le Quart Livre*. Ed. Robert Marichal. Geneva: Droz, 1947.

———. *Le Quart Livre de Pantagruel (edition dite partielle, Lyons, 1548)*. Ed. Jean Plattard. Paris: Champion, 1909.

Rigolot, François. "Cratylisme et pantagruélisme. Rabelais et le statut du signe." *Etudes rabelaisiennes* 13 (1976): 115-32.

———. *Les Langages de Rabelais*. 2nd ed. Geneva: Droz, 1996.

———. *Le Texte de la Renaissance: des Rhétoriquers à Montaigne*. Geneva: Droz, 1972.

Rimbaud, Arthur. *Oeuvres*. Ed. S. Bernard and A. Guyaux. Paris: Garnier, 1981.

Sandy, Gerald N. *Heliodorus*. Boston: Twayne, 1982.

Saulnier, V.-L. *Rabelais II: Rabelais dans son enquête. Etude sur le Quart et le Cinquième Livre*. Paris: SEDES, 1982.

Screech, M. A. *Rabelais*. Ithaca: Cornell UP, 1979.

Scribner, Bob. "Reformation, carnival, and the world turned upside down." *Social History* 3 (1978): 303-29.

Simonin, Michel, ed. *Rabelais pour le XXIe siècle. Actes du colloque du Centre d'Etudes Supérieures de la Renaissance (Chinon-Tours, 1994)*. Geneva: Droz, 1998.

Singleton, Charles S. "In Exitu Israel de Aegypto." *Dante: A Collection of Critical Essays*. Ed. John Freccero. Englewood Cliffs: Prentice Hall, 1965. 102-21.

Smith, Paul J. "'Croquer Pie': *Quart Livre*, Ancient Prologue." *Rabelais-Dionysos: vin, carnaval, ivresse*. Ed. M. Bideaux. Paris: Jeanne Laffitte, 1997.

———. *Voyage et écriture: Etude sur Le Quart Livre de Rabelais*. Geneva: Droz, 1987.

Stalleybrass, Peter and Allon White. *The Politics and Poetics of Transgression*. Ithaca: Cornell UP, 1986.

Starobinski, Jean. "Stendhal pseudonyme." *L'Oeil vivant*. Paris: Gallimard, 1961. 191-244.

Stephens, Walter. *Giants in Those Days. Folklore, Ancient History and Nationalism*. Lincoln: U of Nebraska P, 1989.

Tetel, Marcel. "Carnival and Beyond." *L'Esprit Créateur* 21.1 (1981): 88-104.

———. "Rabelais and Folengo." *Comparative Literature* 15 (1963): 357-64.

Tournon, André. "*En sens agile*". *Les acrobaties de l'esprit selon Rabelais*. Paris: Champion, 1995.

Weinberg, Florence. *The Wine and the Will: Rabelais's Bacchic Christianity*. Detroit: Wayne State UP, 1972.

Wind, Edgar. *Pagan Mysteries in the Renaissance*. Harmondsworth, Eng.: Penguin Books, 1967.

Wittkower, R. "Imitation, Eclecticism, and Genius." *Aspects of the Eighteenth Century*. Ed. Earl R. Wasserman. Baltimore: Johns Hopkins UP, 1965. 143-61.

Zapperi, Roberto. *L'Homme enceint: l'homme, la femme et le pouvoir*. Trans. Marie-Ange Maire Vigueur. Paris: PUF, 1983.

NORTH CAROLINA STUDIES IN THE ROMANCE LANGUAGES AND LITERATURES
I.S.B.N. Prefix 0-8078-

Recent Titles

MYSTIFICATION ET CRÉATIVITÉ DANS L'OEUVRE ROMANESQUE DE MARGUERITE YOURCENAR, par Beatrice Ness. 1994. (No. 247). -9251-3.
TEXT AS TOPOS IN RELIGIOUS LITERATURE OF THE SPANISH GOLDEN AGE, by M. Louise Salstad. 1995. (No. 248). -9252-1.
CALISTO'S DREAM AND THE CELESTINESQUE TRADITION: A REREADING OF CELESTINA, by Ricardo Castells. 1995. (No. 249). -9253-X.
THE ALLEGORICAL IMPULSE IN THE WORKS OF JULIEN GRACQ: HISTORY AS RHETORICAL ENACTMENT IN LE RIVAGE DES SYRTES AND UN BALCON EN FORÊT, by Carol J. Murphy. 1995. (No. 250). -9254-8.
VOID AND VOICE: QUESTIONING NARRATIVE CONVENTIONS IN ANDRÉ GIDE'S MAJOR FIRST-PERSON NARRATIVES, by Charles O'Keefe. 1996. (No. 251). -9255-6.
EL CÍRCULO Y LA FLECHA: PRINCIPIO Y FIN, TRIUNFO Y FRACASO DEL PERSILES, por Julio Baena. 1996. (No. 252). -9256-4.
EL TIEMPO Y LOS MÁRGENES. EUROPA COMO UTOPÍA Y COMO AMENAZA EN LA LITERATURA ESPAÑOLA, por Jesús Torrecilla. 1996. (No. 253). -9257-2.
THE AESTHETICS OF ARTIFICE: VILLIERS'S L'EVE FUTURE, by Marie Lathers. 1996. (No. 254). -9254-8.
DISLOCATIONS OF DESIRE: GENDER, IDENTITY, AND STRATEGY IN LA REGENTA, by Alison Sinclair. 1998. (No. 255). -9259-9.
THE POETICS OF INCONSTANCY, ETIENNE DURAND AND THE END OF RENAISSANCE VERSE, by Hoyt Rogers. 1998. (No. 256). -9260-2.
RONSARD'S CONTENTIOUS SISTERS: THE PARAGONE BETWEEN POETRY AND PAINTING IN THE WORKS OF PIERRE DE RONSARD, by Roberto E. Campo. 1998. (No. 257). -9261-0.
THE RAVISHMENT OF PERSEPHONE: EPISTOLARY LYRIC IN THE SIÈCLE DES LUMIÈRES, by Julia K. De Pree. 1998. (No. 258). -9262-9.
CONVERTING FICTION: COUNTER REFORMATIONAL CLOSURE IN THE SECULAR LITERATURE OF GOLDEN AGE SPAIN, by David H. Darst. 1998. (No. 259). -9263-7.
GALDÓS'S SEGUNDA MANERA: RHETORICAL STRATEGIES AND AFFECTIVE RESPONSE, by Linda M. Willem. 1998. (No. 260). -9264-5.
A MEDIEVAL PILGRIM'S COMPANION. REASSESSING EL LIBRO DE LOS HUÉSPEDES (ESCORIAL MS. h.I.13), by Thomas D. Spaccarelli. 1998. (No. 261). -9265-3.
'PUEBLOS ENFERMOS': THE DISCOURSE OF ILLNESS IN THE TURN-OF-THE-CENTURY SPANISH AND LATIN AMERICAN ESSAY, by Michael Aronna. 1999. (No. 262). -9266-1.
RESONANT THEMES. LITERATURE, HISTORY, AND THE ARTS IN NINETEENTH- AND TWENTIETH-CENTURY EUROPE. ESSAYS IN HONOR OF VICTOR BROMBERT, by Stirling Haig. 1999. (No. 263). -9267-X.
RAZA, GÉNERO E HIBRIDEZ EN EL LAZARILLO DE CIEGOS CAMINANTES, por Mariselle Meléndez. 1999. (No. 264). -9268-8.
DEL ESCENARIO A LA PANTALLA: LA ADAPTACIÓN CINEMATOGRÁFICA DEL TEATRO ESPAÑOL, por María Asunción Gómez. 2000. (No. 265). 9269-6.
THE LEPER IN BLUE: COERCIVE PERFORMANCE AND THE CONTEMPORARY LATIN AMERICAN THEATER, by Amalia Gladhart. 2000. (No. 266). 9270-X.
THE CHARM OF CATASTROPHE: A STUDY OF RABELAIS'S QUART LIVRE, by Alice Fiola Berry. 2000. (No. 267). -9271-8.
PUERTO RICAN CULTURAL IDENTITY AND THE WORK OF LUIS RAFAEL SÁNCHEZ, by John Dimitri Perivolaris. 2000. (No. 268). -9272-6.

When ordering please cite the ISBN Prefix plus the last four digits for each title.

Send orders to: University of North Carolina Press
                     P.O. Box 2288
                     CB# 6215
                     Chapel Hill, NC 27515-2288
                     U.S.A.

www.ingramcontent.com/pod-product-compliance
Lightning Source LLC
Chambersburg PA
CBHW020740230426
43665CB00009B/501